SCIENCE
LEVEL SIX
SECOND EDITION

purposeful design®
publications

Colorado Springs, Colorado

SCIENCE
LEVEL SIX
SECOND EDITION

Vice President for Purposeful Design Publications
Steven Babbitt

Assistant Director for Textbook Development
Don Hulin

Designers
Ana Brodie
Claire Coleman
Susanna Garmany

Editors
Jennifer Bollinger
Gary Brohmer
Barbara Carpenter
Cheryl Chiapperino
Janice Giles
Ellen Johnson
Macki Jones
Kim Pettit
Nancy Sutton
Lorraine Wadman
Lisa Wood

First edition 2009.
Second edition 2014

Printed in the United States of America
20 19 18 17 16 15 14   1 2 3 4 5 6 7

Elementary Science, Level Six – Student Edition
Purposeful Design Elementary Science series
ISBN 978-1-58331-537-8, Catalog #20061

Purposeful Design Publications is the publishing division of the Association of Christian Schools International (ACSI) and is committed to the ministry of Christian school education, to enable Christian educators and schools worldwide to effectively prepare students for life. As the publisher of textbooks, trade books, and other educational resources within ACSI, Purposeful Design Publications strives to produce biblically sound materials that reflect Christian scholarship and stewardship and that address the identified needs of Christian schools around the world.

References to books, computer software, and other ancillary resources in this series are not endorsements by ACSI. These materials were selected to provide teachers with additional resources appropriate to the concepts being taught and to promote student understanding and enjoyment.

Purposeful Design Publications
A Division of ACSI
PO Box 65130 • Colorado Springs, CO • 80962-5130
Customer Service Department: 800/367-0798 • Website: www.purposefuldesign.org

LIFE SCIENCE: DIVERSITY

UNIT 1

Chapter 1 Classification I 2
Domain to Species 4
Bacteria and Archaea 6
Eukarya: Protists and Fungi 8
Plant Kingdom 10
Tropisms 12

Chapter 2 Classification II 14
Vertebrates I 16
Vertebrates II 18
Invertebrates I 20
Invertebrates II 22
Biomes 24

Chapter 3 Cell Processes 26
Cell Structure 28
Cellular Respiration 30
Transport 32
Cell Division 34
Reproduction 36

Chapter 4 Heredity and Genetics 38
Gregor Mendel 40
Basic Genetics 42
Gene Combinations 44
Dominance 46
Animal Breeding 48

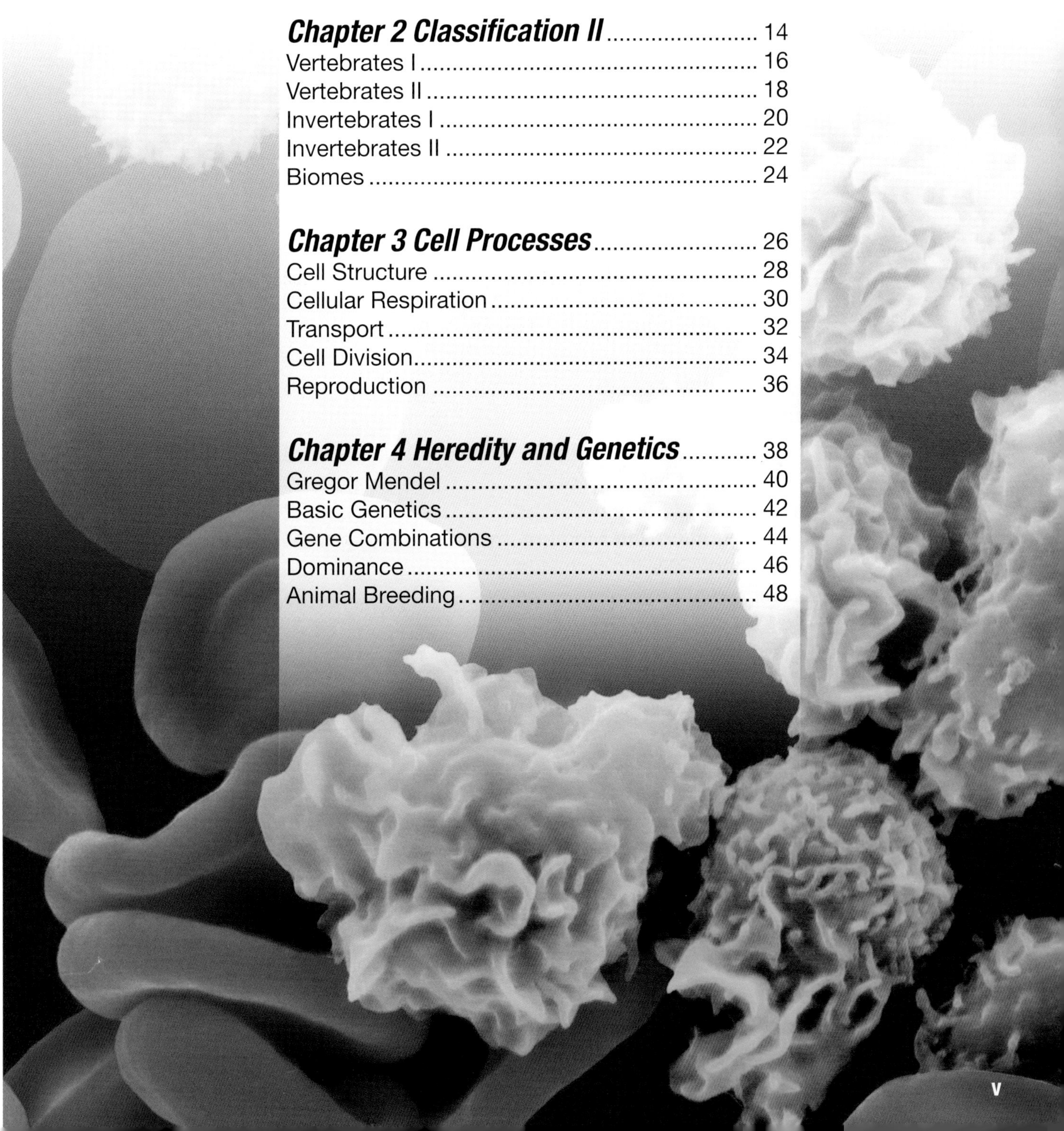

UNIT 2 PHYSICAL SCIENCE: STRUCTURE

Chapter 5 Periodic Table of Elements 52
Atomic Structure 54
Atomic Model 56
Chemical Families 58
Building Molecules 60
Structures and Properties 62

Chapter 6 States of Matter 64
State Changes 66
Temperature Scales 68
Uniqueness of Water 70
pH Scale 72
Heat Technology 74

Chapter 7 Fluids 76
Shape and Volume 78
Properties of Fluids 80
Bernoulli's Principle 82
Flight 84
Applications of Lift 86

Chapter 8 Why Things Move 88
Newton's Laws of Motion 90
Speed and Velocity 92
Acceleration and Momentum 94
Friction 96
Perpetual Motion 98

EARTH AND SPACE SCIENCE: PATTERNS

UNIT 3

Chapter 9 Oceans in Motion 102
Water Movement 104
Currents 106
Ocean Zones 108
Marine Life 110
Brine Pools 112

Chapter 10 Rock Records 114
Rock Cycle 116
Breakdown 118
Deposition 120
Fossil Formation 122
Creation and Evolution 124
Geologic Layers 126

Chapter 11 Violent Motions 128
Earthquakes 130
Volcanoes 132
Thunderstorms and Tornadoes 134
Hurricanes 136
Wildfires 138

Chapter 12 Astronomy 140
Starlight 142
Star Populations 144
Star Life Cycles 146
Celestial Interactions 148
Clusters and Constellations 150

UNIT 4

HUMAN BODY: DECISIONS

Chapter 13 Interaction of Systems 154
Systems Overview 156
Muscular System 158
Skeletal System 160
Nervous System 162
The Senses 164

Chapter 14 Body Stewardship 166
Diet and Exercise 168
System of Supply 170
System of Movement 172
System of Control 174
Healthful Cooking 176

RESOURCES

Scientific Inquiry x
Glossary 179
Index 187

Development Team

First Edition

Vice President of Academic Affairs
Derek Keenan, EdD

Director of Publishing Services
Steven Babbitt

Assistant Director for Textbook Development
Don Hulin

Authors
Chard Berndt, Pat Blackburn, Sandra Burner, Sue Drake, Dr. Diane Foley, Amy Gruetzmacher, Jacqueline Lauriat, Susan Lovelace, Vince Palmer, Elda Robinson, Pam Van der Werff

Editorial Team
Cynthia Behr, Cheryl Chiapperino, Suzanne Clark, John Conaway, Mary Corcoran, Kristi Crosson, Anita Gordon, David Hill, Stephen Johnson, Macki Jones, JoAnn Keenan, Christy Krenek, Sheri Leasure, Wayne Lowe, Zach Moore, Frieda Nossaman, Vanessa Rough, Kara Underwood, Lisa Wood

Design Team
Lindsay Driscoll, Susanna Garmany, Scot McDonald, Kris Orr, Dan Schultz, Sarah Schultz, Chris Tschamler, Shelley Webb

Consultants
Cheryl Blackmon, PhD
Briarwood Christian School

Bob Burtch, EdD
Wheaton College

Don DeYoung, PhD
Grace College

Ruth Ebeling, MS
Biola University

Ray Gates, MS
Cornerstone University

Jerry Johnson, MS
Corban College

Virginia Johnson, PhD
Biola University

James Van Eaton, PhD
Liberty University

Purposeful Design Publications is grateful to Briarwood Christian School in Birmingham, Alabama, for the contributions they made to the original content of the Purposeful Design Science series.

SCIENTIFIC INQUIRY

Scientific inquiry is a way to help you better understand the world God has created. It involves asking questions, making hypotheses, conducting tests, and analyzing results. New discoveries may direct you to make new hypotheses and to conduct additional tests. Communicating and defending your conclusions is another important step in this ongoing process.

Through this process of exploration, you will develop the ability to formulate pertinent questions, conduct appropriate investigations and tests, and generate reasonable explanations for your findings.

1. ASK A QUESTION
2. MAKE A HYPOTHESIS
3. PLAN AND DO A TEST
4. RECORD AND ANALYZE YOUR RESULTS
5. MAKE A CONCLUSION
6. SHARE YOUR RESULTS

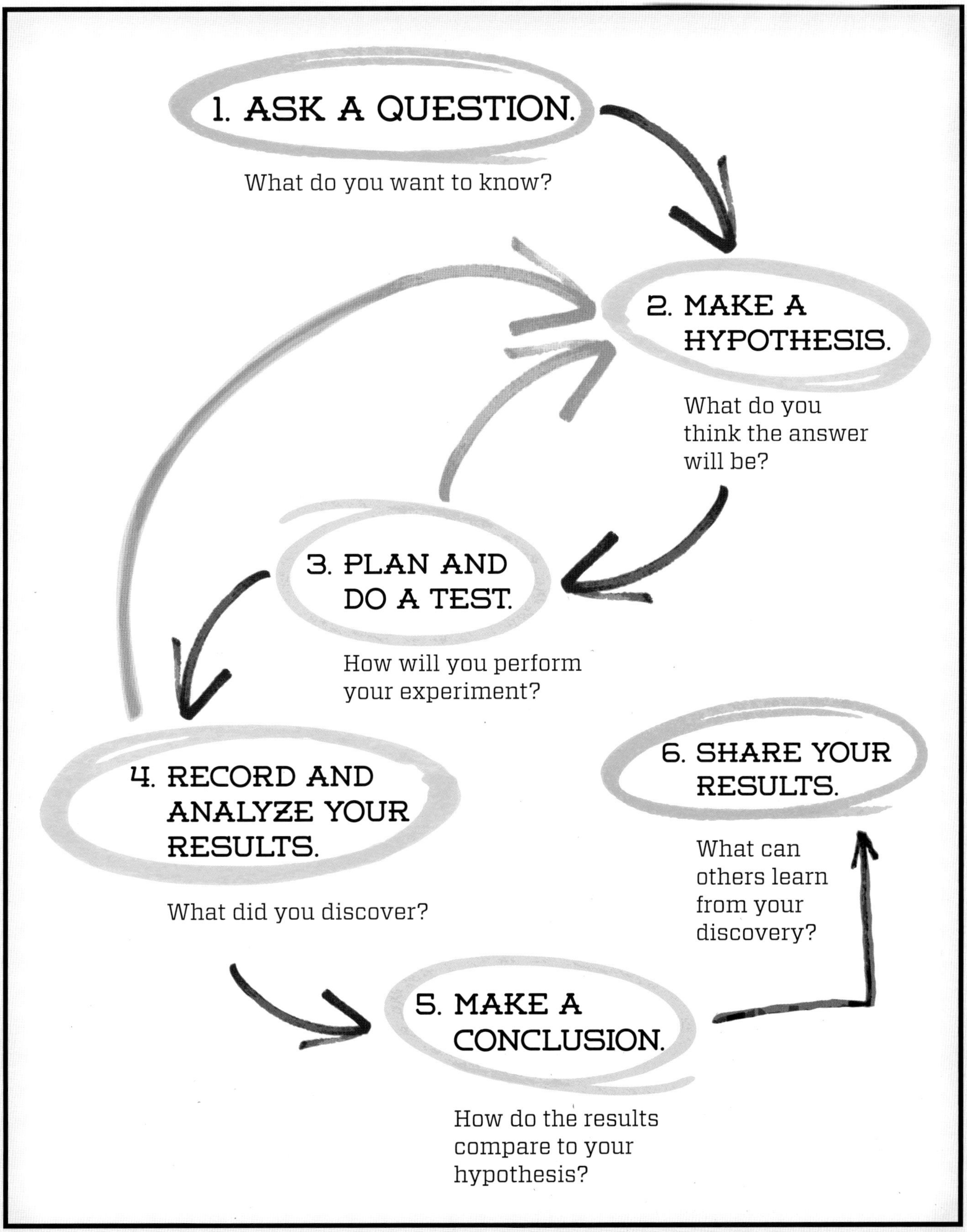
1. ASK A QUESTION.
What do you want to know?
2. MAKE A HYPOTHESIS.
What do you think the answer will be?
3. PLAN AND DO A TEST.
How will you perform your experiment?
4. RECORD AND ANALYZE YOUR RESULTS.
What did you discover?
5. MAKE A CONCLUSION.
How do the results compare to your hypothesis?
6. SHARE YOUR RESULTS.
What can others learn from your discovery?

UNIT 1

LIFE SCIENCE: DIVERSITY

– the study of living things and how they relate to one another

UNIT 2

PHYSICAL SCIENCE: STRUCTURE

UNIT 3

EARTH AND SPACE SCIENCE: PATTERNS

UNIT 4

HUMAN BODY: DECISIONS

CHAPTER

1 CLASSIFICATION I

Taxonomy is a method of organizing information in a way that is orderly and simple to use. When scientists classify organisms, they ask questions such as, what makes these organisms alike? How do they differ? How do these organisms interact with each other? or How do these organisms interact with the environment? Globally, scientists use the same criteria to describe or classify living things as a part of taxonomy. This allows scientists to share information about organisms they have studied. Other scientists around the world are then able to understand the nature of those organisms without firsthand observation.

VOCABULARY

taxonomy (tak·ˈsä·nə·mē) the science of classifying organisms

KEY IDEAS

- Taxonomy enables scientists to classify organisms based on their characteristics.
- Organisms are classified into three domains—Bacteria, Archaea, and Eukarya.
- There are four kingdoms within the eukarya domain—Protist, Fungus, Plant, and Animal.
- Plants respond to environmental factors, including water, light, barriers, and gravity.

QUICK FACT

Around 2650 BC Chinese Emperor Shen Nung cataloged 365 types of medicinal herbs. Later Egyptian writing from 1500 BC identified plants with healing properties. Around 350 BC, Greek philosophers Aristotle and Theophrastus continued the study of plants. Aristotle divided living things into two groups—plants and animals. His pupil Theophrastus began classifying plants as herbs, shrubs, or trees. Classification continued with Dioscorides, a Greek physician in the Roman army. A Greek manuscript that was written around 75 BC identified some 600 medicinal plants.

Strange but True

Is this ooze alive?

DOMAIN TO SPECIES

VOCABULARY

binomial nomenclature
(bī·ˈnō·mē·əl ˈnō·mən·klā·chər)
a two-part naming system that consists of genus and species

IN THE FIELD

John Ray (1627–1705) is known as *the Founder of Biology.* Ray devoted his life not only to following Christ but also to cataloging plants and animals throughout Europe. He published several books of the drawings and descriptions that he and his colleague Francis Willoughby made during their journeys. He especially loved plants. Ray was determined to prove that God created distinct kinds of organisms using his catalog of God's Creation.

Explorers like Ferdinand Magellan traveled around the globe, returning home with new species of plants and animals. The Age of Exploration provided many discoveries that created a need for a catalog of living things. Scientists who studied nature began to form a system of identification. Initially, there was no commonly accepted standard to name these organisms. Eventually, scientists began to use Latin, which was widely accepted.

John Ray, a British naturalist, coined the term *species* to describe a specific kind of organism. He began to develop a system that arranged newly discovered species by appearance and characteristics. Carolus Linnaeus was one of the leading naturalists of the eighteenth century who became known as *the Father of Modern Taxonomy*. He set up the category of genus and placed Ray's category of species into it. He identified all living things by these two categories, and this naming method became known as binomial nomenclature. Some organisms were named after famous people; others were named based on their characteristics. Published in 1758, Linnaeus' book *Systema Naturae* detailed the genus and species of organisms and became the basis for modern taxonomy.

Magellan found a quicker southern route to China in search of spices. Present-day explorers, however, are hoping to find new species of organisms around the world that may hold cures for cancer and other diseases.

The Spanish name for poinsettia is *Flor de Noche Buena*, which translates to *Flower of the Holy Night.* The Latin scientific name is Eukarya Plantae Magnoliophyta Magnoliopsida Euphorbiales Euphorbiaceae *Euphorbia pulcherrima.*

Today, all living organisms are divided into three domains: Bacteria, Archaea, and Eukarya. Only the eukarya domain is further divided into kingdoms. It is traditionally separated into four kingdoms—Protist, Fungus, Plant, and Animal. The bacteria and archaea domains and the eukarya kingdoms are further divided into phylum, class, order, family, genus, and species. The criteria used for classification includes physical characteristics, movement, nourishment, reproduction, presence of a nucleus, number of cells, and genetic makeup. Classification is simply comparing characteristics and grouping similar organisms together. Scientists can then use the classification to better understand each organism's traits.

All life on Earth share similar characteristics because all share a common Creator. When scientists identify and classify organisms, differences and similarities are equally important. Archaea have unique qualities that distinguish them from bacteria. While archaea actually have certain things in common with eukarya, organisms in the eukarya domain have distinctions that separate them from the bacteria and archaea domains.

QUICK FACT

The Bible records that the prophet Isaiah used a lump of figs to treat the Judean King Hezekiah, who was sick to the point of death. (2 Kings 20:7) There appears to be scientific validity to the healing value of figs. Japanese scientists have isolated a chemical in figs that shrinks tumors. Experimenters have proven that fig juice kills bacteria in test-tube studies. According to the US Department of Agriculture, figs contain fiber, vitamins A and C, calcium, magnesium, and potassium, which help control appetite and provide good health.

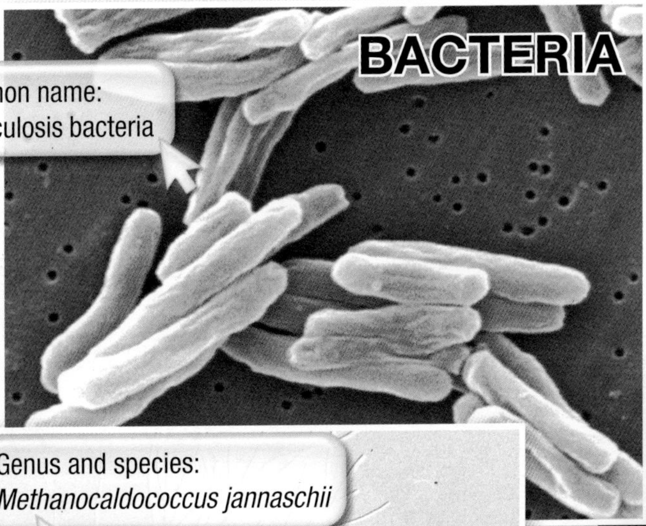

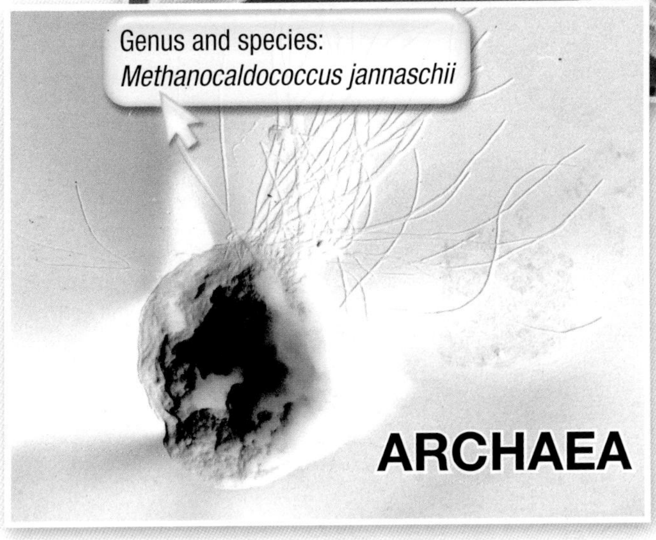

BACTERIA AND ARCHAEA

VOCABULARY

prokaryote (prō·ˈka·rē·ōt) a unicellular microorganism that lacks a distinct nucleus

autotroph (ˈȯ·tə·trōf) an organism that produces its own food

heterotroph (ˈhe·tə·rə·trōf) an organism that obtains food from an outside source

IN THE FIELD

Staining is the first method used by microbiologists to identify and classify bacteria. Hans Christian Gram developed the Gram's stain method to provide a visual aid to see different types of bacteria. During the staining process, the bacteria are bathed in violet dye. If the dye remains even after rinsing and adding another type of stain, the bacteria are purple-colored and gram-positive, such as *Corynebacterium diphtheriae*. If the bacteria do not keep the original dye, the specimen is gram-negative, and pink or red-colored, such as *Legionella pneumophila*. Common gram-positive bacteria are staphylococci that cause certain pimples. Common gram-negative bacteria are the bacilli that cause whooping cough.

Corynebacterium diphtheriae

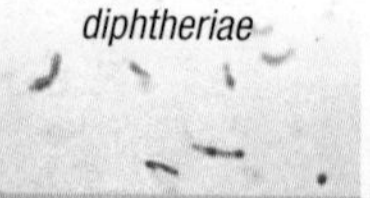

Legionella pneumophila

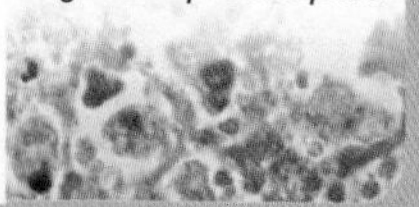

Bacteria and archaea can be found everywhere on Earth, even in extreme environments that other life cannot tolerate. Bacteria are single-celled organisms that do not have a nucleus. They are often thought of as being harmful. However, yogurt, sourdough, some medicines, and vitamins come from helpful bacteria.

The first person to observe bacteria was Antonie van Leeuwenhoek in the 1600s. He called them *animalcules*. His training as a lens grinder enabled him to invent microscopes to explore the world around him. One of Leeuwenhoek's microscopes was slightly bigger than a large postage stamp. A specimen was placed on the needle and positioned with the adjusting screw. The lens was behind the top of the screw.

In 1875, Ferdinand J. Cohn first classified bacteria. He decided to call the rod-shaped bacteria *bacilli*. Other shapes—spherical and spiral—are known as *cocci* and *spirilla*.

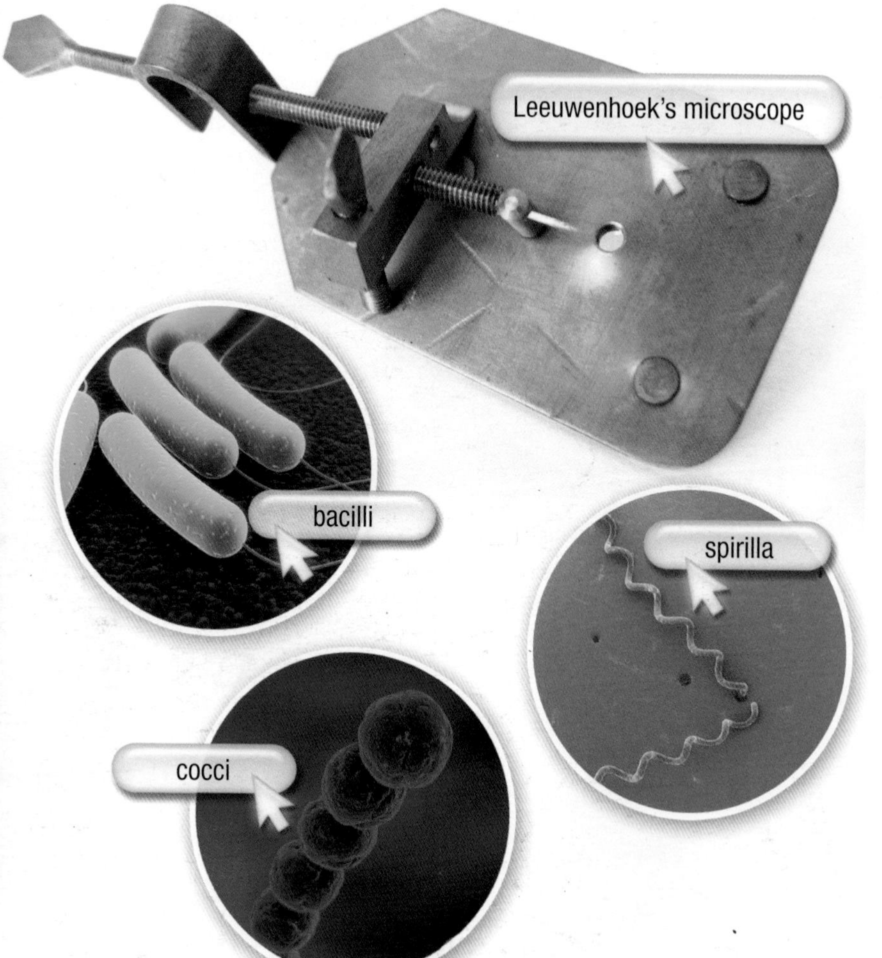

In 1977, Dr. Carl Woese and colleagues at the University of Illinois in the United States discovered organisms now called *archaea*. Initially these organisms were considered a type of bacteria. Although archaea look similar to bacteria, they have different cell structure and chemical makeup. Their genetic information and cell walls are not alike. Archaea also can tolerate extreme conditions that most bacteria cannot and are typically less than 1/1,000 mm (4/100,000 in.) long. They include extremophiles, which thrive in intensely hot, salty, acidic, or alkaline environments. Scientists are investigating the world's extreme environments in search of new species. The study of archaea has improved medicine development and DNA identification tools.

Archaea and bacteria are unicellular, or one-celled, prokaryotes and are important to the life of the planet. Each is classified based upon its need for oxygen. Aerobic organisms need oxygen to make use of energy sources. Anaerobic organisms do not need oxygen and sometimes die if exposed to it. The organisms are also categorized based on how they obtain food. Some archaea are autotrophs, which make their own food. Others are heterotrophs, obtaining food from an outside source. Archaea can be elongated, square, or triangular in shape, as well as rodlike, spherical, and spiral.

A living species of archaea called *snottite* makes a slimy substance that oozes from the ceilings of caves. These caves are toxic to animals because of the presence of sulfuric acid. Snottites use water to break down the sulfur compounds for energy. As a by-product, they release slimy chemicals that form the unusual stalactites.

The Morning Glory Pool in Yellowstone National Park, Wyoming, is an area where scientists study archaea.

EUKARYA: PROTISTS AND FUNGI

VOCABULARY

eukaryote (yo͞o·ˈker·ē·ōt) an organism composed of one or more cells containing a visible nucleus and organelles

The protist kingdom contains organisms which have many characteristics of other kingdoms but which do not completely fit into those categories. Protists are eukaryotes, because their cells have an enclosed, distinct nucleus. They all live in moist habitats, although not all live in water. They can reproduce in various ways. Some are autotrophs (make their own food) while others are heterotrophs (find their food). Protists are the foundation of many food chains.

There are approximately 16 phyla of protists. Some protists are animal-like; some are plantlike. Others are fungus-like. Animal-like protists are heterotrophs called *protozoa*. Examples of these are the amoeba and paramecium. Plantlike protists, often called *algae*, are producers. Most have chlorophyll similar to plants. These include dinoflagellates, a type of plankton; red, green, and brown algae; and diatoms. Diatoms are special microscopic organisms with a glass-like covering. Fungus-like protists are heterotrophs. This group includes slime molds, water molds, and downy mildew.

How are diatoms beneficial to people?

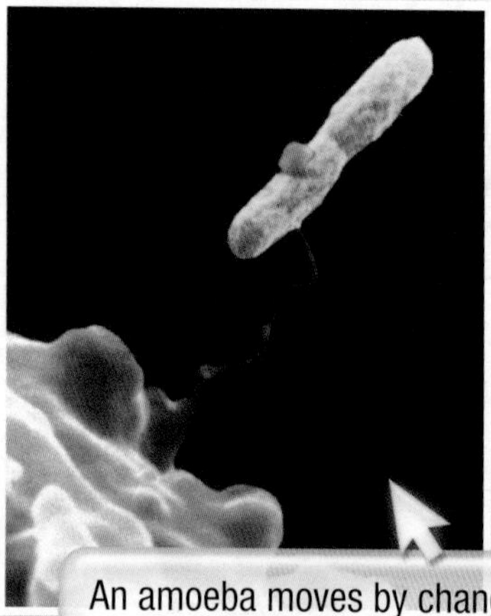

An amoeba moves by changing its shape, creating a pseudopod, which means false foot. This amoeba uses its pseudopod to capture a bacterium.

Downy mildew often damages spinach crops.

Along this shoreline, a chemical reaction is triggered, causing certain plantlike protists to glow. This protist is the dinoflagellate, *Lingulodinium polyedrum*.

The fungus kingdom is also within the eukarya domain. Many people think of mushrooms when they hear the word *fungus*. Some mushrooms are edible, some are very useful for medicines, while others are extremely toxic and deadly. However, there is a wide variety of fascinating fungal species distributed around the world. Some are unicellular, but most are multicellular. Fungi grow in moist areas with little to no sunlight.

Fungi are responsible for many human ailments. Athlete's foot, certain fingernail infections, and some forms of diaper rash are caused by yeast. Farmers must combat rust and smut fungi, which infect plants and grains like wheat. When these rust and smut fungi mature, black, spore-filled masses appear in the grain. These spores are how fungi reproduce. Fungi are considered heterotrophs, since they are decomposers or parasites. Nevertheless, fungi can be useful. Penicillin is produced from a fungus mold. Baker's yeast gives bread its light, fluffy texture.

OUTLOOK

Baker's yeast is a living organism classified in the fungus kingdom. The word *leaven* refers to yeast and other products that make bread rise. Usually a lump of the old dough is kept from the last batch to start the next. Israelites were told to use unleavened bread when they left Egypt. Jesus compared leaven to hypocrisy in Luke 12:1. What characteristic of yeast is important in these examples?

Cyathus olla, or Bird's Nest Fungi, is about the size of a young person's thumbnail. Rain can trigger ejection of the spring-loaded eggs to help disperse the fungi's spores.

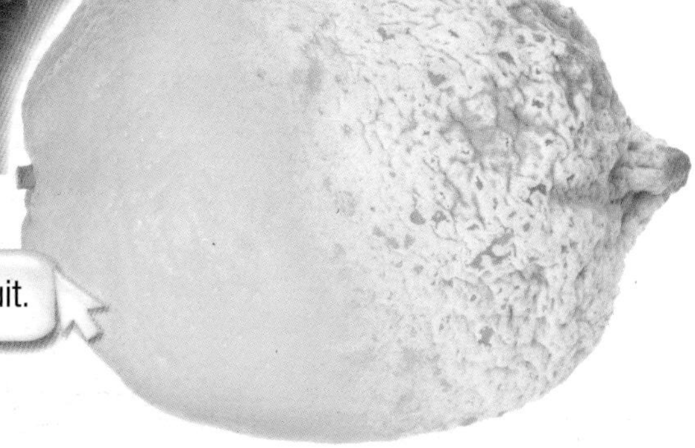

Mold can destroy fruit.

PLANT KINGDOM

VOCABULARY

vascular (ˈvas·kyə·lər) having a system of tubes to transport water and nutrients

angiosperm (ˈan·jē·ə·spərm) a vascular plant that bears flowers and fruit

gymnosperm (ˈjim·nə·spərm) a vascular, cone-bearing plant whose seeds are not enclosed

monocot (ˈmä·nō·kät) a plant having an embryo with a single cotyledon

dicot (ˈdī·kät) a plant having an embryo with two cotyledons

The plant kingdom belongs to the eukarya domain. Plants are autotrophs that have chloroplasts. There are over 250,000 identified species of plants. One characteristic that identifies a plant is the way it moves water and nutrients within itself. Vascular plants have a system of tubes within broad leaves, stems, and roots for water and nutrient transport. Examples of vascular plants include trees, shrubs, and grasses. Nonvascular plants do not have broad leaves or a tube system. Instead, water and nutrients seep from cell to cell within the plant. Moss, liverworts, and green algae are examples of nonvascular plants.

A plant's classification depends on its type of reproductive system. Most vascular plants produce seeds. An angiosperm is a type of vascular plant that produces flowers and has enclosed seeds. A conifer, or cone-bearing plant, is a vascular plant as well. It is a gymnosperm and differs from an angiosperm because its seeds are exposed. The individual seeds are attached to the cones' scales. However, ferns, which are a type of vascular plant, and nonvascular plants have spores rather than seeds. A fern's spore casings open when the spores are mature.

Can you guess how big this tree's cones are?

This is a thalloid liverwort, a nonvascular plant.

Sunflowers are vascular, seed-bearing plants.

QUICK FACT

The Mojave Desert is located in southwestern United States. Scientists believe a creosote bush found there may be one of the oldest living things on Earth. It is over 13.7 m (45 ft) in diameter. The bush has been named *King Clone*. Other bushes in the same area are also very old.

Angiosperms make up almost 90% of the species in the plant kingdom. A plant's flowers help fertilize undeveloped seeds found in the plant's ovary. As the ovary grows, it becomes a fruit. The fruit provides protection and nourishment for the seeds. Another distinguishable feature of flowering plants is seed structure. The seed's leaf and food supply are contained in one or two cotyledons. An angiosperm that has seeds with one cotyledon is a monocot. Seeds with two cotyledons are from a dicot, which can also have a ring of vascular bundles in the stems.

People often observe the leaves of an unknown plant first to identify it. Angiosperms and one type of gymnosperm, *Ginkgo biloba*, have flat leaves with veins. Leaf veins of dicots crisscross like a web through the leaf. Monocots have parallel veins that run the length of the narrow leaf. Nearly all gymnosperms have sharp, slender needles or scales for leaves. Most conifers are considered evergreen because they have leaves year-round.

IN THE FIELD

Caspar Bauhin (1560–1624) was a professor of anatomy, botany, and medicine. His French father fled to Switzerland after becoming a Protestant. He correctly categorized mints, legumes, and grasses. Bauhin personally collected 4,000 plant samples that can be viewed today at the University of Basle in Switzerland. His book, *Pinax theatri botanici*, provided a basis of plant descriptions for Carolus Linnaeus to develop the binomial system of classification. The *Bauhinia variegata*, pictured above, was named in honor of the Bauhin family.

MONOCOT

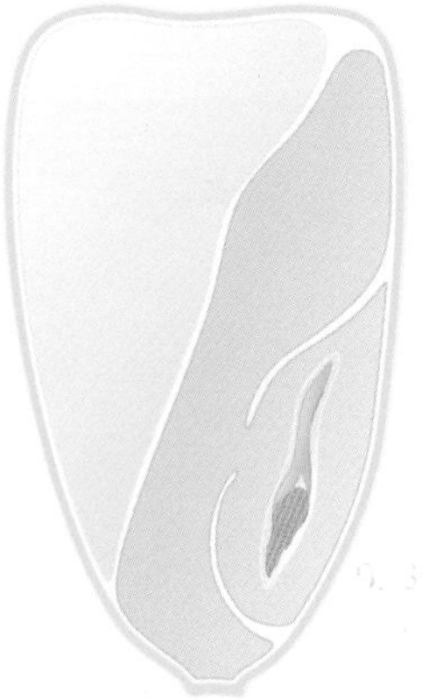

DICOT

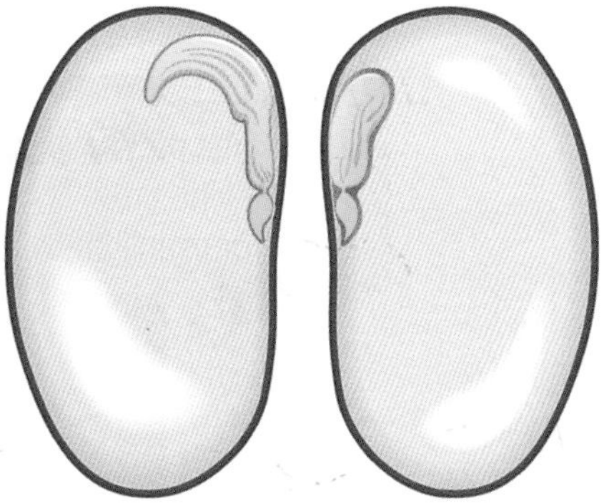

ANGIOSPERMS	
Monocots	**Dicots**
Leaves with parallel veins	Branching veins
Seed with 1 cotyledon	Seed with 2 cotyledons
Scattered vascular bundles in stems	Ring of vascular bundles
Multiples of 3 petals	Multiples of 4 or 5 petals

GYMNOSPERMS	
Conifers	**Other Types**
Needles	Ginkgo leaf and berry
Cones	Juniper berry and leaf
	Cycad cone with frond

VOCABULARY

tropism ('trō·pi·zəm) a positive or negative involuntary reaction of a plant to a stimulus

Plants react to their environments. This response is known as a tropism, which comes from the Greek word *trope* meaning *turn*. The reaction is in direct relationship to a stimulus—light, water, gravity, or a disturbance in the plant's environment.

One common tropism is phototropism. *Photo* is a prefix that means *light*. Phototropism refers to a plant's reaction to light. You may have observed a sunflower turning to face the sun during the day, or a plant placed on a windowsill growing toward the light. These are positive reactions. In contrast, vines growing on walls move away from light toward the darker, solid walls. This is an example of negative phototropism.

Hydrotropism is a plant's response to water that is beyond the normal response of growth. The effect of hydrotropism here on Earth can be seen in root systems of trees that grow along hillsides and beside rivers. Scientists have studied hydrotropism in the past by hanging plants within a cylinder packed with wet sawdust. The roots first grew downward in response to gravity, but then turned and grew upward in response to the moisture. Today, scientists are performing hydrotropic experiments in spaceflight.

QUICK FACT

In 1848, John Curtis of Bangor, Maine, produced the first commercial spruce gum—a chewing gum made of resin from spruce trees. By 1852 the Curtises had built a large chewing gum factory in Portland. As supplies of spruce gum diminished, manufacturers tried other chewables, such as paraffin, eventually turning to the latex of the chicle tree (*Manilkara zapota*). Chicle became the basis of the American Chicle Company, and for their product, Chiclets.

The stems of the trumpet vine grow away from sunlight.

Tree roots will grow toward a water source.

An observable tropism is a plant's response to gravity, known as *gravitropism*. The roots of a plant grow downward with the force of gravity. An opposite reaction known as *negative gravitropism* occurs when the stem and leaves of a plant grow toward the sun against the force of gravity. This is easily observed when a potted plant is turned on its side. In a day, the stems and leaves will begin to turn upward.

One of the most interesting tropisms is thigmotropism. This word comes from the Greek word *thigmo*, meaning *touch*. Some vines, such as sweet peas, need a pole or trellis for support. Scientists have found that when these vines find support, they attach to the surface. One side of the stem grows faster than the other, causing the vine to encircle the pole. Not all plants demonstrate a positive reaction. When a root or stem of a plant encounters an obstacle, it will grow around that object in the same way. Some plants close or curl up when touched.

What tropism is demonstrated by ivy encircling a pole?

LINKS

History Link
Research the history of the modern classification system. Prepare a report or a visual display of a timeline to present the information to the class.

Art Link
Design on paper a small flower garden for the entrance of your school. Your design will include trees, shrubs, and herbaceous plants in a variety of heights and colors. Illustrate each plant and label its common name, genus, and species. You may need to consult a gardening catalog, plant nursery, or the Internet.

Technology Link
Design a computer presentation to summarize the main points of the three domains and the three kingdoms discussed in this chapter.

The jungle has enveloped the Angkor Wat Temples of Cambodia. The Banyan tree roots respond to gravity as well as grow around obstacles.

The leaves of the sensitive plant, *Mimosa pudica*, curl up when lightly touched.

CHAPTER 2

CLASSIFICATION II

VOCABULARY

chordate ('kôr·dāt) an animal that has the beginnings of a backbone during one or more stages of development

exoskeleton (ˌek·sō·'ske·lə·tən) a hard, external covering of an animal

KEY IDEAS

- The animal kingdom consists of vertebrates and invertebrates.
- Ectothermic vertebrates, which include fishes, amphibians, and reptiles, are cold-blooded animals.
- Endothermic vertebrates, which include birds and mammals, are warm-blooded animals.
- Invertebrates are organisms that do not have a spine, but sometimes have an exoskeleton.

Animals are multicellular heterotrophs. The animal kingdom is divided into groups of vertebrates and invertebrates. Vertebrates have an internal spinal column. This joins to an internal skeletal structure that allows the animal to be more complex and support a greater weight. All vertebrates are chordates, which have a simple backbone called a *notochord* during at least one stage of development. This runs internally along the back of the body. Fish, amphibians, reptiles, birds, and mammals are all chordates.

In contrast, invertebrates never have a spinal column. Instead, many have a thick external covering called an exoskeleton. These animals are generally smaller than vertebrates. However, they have a much broader diversity and greater number of species. Scientists estimate that over 95% of animals alive today are invertebrates. There are eight major phyla of invertebrates which include—arthropods, mollusks, echinoderms, cnidarians, poriferans, annelids, platyhelminthes, and nematodes.

Common Name: Bald Eagle
Domain: Eukarya
Kingdom: Animal
Phylum: Chordata
Class: Aves
Order: Falconiformes
Family: Accipitridae
Genus: *Haliaeetus*
Species: *leucocephalus*
Strange but True
How does this fish survive frigid waters?

VERTEBRATES I

VOCABULARY

ectotherm ('ek·tə·thûrm) a cold-blooded animal whose body temperature fluctuates with the temperature of its environment

appendage (ə·'pen·dij) an external structure that extends from the main body

QUICK FACT

Fishes are able to see ultraviolet light, which people cannot see. This ability means colors look different to fish. Male fish usually have brighter coloring than female fish. Colors and patterns are used to hide from predators and to attract a mate. Fish scales are rigid, overlapping plates that contain enamel similar to teeth and allow the fish flexibility. A thin layer of mucous gives added protection.

An animal whose body temperature depends on its surrounding environment is an ectotherm. Three types of ectothermic vertebrates are fishes, amphibians, and reptiles. More than 25,000 species of fish in the waters of the world make up three classes—bony, cartilaginous, and jawless fishes. Bony fishes have a skeleton made of bones. Cartilaginous fishes have a skeleton composed of cartilage rather than bones. As the name implies, jawless fishes, such as the hagfish and the lamprey, have no jaws. These fish do not have hardened bones and are not true vertebrates, since they have no vertebrae. All fishes have appendages called *fins*. Fins are named by their location on the fish. Jawless fishes lack paired fins.

A fish's shape helps it live successfully in its environment. Shapes include depressed, compressed, torpedo, sphere or box, ribbon, and rod. Most fishes lay eggs in the water; however, some sharks carry their eggs internally or give birth to live young. Generally, fishes are covered with scales. Some scales actually have a growth ring that scientists examine to estimate the age of the fish. Fishes breathe with gills, which enable them to obtain oxygen from the water. Their fins provide balance and directional movement.

Anatomy of a Fish

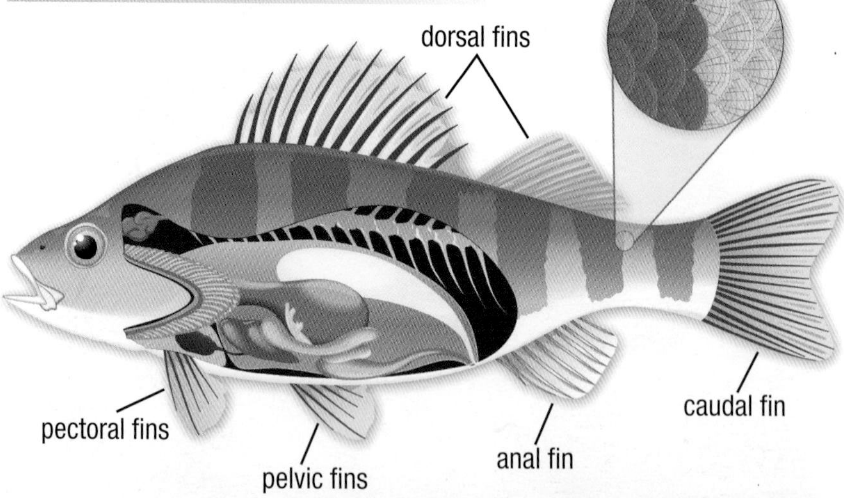

Strange but True

Antarctic fishes, such as the DeVries fish *Paraliparis devriesi*, are able to live in subzero temperatures because their blood contains proteins that work like antifreeze. In subzero temperatures, the water in a fish's blood freezes and begins to form ice crystals. The antifreeze proteins attach to the ice crystals and keep them from binding to other water molecules.

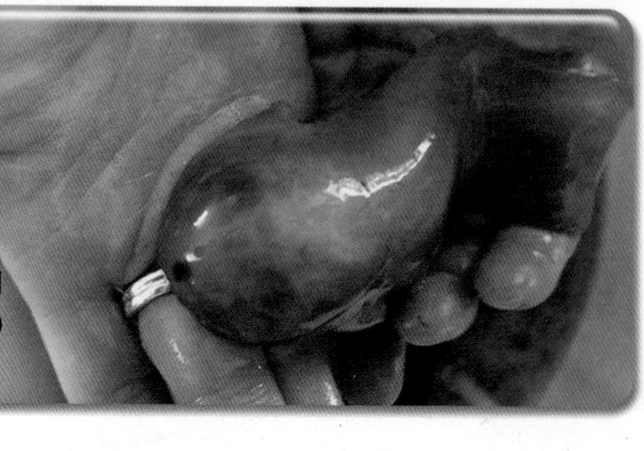

Amphibians are a class of animals defined by their metamorphosis. Early in life, they use gills to breathe. As they transition, lungs take the place of gills to allow amphibians to live on land. Even on land, many still need moisture in order to absorb oxygen through their skin. Three common amphibians are frogs, toads, and salamanders. The skin of both salamanders and frogs is smooth and moist. Toads, however, have dry, rough skin. Both frogs and toads lay their eggs in the water. Frog eggs are typically found in clusters, whereas toad eggs are in chains. Salamanders are tailed amphibians that generally live and lay eggs in or near water.

Reptiles are identified by scaly, waterproof skin. Snakes, turtles, tortoises, crocodiles, alligators, and lizards are all reptiles. Many live in or near water; however, most reptiles cannot breathe underwater. Most lay their eggs on land, but some unusual species produce live offspring. Evidence of reptile diversity is apparent on every continent except Antarctica.

IN THE FIELD

Many species of sea turtles are declining in population. Along with herpetologists who study sea turtle populations and habitats, volunteers rescue turtles and spread public awareness. One volunteer turtle lover was Ila Loetscher, known as the *Turtle Lady from Texas* (1905–2000). After moving to South Padre Island in her early 50s, the Kemp's Ridley turtles captured her attention. She began educating the community while nursing injured turtles back to health. Turtles that she could not release back to the ocean were kept in her yard. Raising support for this cause became her life's passion.

How can you tell the difference between an alligator and a crocodile?

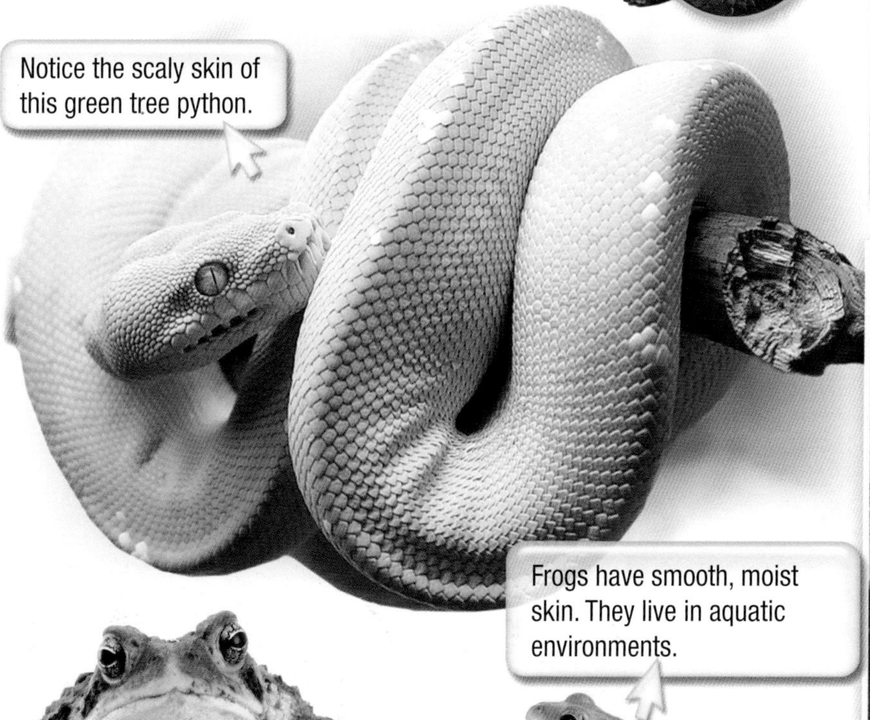

Notice the scaly skin of this green tree python.

A land tortoise may live for 100 years or more. The scaly skin on the legs identifies it as a reptile.

Frogs have smooth, moist skin. They live in aquatic environments.

Toads are very useful garden animals. They eat up to 1,000 insects a day!

VERTEBRATES II

VOCABULARY

endotherm ('en·dō·thûrm) a warm-blooded animal that maintains a constant internal temperature

keratin ('kâr·ə·tən) a strong, structural protein found in skin, hair, nails, and feathers

IN THE FIELD

This blue-footed bird is a native species of the Galapagos Islands. Ornithologists examine the shape, colors, markings, feathers, bills, legs, and feet of birds to identify them. They capture and tag birds to monitor population and migration habits. In addition to identifying birds, an ornithologist will also record the height and weight, determine age and overall health, and inspect them for evidence of disease. Birds are carriers of certain diseases that can be transmitted to humans and other animals.

Birds are one of the five major classes of vertebrates. They are endotherms, or warm-blooded animals, and have bills and wings, lay eggs, and live mostly on land. Birds are identified by their overall shape, their bills, and their feet. A perching bird's foot, with long, thin bones, is made for grasping branches. A predator bird has larger, longer talons for snatching prey. Ducks and other water birds were specially designed for paddling. The penguin foot is uniquely suited for crossing icy, rocky terrain and paddling through water.

A bird's most distinctive characteristic is its feathers. Different types of feathers have different functions. A down feather is fluffy and close to the skin. It helps insulate the bird by trapping body heat close to the skin. Contour feathers give birds shape and include the smooth, stream-lined flight feathers and tail feathers. Besides insulation, movement, and protection, feathers are used to attract mates and discourage or confuse predators. Feathers are made of keratin, which is a tough, fibrous protein found in skin, nails, hair, bills, feathers, horns, and hooves of many mammals.

Do penguins get cold feet?

The bee hummingbird of Cuba, the world's smallest bird, is about 5 cm (2 in.) long and its eggs are the size of a pinky fingernail. Its shape, long bill, and feet help it thrive in its environment.

The trumpeter swan, native to North America, is the largest waterfowl species, weighing 12–14 kg (26–30 lb) and having a wingspan over 2.1 m (7 ft).

Mammals are endotherms. They have common characteristics such as body hair, ear anatomy, and mammary glands. Hair varies in color, density, and function, though it may not be present throughout life. Mammals are also the only animals with three middle ear bones. The hammer, anvil, and stirrup transmit vibrations from the eardrum to the inner ear. All female mammals have mammary glands that produce milk to nourish their offspring.

The smallest mammals are shrews and bats. The Etruscan shrew is about the size of a cricket and lives in the lowlands of the Mediterranean area, from Portugal to the Middle East. Its weight is similar to a lightweight coin such as a dime. The bumblebee bat that lives in the bamboo forests and tea plantations of Thailand is about the size of a bumblebee. It weighs less than three paper clips. The blue whale is the largest mammal and can weigh up to 160 metric tons (176 tons). The largest land mammal is the bull African elephant with a record weight of over 7 metric tons (7.7 tons) and height of nearly 4 m (about 13 ft) at the shoulder.

QUICK FACT

Dairy cows typically have about 5% fat in their milk. However, marine mammals have a higher percentage of fat than land mammals. The hooded seal produces milk with the highest amount of fat—65%—and only nurses her young during the first four days of life. Over those four days, the seal pup typically more than doubles its birth weight from 20 kg (44 lb) to 43 kg (95 lb).

Hedgehogs are native to Africa, Asia, and Europe. They range in size from 16–35 cm (6–14 in.). Hedgehogs are nocturnal and eat insects.

Lions once roamed from Greece to Northern India and Africa. Now a small remnant inhabits India and the sub-Saharan region of Africa. A family of lions is called a *pride*. A lion's roar can be heard up to 8 km (5 mi) away.

INVERTEBRATES I

VOCABULARY

arthropod ('är·thrə·päd) an invertebrate that has a segmented body, jointed appendages, and usually an exoskeleton

crustacean (krəs·'tā·shən) a mainly aquatic arthropod that has a hard exoskeleton and two pairs of antennae

mollusk ('mä·ləsk) an invertebrate with a soft body that is typically enclosed in a shell

echinoderm (i·'kī·nə·dərm) an invertebrate that exhibits radial symmetry and a tough, spiny skin

Invertebrate species make up about 97% of all living animals. There is great diversity in this group. They range in size from as small as a bacteria to the largest of squids. Scientists have classified more than 30 invertebrate phyla. The largest phylum, arthropods, includes invertebrates with jointed appendages, a segmented bilateral body, and, in most species, an exoskeleton. There are more than one million known species in the world today. Arthropods molt their exoskeleton, which enables them to grow.

The insect class makes up over half of the total number of arthropods. Insects have six legs and three body segments. Arachnids are another common class of arthropods. They are distinct from insects, include spiders, and have common characteristics of eight legs and two body segments. Crustaceans are the most abundant class of marine arthropods. These often have harder, thicker exoskeletons called *carapaces*. Crabs, barnacles, shrimp, and lobsters are common examples of marine crustaceans. Barnacles are unique because they are stationary, using feathery tentacles to catch food from the water. Wood lice and land crabs are examples of terrestrial crustaceans.

How many eyes does a jumping spider have?

The loudest insects are male cicadas, which can be heard up to four football fields away. The male cicada attracts a female with his song.

The wood louse, also known as the *pill bug* or *roly-poly*, defends itself by rolling up into a ball. In this image, the louse is molting its exoskeleton.

Crabs have eyes on the ends of stalks as well as the unique ability to walk or run sideways.

The second largest group of invertebrates is the mollusks, which have soft, unsegmented bodies and an organ called a *foot*. Many are covered by one or more shells. Classes of mollusks include gastropods, bivalves, and cephalopods. Gastropods are mollusks with a single shell, such as a sea slug, conch, or snail. Most are carnivores. They all have antennae. Gastropods, such as the snail, have a muscular foot. Bivalves have two matching shells that hinge together and completely protect the animal's body. Oysters, clams, mussels, and scallops are filter-feeding bivalves. They strain food particles out of the water as the water passes over a special filtering structure. Cephalopods, the largest invertebrates, have tentacles and move by pumping water through their bodies. These include the squid, octopus, and nautilus.

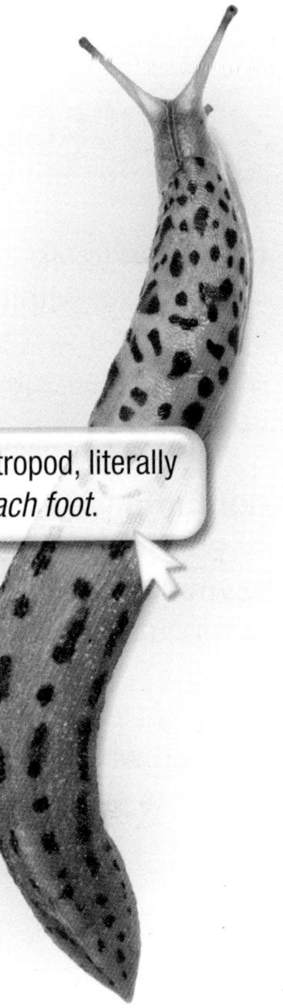

A slug is a gastropod, literally meaning *stomach foot*.

Sea urchins, sand dollars, sea cucumbers, and starfish all belong to the phylum of echinoderms. This term means *spiny skin*. These bottom-feeders only live in marine habitats and utilize water-filled chambers and tubular feet to move around. They feed on worms, mollusks, corals, sponges, crustaceans, and even fish on or near the seafloor. All echinoderms have radial symmetry. This means they have similar sections that are arranged around a central point.

Do clams have eyes?

These sea urchin exoskeletons, also known as *tests*, were found off the coast of Australia. The species *Coelopleurus exquisitus* has been placed on top of *Stereocidaris granularis*.

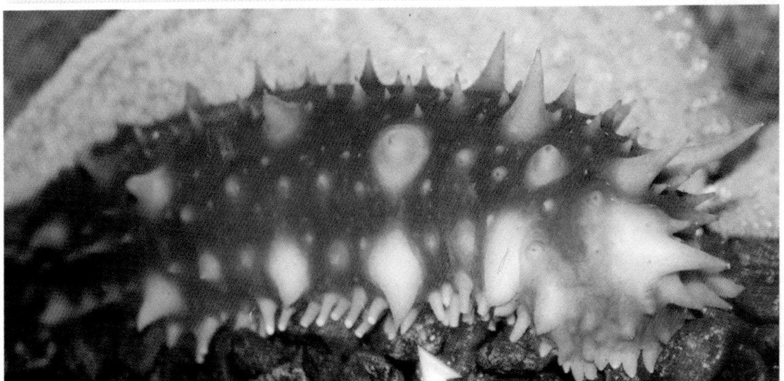

Sea cucumbers have skin covered with bumps or soft spines. When they are threatened, sea cucumbers constrict their muscles and shoot water from their body.

INVERTEBRATES II

VOCABULARY

cnidarian (nī·ˈdâr·ē·ən) an invertebrate with radial symmetry, a soft body, and tentacles with stinging capability

poriferan (pə·ˈrif·ə·rən) an invertebrate with a porous, asymmetrical body that pumps and filters water

ostia (ˈäs·tē·ə) the small pores through which water and nutrients enter a sponge

The word cnidarian comes from the Greek meaning *stinging nettle*. Animals in the cnidarian phylum possess the ability to sting as a way to obtain food and defend themselves. They have soft, radial-symmetric bodies that have two basic shapes—medusa and polyp. The medusa is bowl-shaped with tentacles and mouth pointing down, and the polyp has a can shape with tentacles and mouth pointing up. Most cnidarians are marine creatures, such as the jellyfish and the sea anemone. The smallest jellyfish, the Irukandji, is only 3.8 cm ($1\frac{1}{2}$ in.) across and nearly transparent. It lives near Australia and is very poisonous. The lion's mane jellyfish, which lives in the Arctic, can be up to 2.4 m (8 ft) across, with tentacles reaching 61 m (200 ft) long, making it the longest animal.

Poriferans are sponges. These aquatic animals come in a variety of shapes and colors. They attach themselves to solid objects, and most are found in shallow water in reefs. Sponges feed by drawing water in through their ostia, or small holes, and filtering out the nutrients. The water is then forced out through a larger opening. Sponges have only two layers of cells and spicules, or spikelike structures.

What relationship do these leatherback turtles have with jellyfish?

The mouth and tentacles of the medusa-shaped jellyfish point down. Those of the sea anemone point upward because of its polyp shape. When prey venture near, they are stung by the tentacles, paralyzed, and eaten.

A vase sponge is often home to shrimp and small crabs.

The most familiar kinds of worms are in the annelid phylum. Annelids, or segmented worms, have tube-shaped bodies that are divided into sections and contain a nerve center and digestive system. Similar to amphibians, they can breathe through their skin. This is one reason why they must stay moist. Annelids feed on plants and decayed animals called *carrion*. All these segmented worms use bristles to move. A common annelid is the earthworm. Other worms in this phylum include marine worms and leeches.

The platyhelminthes phylum contains unsegmented, flat-shaped worms, which can be found mostly in freshwater and saltwater, but sometimes in moist ground. The most familiar worms in this phylum are the parasitic tapeworm and the fluke. Not all platyhelminthes are parasitic, though. For example, some planarians eat decayed meat, live in freshwater, and have the ability to regenerate. Nematodes, or round worms, make up another phylum. They have a narrow, tubelike, unsegmented body and live in water and soil. Many nematodes are parasitic, such as the pinworm and ascaris.

What does this animal have in common with a popular holiday?

IN THE FIELD

The European Space Agency and NASA are studying the effects of cosmic radiation to understand what happens to astronauts in space. As a part of this study, worms smaller than grains of salt were carried aboard the International Space Station during 2007–2011. This species was selected because it has a short life span, making it easier to detect mutations in its DNA. Scientists noted no additional mutations due to the radiation in space, but observed that some worms experienced changes in their movement upon return to Earth.

This marine fireworm is classified with earthworms. Its name comes from the burning sensation felt if touched.

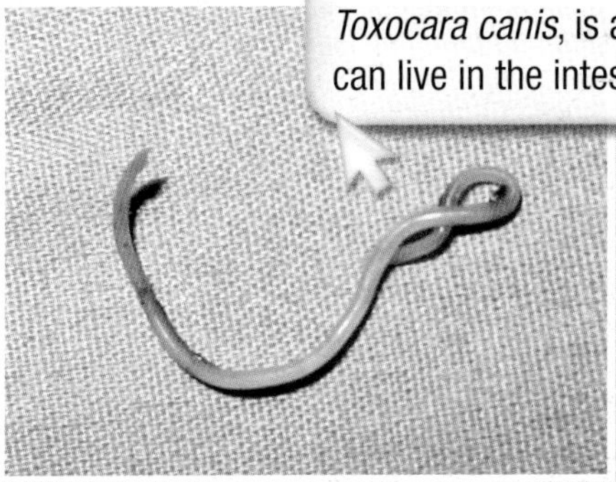

This nematode species, *Toxocara canis*, is a parasite that can live in the intestines of dogs.

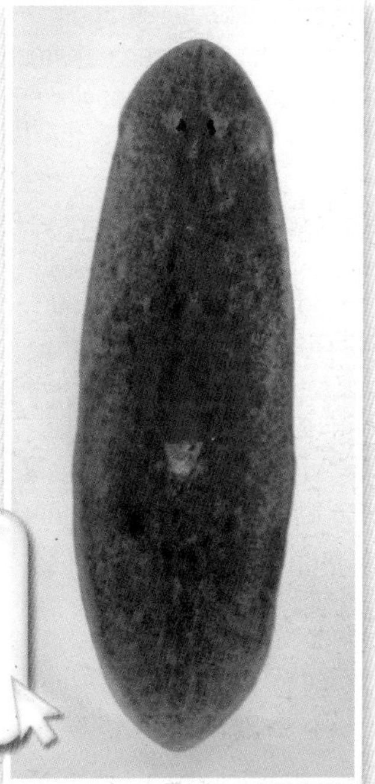

This is a flatworm in the platyhelminthes phylum. It is called a *planarian* and ranges in size from 3 to 12 mm ($\frac{1}{10}$ to $\frac{1}{2}$ in.).

VOCABULARY

biome (ˈbī·ōm) a large region that has a particular climate and specific plants and animals

QUICK FACT

The world's largest living lizard, *Varanus komodoensis*, is the carnivorous Komodo dragon. These beasts will even eat smaller Komodo dragons, a behavior called *cannibalism*. It has the ability to smell a rotting carcass as far away as 4 km (2.5 mi). The dragon flicks its tongue to sense chemicals in the air. When the tongue touches the roof of its mouth, the Jacobson's organ detects the chemical scent of other animals. The side of the tongue that has a higher concentration of scent indicates the direction of the animal. Native to Indonesia, Komodo dragons are a protected species that lives in the grasslands and forests.

A biome is a major life zone or vast ecological community. The temperature and amount of rainfall are the key elements of determining a biome. Due to these two factors, only certain plants can grow. The plant life then limits the variety of animals that can live in each region. There are six basic land biomes—arctic, taiga, temperate forest, grassland, tropical rain forest, and desert.

The arctic biome is the coldest and experiences strong, dry winds. The subsoil there is permanently frozen. Because of the tilt of the earth, this area undergoes prolonged times of darkness and light. Moss, lichen, cotton grass, sedge, and dwarf heath are common plants. Polar bears, penguins, walrus, seals, caribou, and mosquitoes are all classified as arctic animals, although mosquitoes live in almost every land biome.

The taiga, also known as the *boreal forest*, is the biome that is almost exclusively conifers. It occurs just below the timberline on a mountain or south of the arctic biome in the northern parts of North America, Europe, and Asia. Taigas are the largest land biome. Harsh coldness and low precipitation characterize this region. Moss covers the forest floor. Moose, reindeer, wolves, white owls, and ravens live there.

The polar bear lives in the arctic biome.

The temperate forest experiences four distinct seasons, where plant growth occurs during a four- to six-month span. Typical plants include maple, oak, elm, spruce, azalea, herbs, moss, and lichen. Squirrels, skunks, birds, deer, bobcat, wolf, fox, and black bear live there.

Grasslands are rolling hills of grasses and wildflowers and exist on every continent but Antarctica. Rainfall ranges from 25 to 76 cm (10 to 30 in.) annually while temperature varies from –40°C to 38°C (–40°F to 100°F). Grasshoppers, birds, rabbits, lions, rhinoceroses, and gazelles live in this biome.

Tropical rain forests have a thick canopy that does not let much light through to the dense vegetation below. The temperature only varies slightly, from 20° to 25°C (68° to 77°F). This biome contains a diverse selection of trees, as well as orchids, ferns, and moss, and is home to birds, bats, small mammals, insects, reptiles, and amphibians.

Deserts and arid regions cover 20% of the earth's surface and receive less than 50 cm (20 in.) of rain per year. Cactus, shrubs, and low-lying woody trees can exist in this harsh environment. Reptiles and kangaroo mice are some animals that survive there.

LINKS

Math Link
Choose an herbivore, carnivore, and omnivore from a particular biome. Research the average amount of food eaten in a day by each animal. Create a chart showing the differences in amounts of food consumed. Develop a graph that shows the average weight of the animals compared to the type and amount of food eaten.

Art Link
Create a poster or diorama of a biome, showing native plants and animals. Include one animal from each of the nine major phyla of the Animal Kingdom.

Geography Link
Select any migratory animal, such as the swallow or the wapiti, and chart its migration on a world map. Calculate the distance covered. Describe five characteristics of the animal as well as its full classification.

The omnivorous meerkats, which live in African grasslands, eat fruits, roots, eggs, grubs, beetles, and even scorpions.

CHAPTER 3

CELL PROCESSES

KEY IDEAS

- Organelles perform specific functions in cells.
- Materials pass through the cell membrane by passive and active transport.
- Cells reproduce by mitosis, and reproductive cells are formed during meiosis.
- Cells produce energy through cellular respiration or fermentation.

Cells are the basic units of life. They are complex in structure and function. They contain cytoplasm and organelles, enclosed by a cell membrane. Cells have intricate communication systems that use chemical and electrical signals. These signals can be sent to nearby cells or directed to a target cell or organ in the body. They also respond to their environment. DNA provides the genetic information that directs cell processes. Much like organs in a human body, organelles have specific functions that maintain homeostasis, or balanced cell health, within the cell. Energy is produced in the cell and is used as fuel to help the cell function. All cells undergo a sequence of events called *the cell cycle*. Once a healthy cell matures, it will produce an exact copy of itself through mitosis, which is required for growth and replacement of older cells.

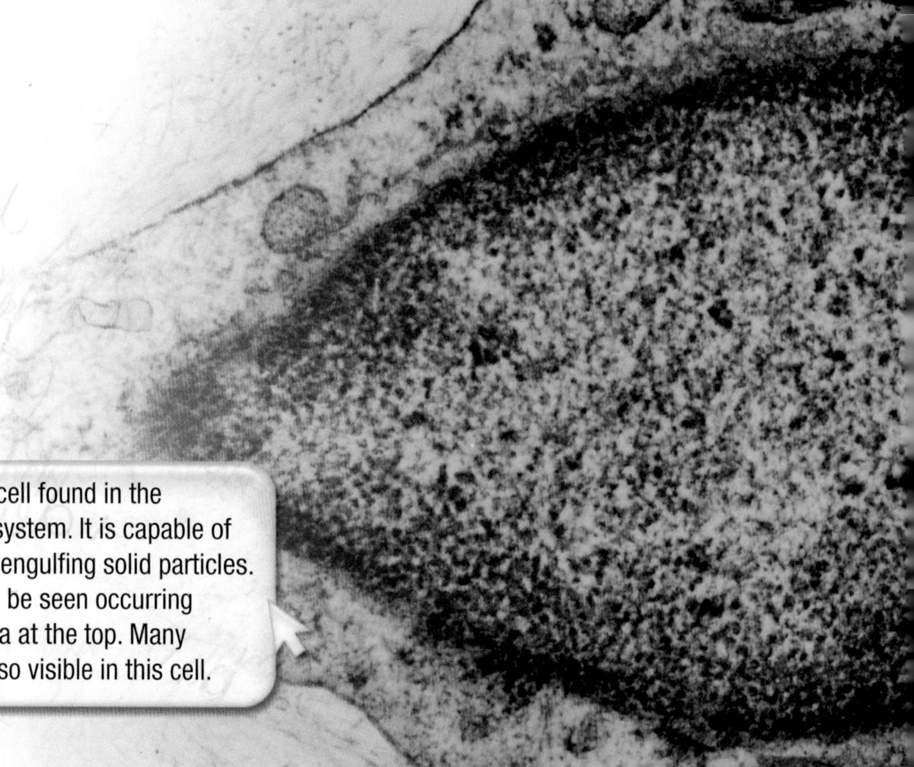

This is a type of cell found in the central nervous system. It is capable of phagocytosis, or engulfing solid particles. This process can be seen occurring in the circled area at the top. Many organelles are also visible in this cell.

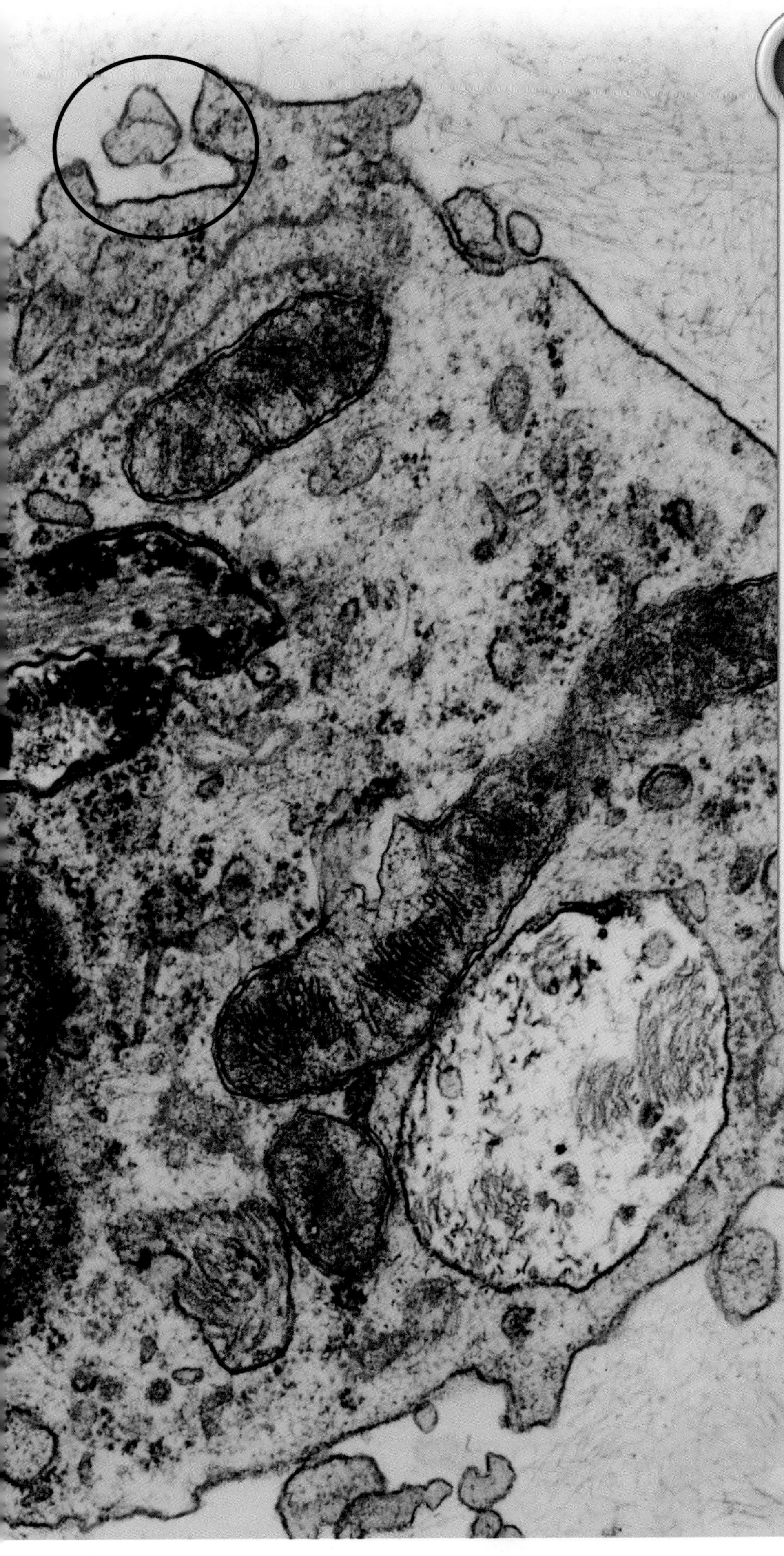

QUICK FACT

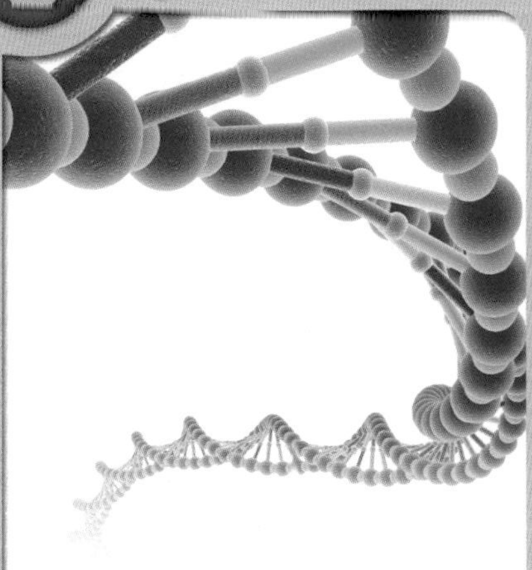

Deoxyribonucleic acid, or DNA, is made of a combination of paired molecules called *nitrogen bases.* There are four different types of these bases that form the rungs of the DNA ladder. They are arranged in specific order and provide the genetic information found in genes that specifies what type of protein will be made. Proteins are made of amino acids. The sequence of the nitrogen bases in the gene determines the order in which the amino acids are put together to form the protein. Proteins, in turn, determine the characteristics of the organism.

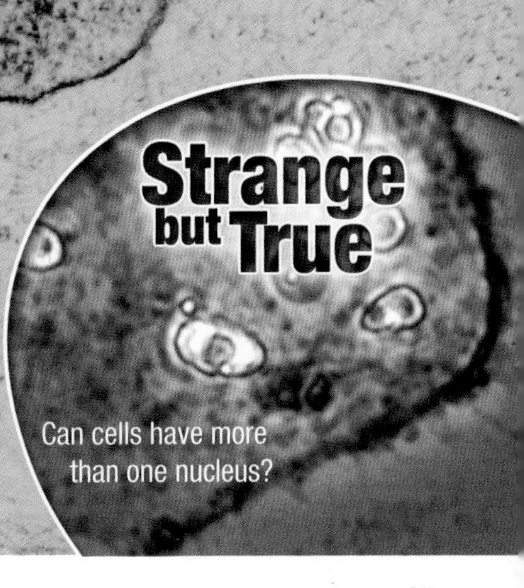

CELL STRUCTURE

VOCABULARY

mitochondrion (ˌmī·tə·ˈkän·drē·ən) an organelle that produces energy from food

vacuole (ˈva·kyə·wōl) a membrane-bound sac within a cell or tissues that stores water or other materials

ribosome (ˈrī·bə·sōm) an organelle responsible for protein synthesis

endoplasmic reticulum (ˈen·də·plaz·mik ri·ˈti·kyə·ləm) a network of passageways within a cell that transports materials

All cells contain organelles that perform different functions within the cell. The nucleus contains DNA and directs all the cell's activities. The cell membrane controls what enters and exits the cell. Each mitochondrion converts glucose, or sugar, into energy and is often called *the powerhouse of the cell*. Water, wastes, food, and other materials are stored in a vacuole until they are needed or released through the cell membrane. A plant cell usually has one large vacuole. Animal cells may or may not have vacuoles. A ribosome is the site of protein production. Some ribosomes are found floating in the cytoplasm. Others are attached to some of the surfaces of the endoplasmic reticulum, which is like a maze of passageways that carries materials throughout the cell. The Golgi body receives materials from the endoplasmic reticulum, then packages and sends them to other parts of the cell. The lysosome contains digestive enzymes that break down food particles as well as old cell parts. The substances are then released and used again by the cell. In plant cells, photosynthesis takes place in the chloroplasts, which contain chlorophyll, a chemical that absorbs light energy and gives leaves their green color. Plant cells also have a cell wall made of cellulose that helps support and protect the cell.

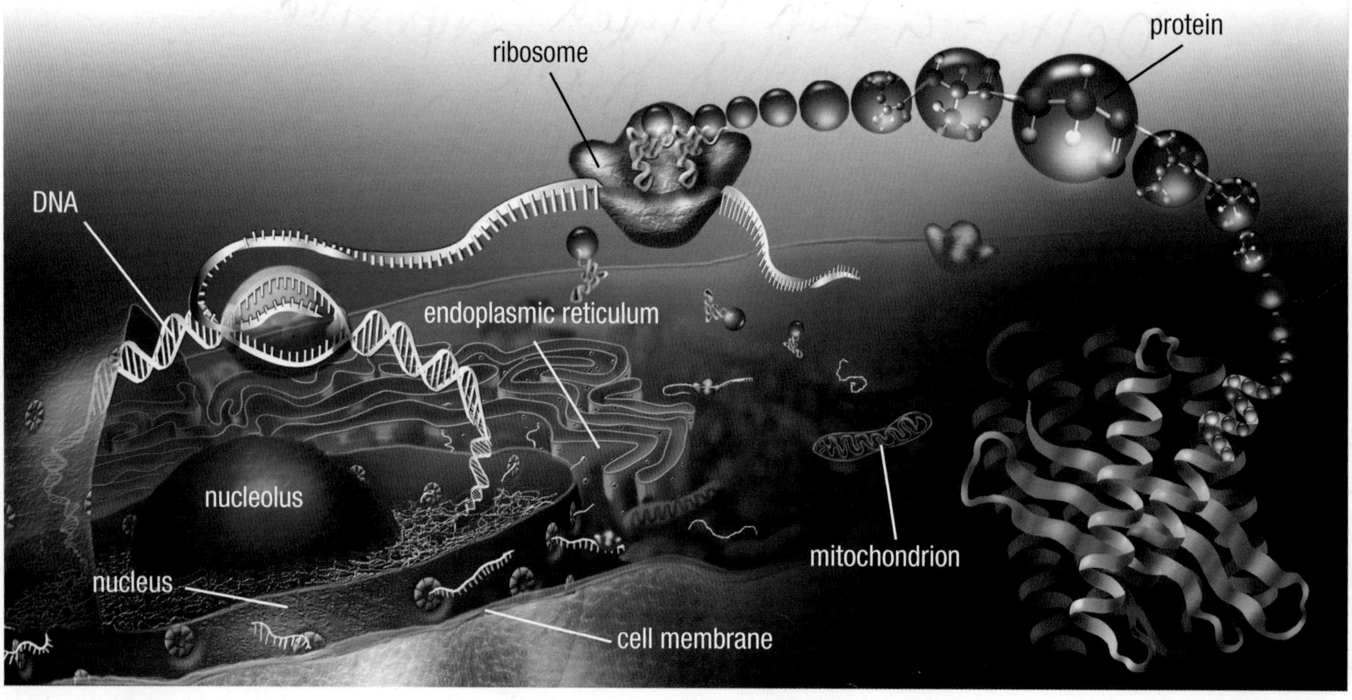

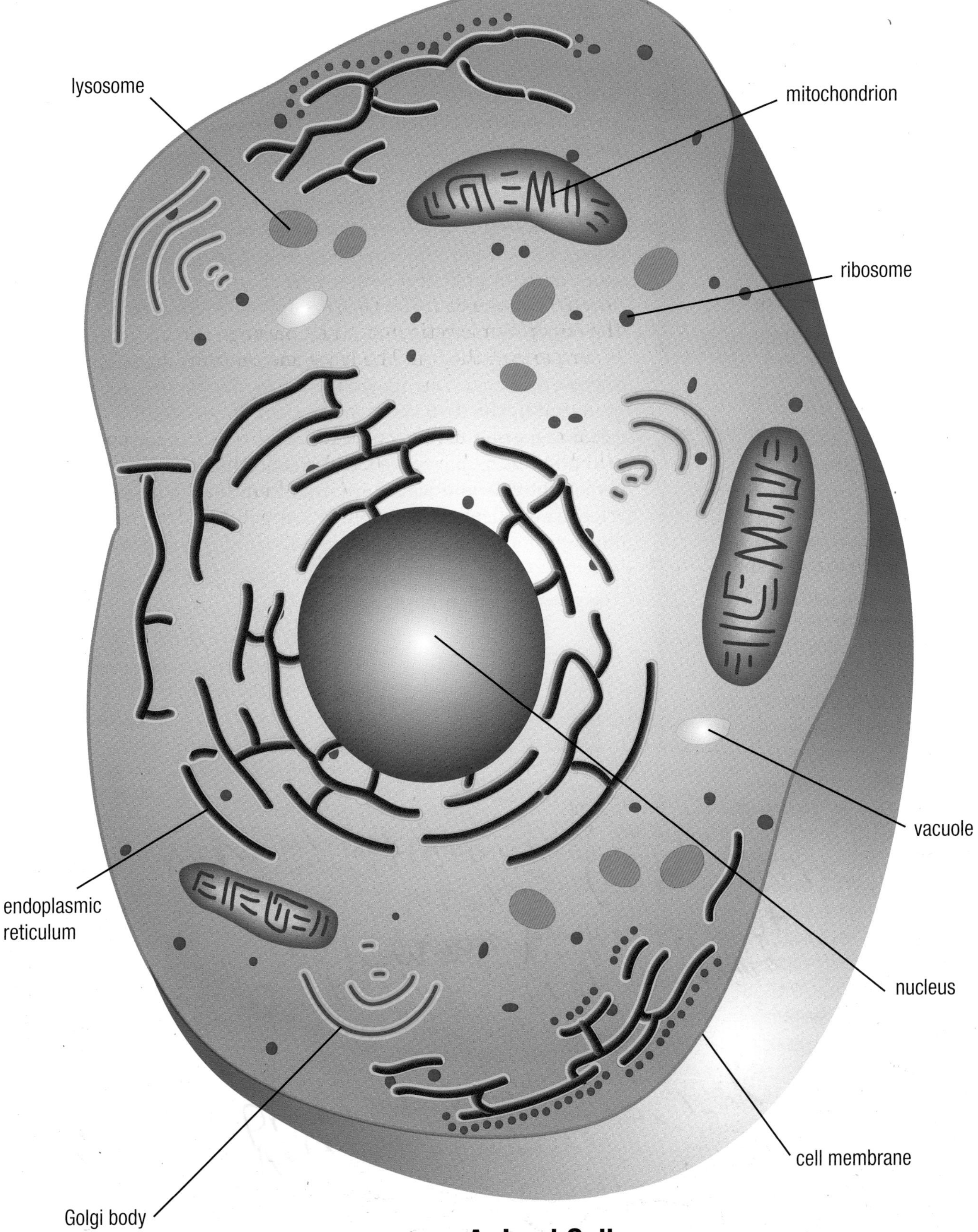
lysosome
mitochondrion
ribosome
vacuole
endoplasmic
reticulum
nucleus
cell membrane
Golgi body

Animal Cell

CELLULAR RESPIRATION

VOCABULARY

glucose ('glo͞o·kōs) the simplest form of sugar, used as a source of energy

fermentation (fər·mən·'tā·shən) the process in which cells break down molecules without the use of oxygen

QUICK FACT

Glucose is also known as *blood sugar*. It is the fuel for cells that comes from food eaten. If the blood sugar level drops to lower than normal levels, hypoglycemia results. This is evidenced by symptoms such as dizziness, shakiness, nervousness, sleepiness, and weakness. Eating small meals every few hours can help alleviate hypoglycemia. Diabetes, on the other hand, occurs when glucose levels are higher than normal. Insulin, the hormone needed to convert sugar into energy, is not being produced or used by the body sufficiently. This causes glucose levels to spike. Medical professionals should monitor both conditions.

Plant cells use carbon dioxide, water, and light to make food, or glucose. The production of glucose in plants is known as *photosynthesis*. Cellular respiration occurs when bacteria, plant, fungi, and animal cells convert this simple sugar of plants to make energy. During cellular respiration, cells break down food molecules and release their stored energy. This occurs in three main stages.

The first stage of cellular respiration takes place in the cytoplasm of the cell. Here, molecules of glucose are broken down into smaller molecules. Oxygen is not involved. Only a small amount of energy is released. The next two stages require oxygen. In eukaryotes—those organisms having both a nucleus and organelles—these two stages occur in the mitochondria. In prokaryotes—bacteria and archaea—the process continues in the cytoplasm. During these stages, the smaller molecules produced in the first stage are broken down even further, which releases a great deal of energy. This is why the mitochondria are called *the powerhouses* of the cell. In addition to energy, carbon dioxide and water are produced. This is what a person releases into the air when he or she exhales. Oxygen is taken in during inhalation and is a raw material for respiration.

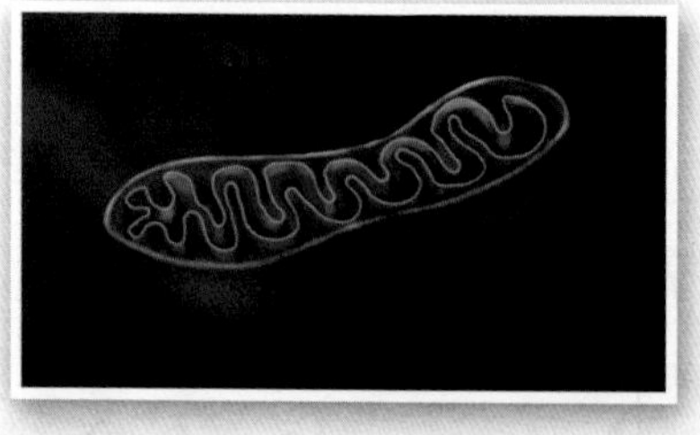

During respiration, the mitochondria of animal cells use glucose and oxygen. Carbon dioxide and water are released.

$$C_6H_{12}O_6 + 6\ O_2 \longrightarrow 6\ CO_2 + 6\ H_2O$$

Plants cells use carbon dioxide and water plus light energy to produce glucose and oxygen in the chloroplasts during photosynthesis.

$$6\ CO_2 + 6\ H_2O \xrightarrow{\text{(+ light energy)}} C_6H_{12}O_6 + 6\ O_2$$

Sometimes not enough oxygen is available for cellular respiration to occur. For example, some single-celled organisms live in the depths of the ocean or deep within Earth's crust where there is no oxygen. In these situations, cells are still able to obtain energy through **fermentation**. In this process, oxygen is not required to produce energy. However, the amount of energy released is much less than the amount released during cellular respiration. There are two common types of fermentation—lactic acid fermentation and alcohol fermentation.

The entire process of fermentation takes place in the cytoplasm. Glucose molecules are first broken down into smaller molecules. In lactic acid fermentation, the molecules are further broken down and make the by-product lactic acid—a toxic substance to the cells. This type of fermentation is performed by some fungi and bacteria and occasionally by the muscles in humans. Alcohol fermentation occurs in yeast and certain kinds of bacteria. The waste products in this process are alcohol and carbon dioxide. Both types of fermentation occur naturally in many different types of foods. Humans have used these processes for thousands of years to produce items like pickles and yogurt.

IN THE FIELD

Normally, muscles perform cellular respiration, using oxygen to supply the energy needed for them to function. However, during strenuous exercise or great exertion, the oxygen supplied by the lungs and blood cannot get to the muscles fast enough. In these cases, the muscle cells switch to lactic acid fermentation. During this process, the production of energy occurs without oxygen. Lactic acid is a by-product. The presence of lactic acid in the muscles causes a stiff and sore feeling the next day. The soreness goes away after a few days of oxygen-rich respiration.

Cellular respiration, or aerobic respiration, requires oxygen. Yeast can produce energy without oxygen through fermentation, or anaerobic respiration. The carbon dioxide that is released causes bread dough to rise, leaving tiny holes after it is baked. All alcohol evaporates when the bread is baked.

VOCABULARY

diffusion (di·ˈfo͞o·zhen) the movement of molecules from an area of higher concentration to an area of lower concentration

osmosis (äz·ˈmō·səs) the diffusion of water through a membrane that allows specific substances to pass through

The flexible cell membrane separates the cell's contents from the environment around it. It surrounds the cell and provides shape, support, and protection. It also determines what can enter and exit the cell. The cell membrane is selectively permeable. This means it has openings that allow only specific particles to pass through. These particles move through the cell membrane in one of two ways—either passive or active transport. Passive transport does not require the cell to use energy to help move the particles. Active transport does require extra energy.

Diffusion is a type of passive transport. It is the process by which particles move from an area of higher concentration of substances to an area of lower concentration. Oxygen enters and carbon dioxide exits the cell by diffusion. Osmosis is another form of passive transport that involves the movement of water molecules across a membrane. If a cell is placed in pure water, the water will move into the cell until equilibrium is reached or the membrane bursts. In contrast, if the concentration of water is higher inside the cell than outside, water leaves the cell. This can lead to dehydration. Equilibrium occurs when the concentration of water inside the cell matches that outside the cell.

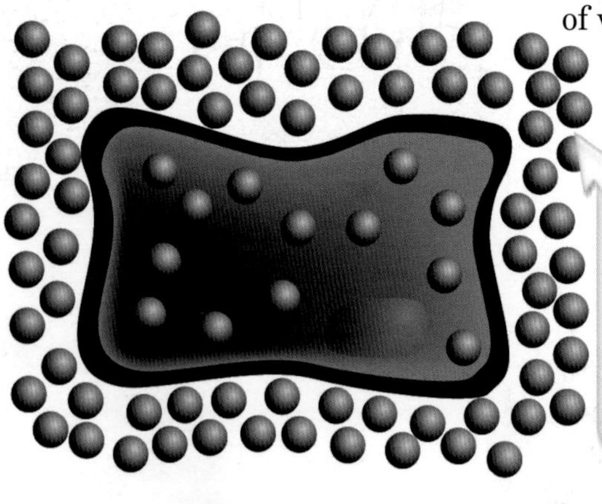

The concentration of particles before diffusion is greater outside the cell than inside. Diffusion moves particles from the area of higher concentration to the area of lower concentration until equilibrium is reached.

Before

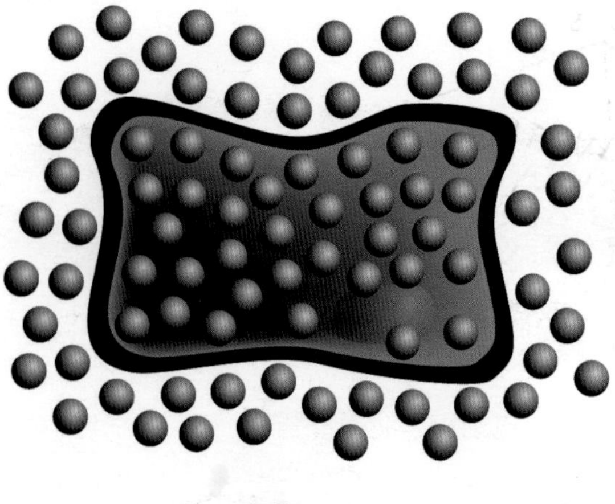

After

Wilting is evidence that water inside the cells has moved through the cell membranes and out of the cells.

Glucose and some types of sodium, potassium, and chlorine molecules cannot diffuse through membranes. However, in a type of passive transport called *facilitated diffusion,* molecules are able to cross the cell membrane because they are helped, or facilitated, by transport proteins. These special proteins are located throughout the cell membrane. The molecules bind to the proteins, which then transport them into or out of the cell. Once the substance is bound, the transport protein changes shape and carries the substance across the cell membrane.

Sometimes a cell needs more of a substance that has a higher concentration inside the cell than outside. To move that material into the cell requires extra energy. Active transport is the process by which materials are actively pumped through the cell membrane. Often other cells, fragments, or proteins may be too large to pass through the membrane. Instead, the membrane will engulf these large particles. This form of active transport occasionally involves the cell creating a vacuole around the engulfed materials. Lysosomes then break down the materials so that they are digestible. A cell can also actively move wastes or other unwanted materials outside the cell. The cell membrane wraps around the vacuole and pinches off, releasing the vacuole and its contents outside the cell.

OUTLOOK

Without water, life ceases. Water accounts for approximately 66% of the human body and 75% of the human brain. Throughout the Scriptures, God compares Himself with water. In Jeremiah 2, God is referred to as *the spring of living water.* Jesus said that whoever drinks of the water He gives will never thirst again. Based on what you have learned, why do you think God would compare Himself to water?

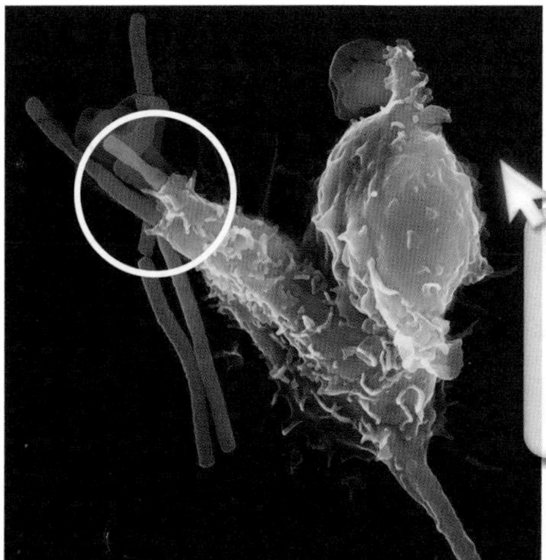

Cells perform a special form of active transport to bring other live cells or fragments into the cytoplasm. This engulfing action is called *phagocytosis,* which means *cell-eating.*

The cell membrane is a two-layered structure with proteins embedded throughout the membrane. These proteins act as gatekeepers, carrying substances of specific sizes and shapes in and out of the membrane.

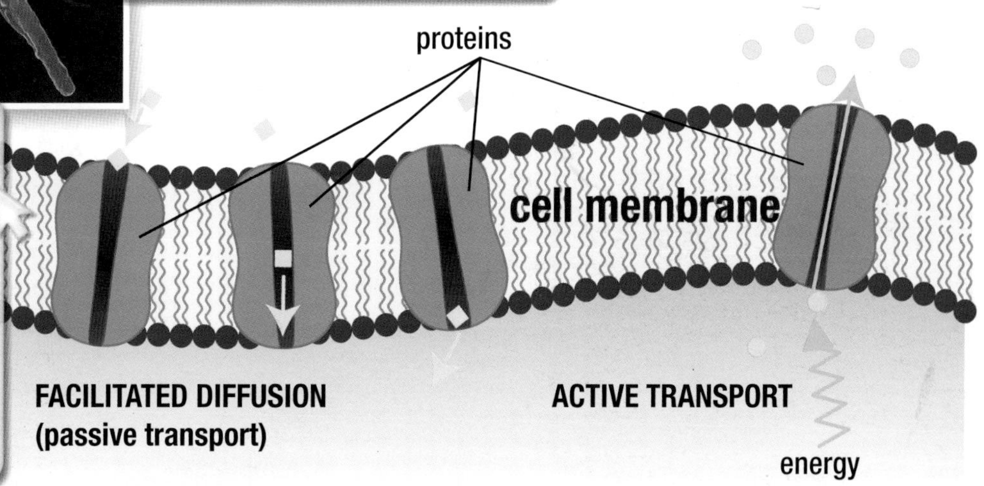

CELL DIVISION

VOCABULARY

somatic cell (sō·ˈma·tik ˈsel) a body cell other than a reproductive cell

chromatid (ˈkrō·mə·təd) one of the two strands of a duplicated chromosome

meiosis (mī·ˈō·səs) the type of cell division that produces reproductive cells

gamete (ˈga·mēt) a mature male or female reproductive cell

QUICK FACT

Cells undergo mitosis to reproduce, for growth and development, and to replace dead or damaged cells. The cells of your skin and intestine are replaced every few days. There are more than 25 million cell divisions occurring in mitosis every second in the human body. Research indicates that even some brain cells may undergo mitosis.

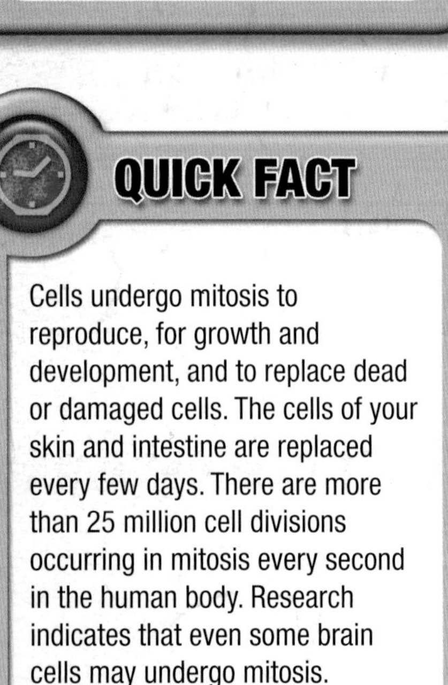

There are two types of cells in the human body—somatic cells and gametes. A somatic cell makes up body tissues and organs. It contains two sets of chromosomes. Somatic cells duplicate themselves by dividing into two new cells. The two daughter cells are exact copies of the original parent cell. This cell division involves three stages: interphase, mitosis, and cytokinesis. Interphase is the first and longest stage. The cell grows, makes a copy of its DNA, and prepares for division.

The nucleus divides during the second stage called *mitosis*. Mitosis has four phases of its own. The first is prophase, in which the duplicated DNA condenses to form X-shaped chromosomes. Each strand in the chromosome is called a chromatid. Paired chromatids are held together in the middle by a structure called a *centromere,* which gives them an *X* shape. The nuclear membrane breaks down and spindle fibers appear. The second phase is metaphase. The chromosomes line up along the middle of the cell and attach to spindle fibers. The third phase is anaphase. The chromosomes separate at their centromeres and move toward the opposite sides of the cell. In the fourth phase—telophase—the chromosomes uncoil, two new nuclear membranes form, and the spindle fibers disappear.

Cytokinesis is the final stage of cell division. The cytoplasm separates into two parts, forming two identical daughter cells with separate cell membranes. This cycle of cell division involving mitosis continues throughout the life of the organism, multiplying body cells for growth, development, and repair.

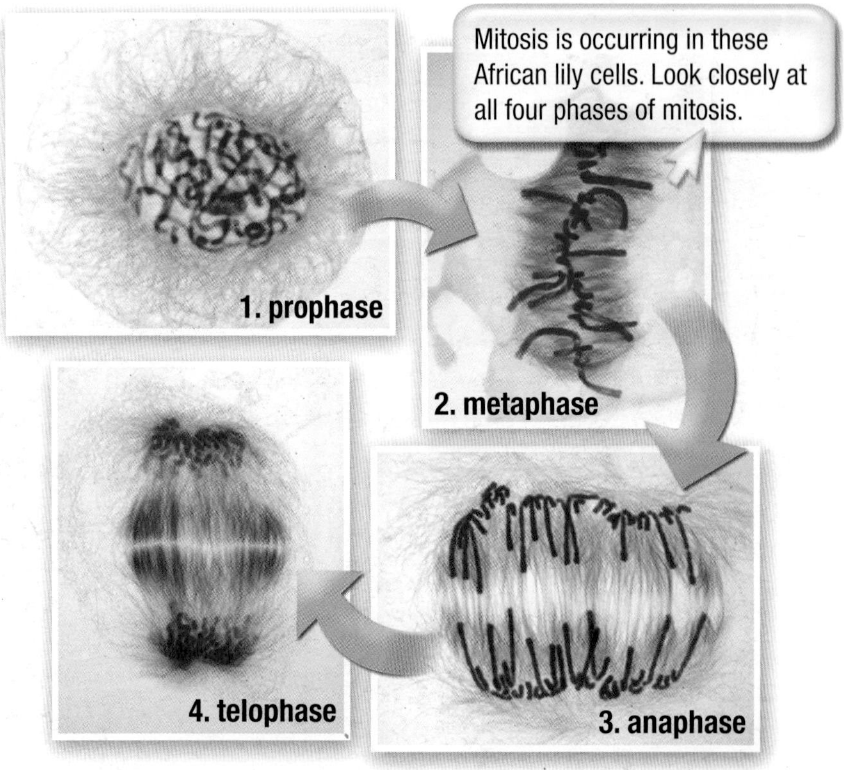

Meiosis is also a process of cell division, but it produces reproductive cells. It differs from mitosis in several ways. At the end of mitosis, the two daughter cells, which are identical, each contain two complete sets of chromosomes, for a total of 46 chromosomes. In meiosis, a cell divides two times, ending with four daughter cells that are not identical. Each daughter cell is a gamete that contains only one set of 23 chromosomes. During sexual reproduction, a male gamete joins with a female gamete. When these two gametes combine to form one new, unique cell, their number of chromosomes equals those found in a somatic cell.

Meiosis occurs in two stages—meiosis I and meiosis II. In meiosis I, the DNA replicates to have 46 chromosomes in each daughter cell. Their chromatids are held together by centromeres. In humans, each cell has two sets of 23 chromosomes—one maternal set from the female cell and one paternal set from the male cell. When the chromosomes line up down the middle in meiosis I, each maternal chromosome pairs up with its similar paternal chromosome. The pairs of like chromosomes separate, but the centromeres remain intact. Then the chromosomes, each still with two chromatids, migrate to opposite poles. Two new cells form, each having 46 chromosomes. In meiosis II, the chromosomes align down the middle. The chromatids separate at their centromeres and migrate to opposite poles. The result is four gametes that have one set of 23 chromosomes each.

IN THE FIELD

Occasionally, during meiosis I, paired chromosomes fail to separate. Both chromosomes may migrate together to one pole. A gamete with a missing or extra chromosome can cause serious abnormalities known as *genetic disorders*. Geneticists analyze the chromosomes of a cell by arranging them in pairs. The chart they use is called a *karyotype*.

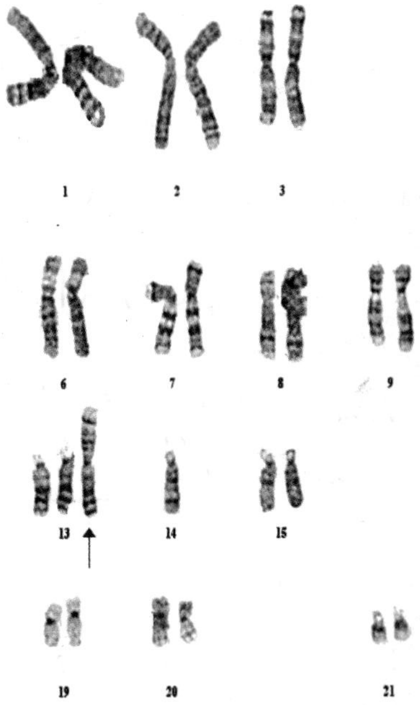

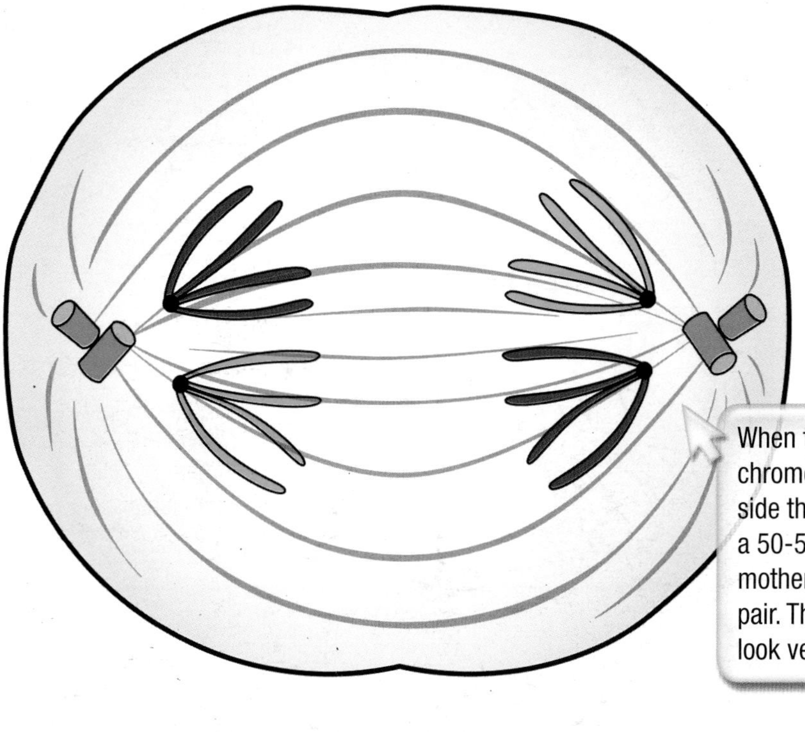

When the paternal and maternal chromosomes pair up during meiosis I, the side they end up on is random. This gives a 50-50 chance for the gamete to get the mother's or father's chromosome for each pair. This explains why some siblings may look very different from one another.

REPRODUCTION

VOCABULARY

binary fission ('bī·nə·rē 'fi·shən) a type of asexual reproduction in which a cell divides into two parts

budding ('bə·ding) a type of asexual reproduction that involves the outgrowth of a small part of the parent, which develops into a new organism

IN THE FIELD

Genetic engineers use bacterial cells to produce human proteins like insulin. These scientists remove DNA from the bacterial cells, use enzymes to open the DNA, and insert the gene for the protein they want produced. The human gene and the bacterial DNA fuse before being reinserted into the bacteria. As bacteria grow and reproduce, they produce the human protein that scientists then harvest for human use.

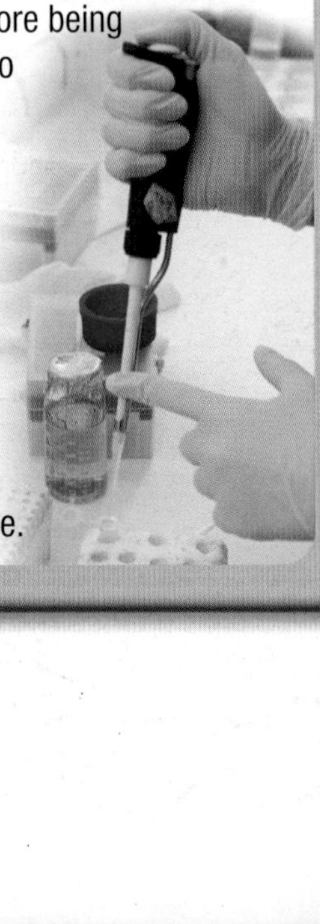

Most multicellular organisms reproduce when a male and a female gamete join and form a zygote. This is called *sexual reproduction*. Most unicellular organisms reproduce by a process called *asexual reproduction*. This means they form offspring from parent cells without forming a zygote. Prokaryotes, or bacteria, many protists, and even some algae and worms reproduce asexually using a process called binary fission. Binary fission occurs when one parent cell grows to about twice its normal size. After this, a copy of the DNA is made and the parent cell begins to split in two. The cell membrane surrounds each half, forming two identical new cells. Numerous bacterial cells complete binary fission in just a matter of minutes.

Spores are another way in which bacteria, fungi, and some plants can reproduce asexually. In this case, capsule-shaped spores, which contain DNA, sprout new organisms on their own. This is in contrast to the production of most seeds, which are produced from sexual reproduction.

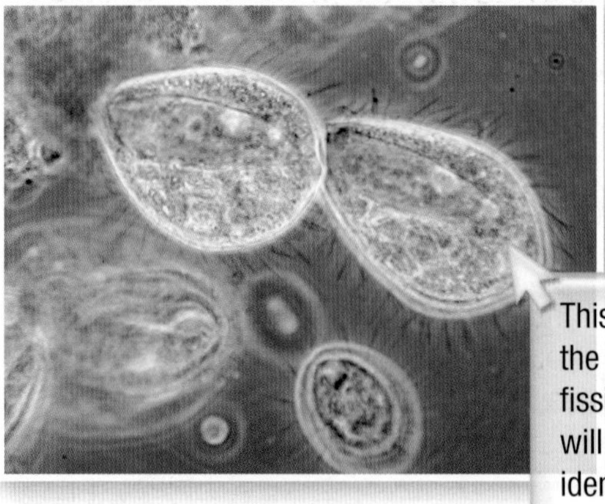

This ciliated protist is in the final stages of binary fission. Two new organisms will be produced, each identical to the original parent cell.

Strange but True

A cell that has many nuclei is called a *syncytium*. Skeletal muscle cells, slime molds, and cancer cells have multiple nuclei.

Asexual reproduction is not limited to unicellular organisms. Some multicellular organisms can also reproduce without using gametes. Corals, sponges, tapeworms, some fungi, and certain cnidarians, such as the hydra, are examples of multicellular organisms that can reproduce through budding. The budding process involves a part of the parent's body breaking away. The released bud becomes an entirely new organism that is genetically identical to the parent. In some species, such as corals, the new organism remains attached to the parent. Budding is also commonly seen in yeast, a unicellular fungus.

Vegetative reproduction is a common type of asexual reproduction found in plants. Here, growth from the parent plant eventually becomes new individual plants. Strawberries, potatoes, and onions reproduce in this manner.

The process of asexual reproduction is efficient and fast. Organisms do not use their cellular energy to make gametes or find mates. Offspring are genetically identical to the parent, which means if the parents could survive in the surrounding environment, the offspring can too—as long as there is not much change in the environment.

LINKS

Language Arts Link
Write a story that compares a cell and the functions of its organelles with a factory, a city, a household, or a school. Include analogies of the parts of the cell and the parts of the example you are using for comparison.

Music Link
Write a song about mitosis or meiosis. Be sure to use the words *prophase, metaphase, anaphase,* and *telophase.* Your lyrics should explain why the cell goes through these processes and the results of each type of division. Perform your song for the class.

History Link
Research the work of James Watson and Francis Crick. Also search for information regarding the work of Rosalind Franklin and how it contributed to Watson and Crick's landmark announcement about DNA. Write an essay about your findings and include a bibliography.

The eyes on these potatoes are growths for vegetative reproduction.

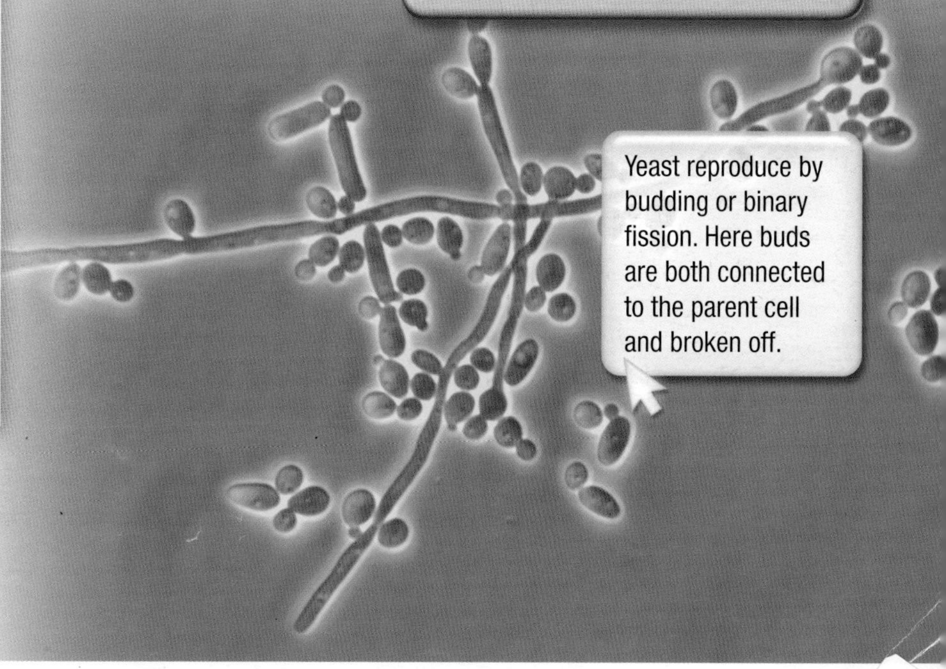

Yeast reproduce by budding or binary fission. Here buds are both connected to the parent cell and broken off.

HEREDITY AND GENETICS

CHAPTER 4

It may not always be obvious, but every individual receives an inheritance from his or her natural parents. Each person has thousands of genes—codes that determine appearance, development, and the formation of individual proteins. Each gene has been contributed by the father and mother. The characteristics that are passed down from the parents to their offspring are traits. The passing of traits is called heredity. The field of science that researches heredity is called *genetics*. Geneticists sometimes study organisms that reproduce asexually. The main focus of their study, however, is offspring resulting from sexual reproduction. In most instances, genes can only continue to be successfully passed on if the offspring are produced by parents who are of the same species.

VOCABULARY

trait ('trāt) a characteristic that is inherited

heredity (hə·'re·də·tē) the passing of traits from parent to offspring

KEY IDEAS

- God designed living things to reproduce with their own kind.
- Genetics is the study of how traits are passed from parents to their offspring.
- Traits are determined by genes that are contained in DNA and carried on chromosomes.

Diversity is found all around the world in living and nonliving things. While humans are made in God's image, each individual has his or her own unique traits. These traits are passed from parent to offspring through genetic information. Genes determine an organism's characteristics.

QUICK FACT

Throughout history, the definition of the word *species* has changed. Today, it is generally understood that animals of the same species are those that are similar enough to each other that they can mate and produce fertile offspring. While a donkey and a horse are similar, they are not a single species since their offspring are generally infertile. A mule is the offspring of a male donkey and a female horse. Although the mule is a genetic recombination of its parents, it is naturally infertile. A hinny is the offspring of a female donkey and a male horse. It is usually infertile.

Strange but True

Are fingerprints inherited?

GREGOR MENDEL

VOCABULARY

genotype ('jē·nə·tīp) the set of genes that make up an organism

phenotype ('fē·nə·tīp) the observable characteristics of an organism's genotype

IN THE FIELD

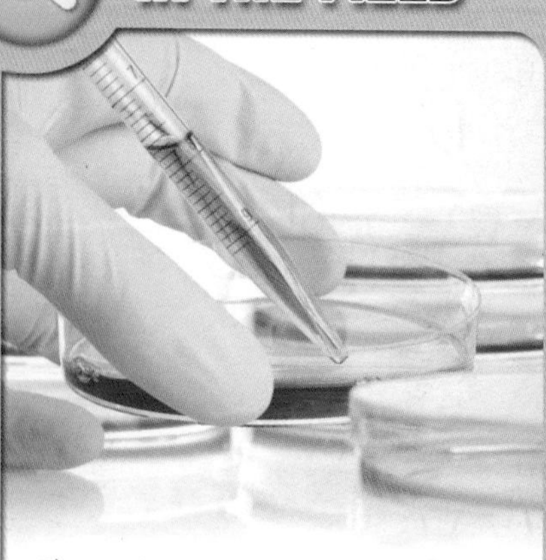

Geneticists study heredity. Modern geneticists are research scientists who study family traits and DNA to analyze a genetic disease. They compare the DNA of individuals affected with a particular genetic disease to those who are unaffected. Geneticists often work for many years, or even their entire careers, attempting to answer the question of which gene causes a particular disease.

In the 1850s, a young priest named Gregor Mendel tended a garden in an Augustinian monastery in Austria. Mendel, who would later be considered *the Father of Genetics*, noticed that both animals and plants pass certain traits to their offspring. He also observed that other traits do not seem to be inherited by offspring.

Mendel began experimenting and observing traits in mice. When he was forced by the monastery to stop using mice, he had to find an alternative. He fertilized plants by hand, transferring the pollen from one plant to the pollen-receiving stigma of another. With this knowledge, he began to study pea plants. The pea plants grew and reproduced quickly. They also exhibited traits that were easily observed and only occurred in one of two forms. Height was either tall or short. The seeds could only be round or wrinkled, and yellow or green. The pods were either smooth or pinched. The rapidly reproducing and numerous pea plants allowed large amounts of data to be collected in a relatively short amount of time. Mendel hypothesized that factors controlled traits and he documented two laws that were at work during his research.

Mendel's Pea Plant Traits

Plant Height	Seed Shape	Seed Color	Pod Shape
tall 	*round* 	*yellow* 	*smooth* 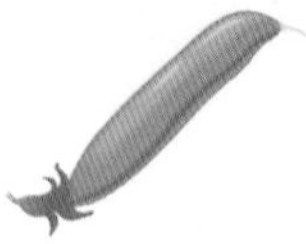
short 	*wrinkled* 	*green* 	*pinched* 

Mendel observed the inherited traits of over 28,000 pea plants.

MENDEL'S LAWS

LAW OF SEGREGATION

EACH PARENT CONTRIBUTES ONE FACTOR TO A PAIR OF FACTORS.

LAW OF INDEPENDENT ASSORTMENT

PAIRS OF FACTORS NEEDED FOR EACH TRAIT ARE PASSED ON TO OFFSPRING INDEPENDENTLY OF EACH OTHER.

Mendel categorized his pea plants based on their appearance. Each pea plant has its own set of factors received from the parent plants. These factors, or gene sets, are called the organism's genotype. They are the DNA coding that make up an organism. The observable characteristics of an organism are called the phenotype. For pea plants, this includes traits such as height—tall or short, or seed color—green or yellow. The genotype determines what is seen in the phenotype.

Mendel fertilized, or crossed, tall pea plants until the offspring were always tall. He did the same with short pea plants. He then crossed these tall and short offspring to determine what would happen. Surprisingly, the result was always tall pea plants. Once these first generation plants matured, they were allowed to pollinate naturally to produce a second generation. Certain traits occurred more frequently than others. For every three tall plants that resulted, there was also one short plant.

OUTLOOK

Gregor Mendel's first name was actually Johann, but when he became a monk, Johann changed his name to Gregor. This act symbolized the start of his new life. The Augustinian monks followed the teachings of St. Augustine, who encouraged people to pray and read the Bible. He believed that people could talk to God through prayer and that God could talk to people through the printed Word. How do you believe God speaks to people through His Word?

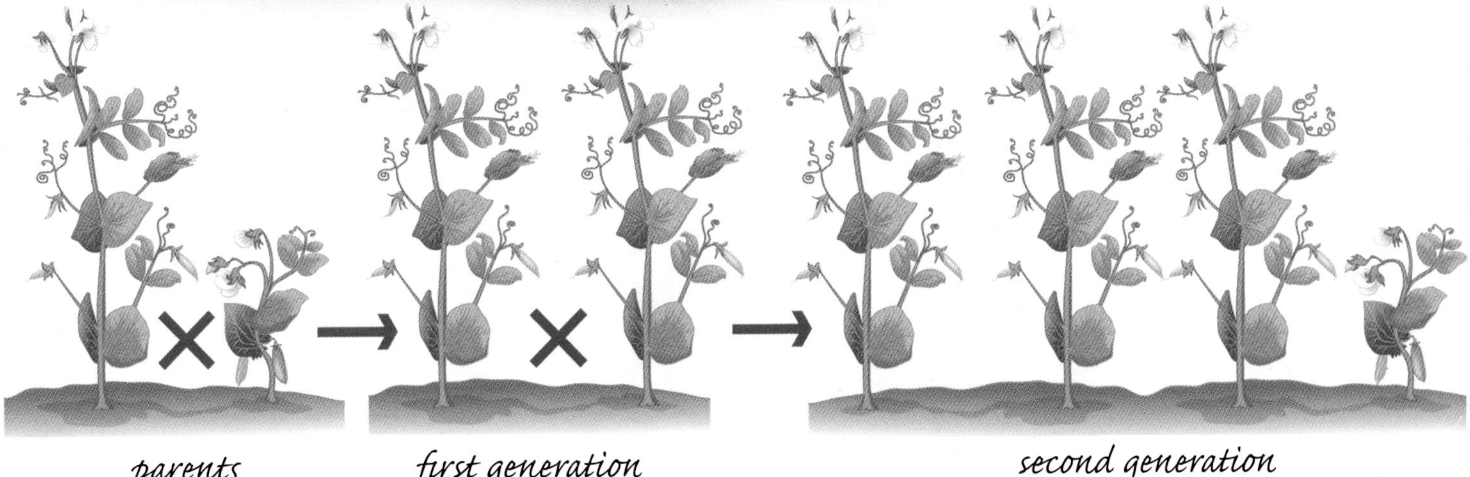

BASIC GENETICS

VOCABULARY

allele (ə·ˈlēl) a different form of a single gene that controls an inherited characteristic

dominant allele (ˈdä·mə·nənt ə·ˈlēl) the allele that hides the effects of another allele

recessive allele (ri·ˈse·siv ə·ˈlēl) the allele whose effect is hidden when paired with a dominant allele

purebred (ˈpyo͞or·bred) an organism with identical alleles for a particular trait

hybrid (ˈhī·brəd) an organism that has two different alleles for a particular trait

Mendel discovered that there were two factors that controlled each of the traits displayed in his pea plants. One factor was contributed by each of the two parents. He also noted that one factor in a pair could mask or hide the other factor. Today the factors are called alleles, which are different forms of the same gene. They determine the traits that an organism has. The phenotype of a dominant allele shows up regardless of the other allele it is paired with. The display of a recessive allele can only be observed if both alleles for that particular trait are recessive.

When an organism's genetic coding contains two like alleles for the same trait—either two dominant or two recessive alleles—the organism is called a purebred. The offspring of two purebreds that have dominant alleles always show the dominant trait. Purebred parents with recessive alleles always produce offspring with recessive traits. Organisms containing one dominant and one recessive allele are called hybrids. Although hybrids display the dominant phenotype, they can pass on either the dominant or the recessive allele to their offspring.

What is the most popular purebred dog in the United States?

Traits Controlled by Dominant and Recessive Alleles

	Plant Height	Seed Shape	Seed Color	Pod Shape
dominant	*tall*	*round*	*yellow*	*smooth*
recessive	*short*	*wrinkled*	*green*	*wrinkled*

IN THE FIELD

Geneticists have studied inheritance patterns in numerous organisms, including pea plants, fruit flies, and worms. Geneticists who focus on cancer research, often study human cancer cells grown in the laboratory. They may also use animal subjects. The most commonly used animal in cancer research is the mouse. Mice reproduce rapidly and their genes are approximately 90% the same as the human genome.

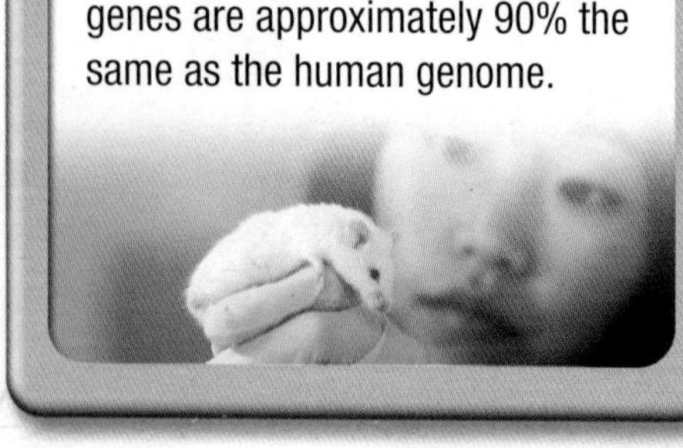

Fruit can be purebred or hybrid. The nectarine is a hybrid fruit, a variety of the common peach. Nectarines lack the fuzzy outer skin found on regular peaches.

Mendel used symbols to understand and calculate expected genetic outcomes. Scientists today still use symbols, but not in the same way that Mendel did. Alleles that are dominant are symbolized by capital letters. For example, the allele for tall plants is symbolized as *T*. Alleles for recessive traits are shown as lower case of the same letter. The allele for a short plant is written as *t*.

A purebred dominant genotype is recorded as *TT* and a purebred recessive genotype as *tt*. A hybrid has one of each allele, *Tt*. The coding for a hybrid's genetic makeup contains both a dominant and a recessive allele. Its phenotype, however, shows only the dominant trait. Two parent hybrids would have some purebred dominant offspring (*TT*), some purebred recessive offspring (*tt*), and some hybrids (*Tt*). The purebred dominant offspring and the hybrid offspring would all be tall plants while the purebred recessive would be short.

How is the offspring of a wolf and a dog unique?

QUICK FACT

Many roses are hybrids formed by combining the genes and traits of two or more rose types. Most roses are native to Asia, with very few originating in North America, Europe, and Africa. The most popular rose is the hybrid tea rose, which is commonly grown in greenhouses and gardens, and is sold in flower shops. It comes in a wide variety of colors and has large, proportioned blossoms.

The gene for blue eyes is recessive. The only genotype it can have is a purebred recessive such as *bb*.

A poison ivy plant can cause severe rashes and allergic reactions for many people. There are people, however, who have a genetic immunity to the oil that causes the rash. This immunity trait is dominant, so only one allele would be required to gain immunity.

GENE COMBINATIONS

VOCABULARY

Punnett square ('pə·nət 'skwâr) a diagram used to show all the possible allele combinations of a genetic cross

homozygous ('hō·mō·zī·gəs) having the presence of the same two alleles for the same gene

heterozygous ('he·tə·rō·ˌzī·gəs) having the presence of two different alleles for the same gene

pedigree ('pe·də·grē) a record that shows a pattern of genetic inheritance in a family

Scientists who study genes use Punnett squares as a tool to help predict the possible outcomes of allele combinations. These charts help determine if the offspring will inherit a specific trait. The likelihood of the trait being inherited depends upon the combinations of the parents' alleles. Two recessive purebred parents will always produce recessive purebred offspring. Two dominant purebred parents will always produce dominant purebred offspring. If one parent is recessive purebred and the other is hybrid, 50% of the offspring will be recessive purebred and 50% will be hybrid. The offspring of two hybrid parents are 25% dominant purebred, 25% recessive purebred, and 50% hybrid.

If offspring have the same two alleles for a particular gene—either all dominant or all recessive—then the offspring is homozygous for that gene. If the offspring is a hybrid with one dominant and one recessive allele, then the offspring is heterozygous for the gene. In evaluating Punnett squares, scientists look for the percentage of heterozygous or homozygous possibilities.

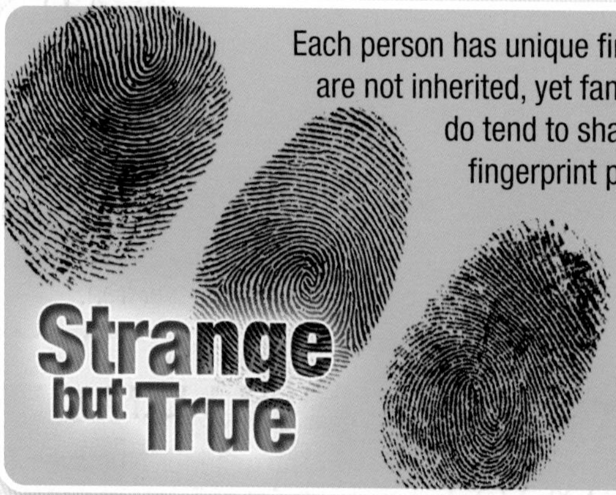

Each person has unique fingerprints. They are not inherited, yet family members do tend to share similar fingerprint patterns.

The top of the Punnett square shows the mother's genotype, and the left-hand side shows the father's genotype for a particular trait. The boxes show the possible allele combinations of the offspring.

cross of two homozygous recessive parents

Father	Mother: b	Mother: b
b	bb	bb
b	bb	bb

cross of two heterozygous parents

Father	Mother: B	Mother: b
B	BB	Bb
b	Bb	bb

cross of a homozygous dominant mother, with a heterozygous father

Father	Mother: B	Mother: B
B	BB	BB
b	Bb	Bb

Punnett squares are also used to predict possible patterns of heredity within a family line. They can be useful for an individual to know whether or not a harmful genetic disorder could be passed on to an offspring. A pedigree is another type of chart that records the inheritance of traits in a family. Pedigrees are like genetic family trees. Although a Punnett square is used to predict if future generations would display a gene, pedigrees track the gene through several generations in the past to predict future probabilities. It is possible to pass along a gene to the next generation even if neither parent in the current generation displays the trait. For instance, two brown-eyed parents can produce a child with blue eyes. If this gene for blue eyes were tracked back through past generations, it would show the last time an ancestor had blue eyes. The traits that a pedigree keeps track of can be something common, such as eye color, or something unusual, such as sickle cell anemia or color blindness.

What are the chances that an individual who was a twin will produce a set of twins?

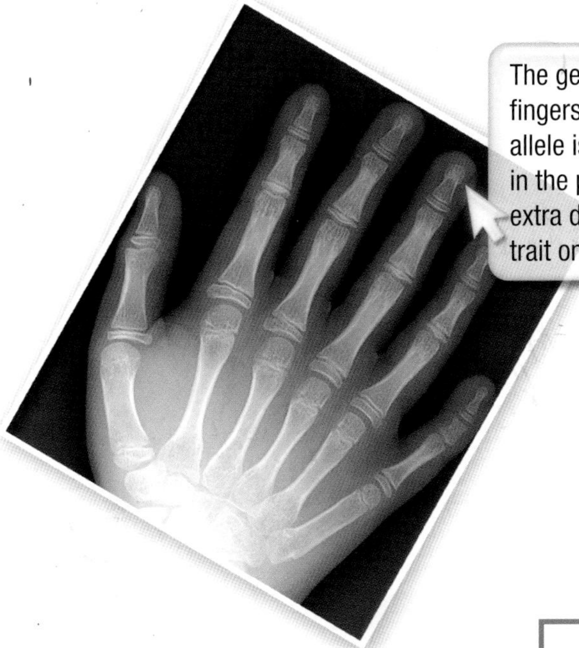

The gene that codes for extra fingers is a dominant trait. Only one allele is necessary for this to appear in the phenotype. If a parent has an extra digit, he or she could pass the trait on to his or her children.

IN THE FIELD

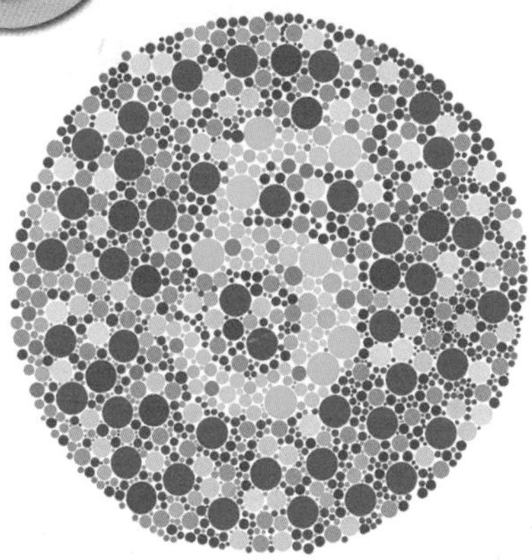

Each person has 23 pairs of chromosomes. One of these pairs determines whether the person is male or female. If the two sex-determining chromosomes match, the person is a female. Those chromosomes are labeled XX. If they do not match, then that individual is a male, and the chromosomes are labeled XY. Hemophilia and color-blindness are genetic disorders that are linked to the X chromosome. Doctors use images like the one shown here to help determine the level of color-blindness of an individual.

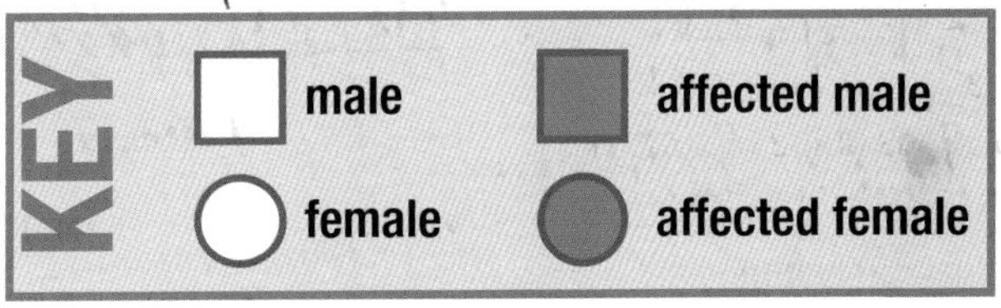

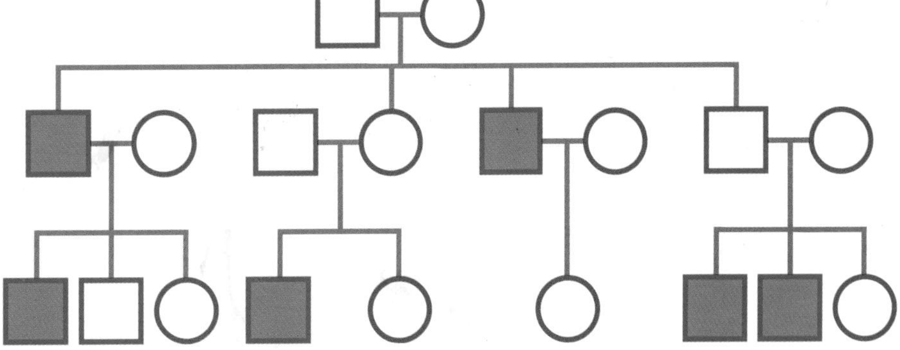

In this pedigree, the occurrence of a particular trait appears only in males. A male and female who do not show the trait in their phenotypes could still produce offspring who are affected by the gene.

VOCABULARY

codominance
(kō·ˈdä·mə·nənts) the condition in which both alleles of a gene are actively expressed and neither is dominant or recessive

incomplete dominance
(in·kəm·ˈplēt ˈdä·mə·nənts) the condition in which both alleles are partially expressed in a blended appearance of the trait

QUICK FACT

In humans, there are specific molecules called *antigens* found on blood cells that determine its type. Type A blood has the A antigen, type B has the B antigen, type AB has both the A and B antigens, and type O has neither antigen present. The AB blood type is a codominant trait. When an individual receives the allele for A and for B, instead of producing only one dominant antigen, both antigens share dominance and are therefore both expressed in the phenotype.

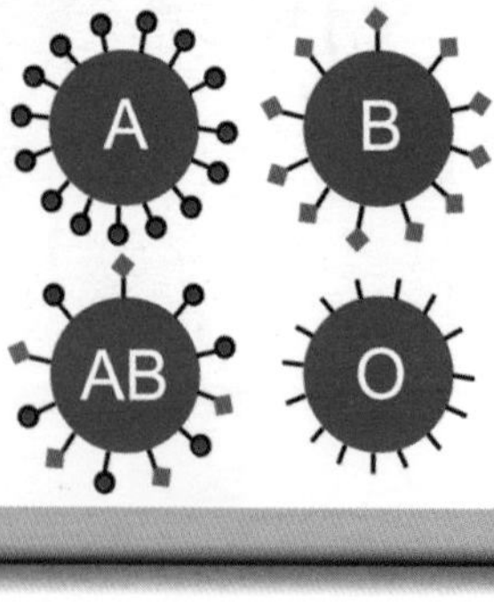

The thousands of plants that Mendel studied had very basic gene combinations. There was always a dominant gene that could mask the presence of the recessive gene. This is not the case with all traits. It was later discovered that many alleles are able to share dominance. This is very different from the pattern of inheritance that Mendel discovered. Sometimes an offspring expresses, or shows, both alleles. This condition is called codominance. Neither allele is completely dominant over the other, which results in many possibilities for the trait to be displayed. Chickens and roosters, for instance, have feathers that can appear in several colors. If a white chicken and a black rooster had a chick, it would express both colors. This means that the chick would have both white feathers and black feathers, instead of expressing only one color or the other. This codominant effect helps explain the variety seen in the traits of different organisms.

When codominant alleles are present, a capital letter is written to signify the trait, with a superscript letter above and to the right to represent the phenotype that is displayed. Since the offspring from a white chicken and a black rooster contains both black and white feathers, its allele combination would be F^WF^B, where *F* stands for the trait of feather color and the superscript *W* and *B* represent the actual codominant colors.

Are black and white cows the result of a codominant trait?

In addition to codominance, some offspring appear as a blending of their parents' traits. When this occurs, there is an incomplete dominance in effect. When different-colored snapdragon flowers are cross-fertilized, the resulting offspring have a blended-colored flower. For example, if white-flowered and red-flowered snapdragons are both homozygous for color, their genotypes would be written as *WW* for white and *RR* for red. If someone used Mendel's results from his pea plant experiments to predict the outcome, he or she might expect that the offspring would be either red or white, depending upon the dominance of the genes. However, the resulting offspring are pink. The genotype for this cross is written as *WR*.

Codominance and incomplete dominance show that there is more to genetics than what Mendel discovered. In humans and other more complex organisms, most traits are determined by several different factors. Certain traits may simply share a dominant/recessive relationship. Other traits are more complicated, with the alleles interacting to create different combinations of the parent phenotypes.

IN THE FIELD

Sickle cell anemia is a genetic disorder that affects a protein in the red blood cells. If a person has both alleles for the sickle cell trait, they will have the disease that causes sickle, or crescent-shaped, blood cells. If a person has one sickle cell allele, they will produce normal and abnormal proteins in the red blood, but will most likely not have the disease. This is because the allele for this disease is codominant with the normal allele.

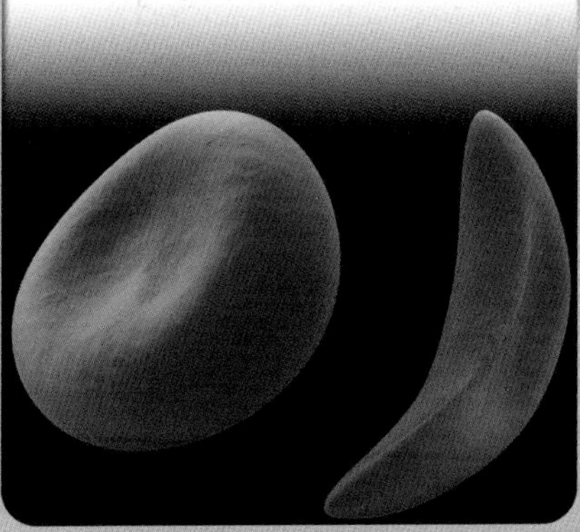

What causes genetic disorders?

ANIMAL BREEDING

IN THE FIELD

Genetic engineering is a technique used by scientists to transfer the DNA from one organism to another. It is used to produce offspring that have incorporated the new DNA into their own genetic code. For instance, scientists have been able to produce crops that have a natural ability to ward off insects, which allows fewer harmful pesticides to be used. Corn, cotton, and potato plants are examples of common crops that have had their genes modified to resist different insect species.

In the 1700s, agriculturist Robert Bakewell became one of the first in English history to breed animals for a specific, desirable trait. It was common practice for farmers at the time to breed sheep and cattle. The breeding was random and produced a wide variety of traits. These animals were used primarily for work and for wool. Bakewell determined that if he separated the males from the females, he could mate specific pairs to produce outward appearances, or phenotypes, that were desirable. He crossbred selected animals to weed out the undesirable traits as well as to promote and amplify the desired qualities.

Bakewell is well known for breeding cattle and sheep for food purposes. By inbreeding his animals, his longhorn cattle were able to eat less and yet grow larger. This trait was desirable because Bakewell did not have to feed them as much and yet yielded more meat. He bred his sheep to have longer and coarser wool and large amounts of high-quality meat.

Does inbreeding always produce beneficial qualities?

Bakewell's cows were longhorns, which may have looked much like this modern longhorn.

Sheep on a livestock farm are raised for a variety of reasons. Their wool can be sheared and then used to make fabric, and they can also be raised for food.

Bakewell's techniques can be seen in today's horse and dog breeding. Typically, horse breeders are looking for traits such as speed, temperament, size, and physical appearance. The most profitable horses are purebred and come from an established line of award-winning parentage. Racehorses in particular need to have recorded purebred lines and registration with the appropriate breed organization to be eligible to race.

Dog breeding produces animals that can be used for a variety of purposes. Hunting dogs, for instance, are bred for their toughness in changing environments and can either be scent dogs or sight dogs. Scent dogs have several features that enhance their sense of smell in tracking animals on land and even over moving water. Sight dogs are quick, lean, and have an excellent ability to see. Dogs are also bred to be family pets. Breeders choose dogs that are good-natured as well as gentle with children.

LINKS

Art Links
Create a collage displaying five dog breeds that are either hunting dogs, working dogs, or great family dogs. Include at least two beneficial phenotypic traits for each dog.

Language Arts Link
There are many diseases caused by genetic defects in the DNA. These diseases can cause a wide range of difficulties and may eventually lead to death. Research and write a report about a genetic disorder. Include its hereditary pattern, as well as it symptoms and the treatments that may be available.

Bible Link
The Bible is filled with several lineage accounts. Jesus' lineage is described in Matthew 1 and in Luke 3. Abraham is listed in both lineage accounts. Describe the promises God made to Abraham in Genesis 12:1–4. Include Abraham's response.

What kind of animal is this?

A jockey is a person who is paid a fee to ride a horse during a race. The fee is paid regardless of the race outcome. The jockey earns more if the horse wins.

Beagles are one of several breeds of hunting dogs. Their long ears help trap and funnel scents toward the nose, making them excellent at sniffing out anything from quail to rabbits.

UNIT 1

LIFE SCIENCE: DIVERSITY

UNIT 2

PHYSICAL SCIENCE: STRUCTURE

– the study of elements, states of matter, and movement

UNIT 3

EARTH AND SPACE SCIENCE: PATTERNS

UNIT 4

HUMAN BODY: DECISIONS

CHAPTER 5

PERIODIC TABLE OF ELEMENTS

VOCABULARY

periodic table (pir·ē·'ä·dik 'tā·bəl) a chart that arranges elements having similar properties into the same groups

KEY IDEAS

- An element's atomic number, atomic mass, and position on the periodic table reveal its atomic structure and chemical properties.
- Atoms are held together by electrostatic charge and the strong force.
- Electrons are located in energy levels modeled by electron dot diagrams that predict properties and represent valence electrons.
- Metals and nonmetals have unique structures and properties.

All matter in the universe, including all living things, is made up of one or more of over 100 elements. These elements, such as carbon and potassium, are organized into the chart that is covering these pages. This chart is known as the periodic table of elements. It arranges the elements into vertical groups, or columns, having similar properties.

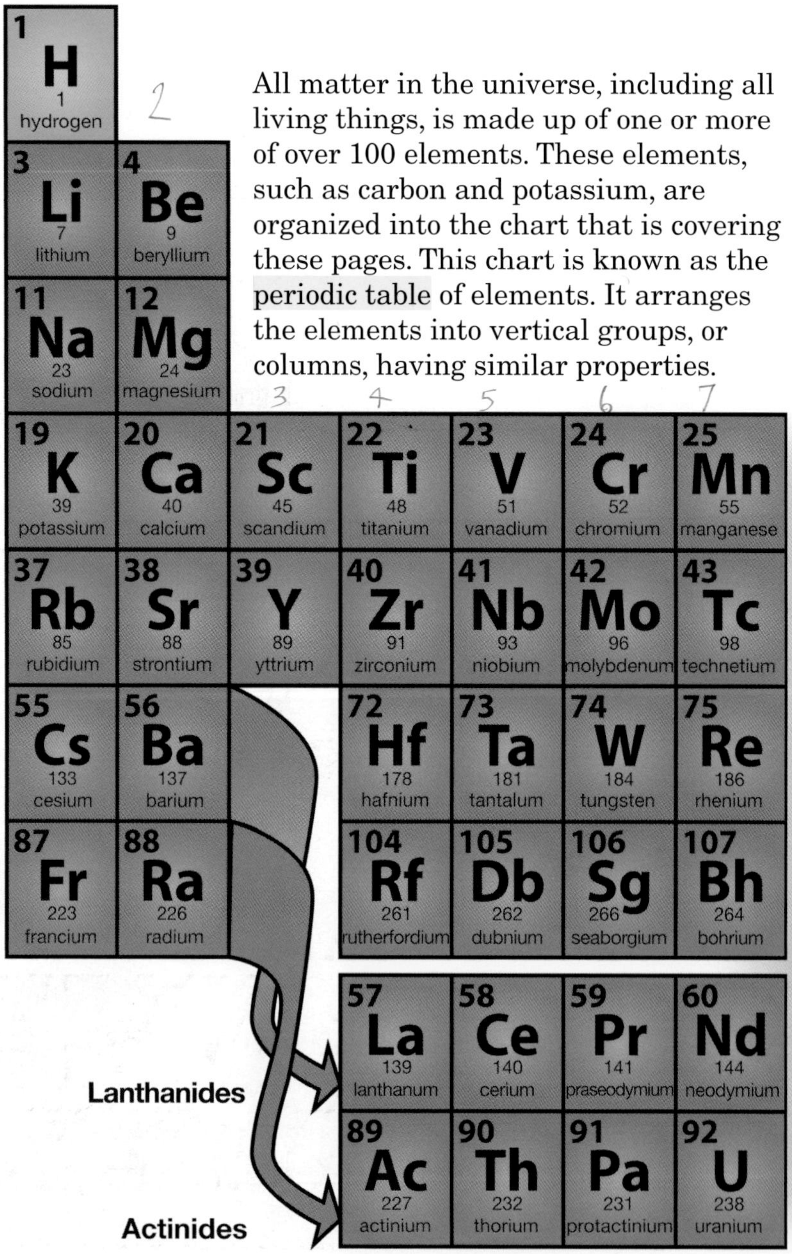

An element is a substance that is made of only one particular type of atom and cannot be broken down into simpler substances. The basic building block of each element is the atom. Atoms are the smallest units of an element that retain the properties of that element. If an atom is broken apart, it no longer functions like the same element.

The atoms of all elements contain the same three particles—protons, neutrons, and electrons. Different elements have different numbers of these particles. Atoms are extremely small. Imagine counting the number of atoms in an object the size of the period that ends this sentence. Even if a person could count one million atoms every second for 100 years, he or she still would not be finished counting all of the atoms in one period!

8	9	10	11	12	13	14	15	16	17	18
										2 He 4 helium
					5 B 11 boron	6 C 12 carbon	7 N 14 nitrogen	8 O 16 oxygen	9 F 19 fluorine	10 Ne 20 neon
					13 Al 27 aluminum	14 Si 28 silicon	15 P 31 phosphorus	16 S 32 sulfur	17 Cl 35 chlorine	18 Ar 40 argon
26 Fe 56 iron	27 Co 59 cobalt	28 Ni 59 nickel	29 Cu 64 copper	30 Zn 65 zinc	31 Ga 70 gallium	32 Ge 73 germanium	33 As 75 arsenic	34 Se 79 selenium	35 Br 80 bromine	36 Kr 84 krypton
44 Ru 101 ruthenium	45 Rh 103 rhodium	46 Pd 106 palladium	47 Ag 108 silver	48 Cd 112 cadmium	49 In 115 indium	50 Sn 119 tin	51 Sb 122 antimony	52 Te 128 tellurium	53 I 127 iodine	54 Xe 131 xenon
76 Os 190 osmium	77 Ir 192 iridium	78 Pt 195 platinum	79 Au 197 gold	80 Hg 201 mercury	81 Tl 204 thallium	82 Pb 207 lead	83 Bi 209 bismuth	84 Po 209 polonium	85 At 210 astatine	86 Rn 222 radon
108 Hs (277) hassium	109 Mt (276) meitnerium	110 Ds 281 darmstadtium	111 Rg 280 roentgenium	112 Cn 285 copernicium	113 Uut (...) ununtrium	114 Fl (287) flerovium	115 Uup (...) ununpentium	116 Lv (291) livermorium	117 Uus (...) ununseptium	118 Uuo (...) ununoctium

61 Pm 145 promethium	62 Sm 150 samarium	63 Eu 152 europium	64 Gd 157 gadolinium	65 Tb 159 terbium	66 Dy 163 dysprosium	67 Ho 165 holmium	68 Er 167 erbium	69 Tm 169 thulium	70 Yb 173 ytterbium	71 Lu 175 lutetium
93 Np 237 neptunium	94 Pu 244 plutonium	95 Am 243 americium	96 Cm 247 curium	97 Bk 247 berkelium	98 Cf 251 californium	99 Es 252 einsteinium	100 Fm 257 fermium	101 Md 258 mendelevium	102 No 259 nobelium	103 Lr 262 lawrencium

Note: Brackets indicate uncertain count. Elements 113, 115, 117, and 118 have been identified but not officially recognized.

1 H 1 hydrogen

- 1 ← atomic number
- H ← symbol
- 1 ← atomic mass
- hydrogen ← name

metals | metalloids | nonmetals

ATOMIC STRUCTURE

VOCABULARY

electrostatic charge (i-ˌlek·trə-ˈsta·tik ˈchärj) a property of matter that can be either positive, negative, or neutral

strong force (ˈsträng ˈfors) the attractive force that holds the nucleus of an atom together

atomic number (ə-ˈtä·mik ˈnəm·bər) the number of protons in one atom of a particular element

atomic mass (ə-ˈtä·mik ˈmas) the number of protons plus the number of neutrons in one atom

An important property of all matter is electrostatic charge. It can be positive, negative, or neutral. Neutrons are neutral, which means *having no charge*. Protons have a positive charge, and electrons have a negative charge. Normally, an atom has the same number of protons as electrons, making it neutral. Both protons and neutrons are in the nucleus, giving the nucleus a positive charge. Electrons exist in motion around the nucleus and have almost no mass.

Opposite charges attract each other. Therefore, electrons stay around the atom because of the attractive force between their negative charge and the positive charge of the protons. Like charges repel each other. The force pushing them apart is called *repulsion*. What holds the nucleus together? The protons push apart because of their positive charges. But the neutrons help produce the strong force, which holds the nucleus together.

How does static cling work?

These balloons were rubbed against a person's hair. This gave them the same charge. Since like charges repel each other, the force of repulsion keeps the balloons apart.

Atomic Model

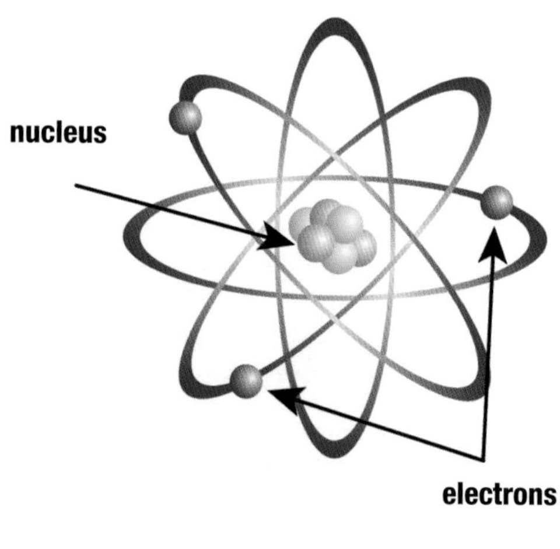

Each type of atom has a symbol like ${}^{3}_{7}Li$. The upper number is the atomic number. It represents the number of protons, which is the same as the number of electrons, in one atom of that element. Lithium has an atomic number of 3. One atom of lithium has 3 protons in its nucleus. It also has 3 electrons outside of the nucleus. The bottom number is the atomic mass. It gives the sum of protons and neutrons in the nucleus of one atom. Lithium has an atomic mass of 7. This means that lithium has a total of 7 protons and neutrons. Since the atomic number shows that lithium has only 3 protons, that means there must be 4 neutrons in the atom. The element ${}^{8}_{16}O$ has 8 protons, 8 electrons, and 8 neutrons in one atom. The element ${}^{92}_{238}U$ has 92 protons, 92 electrons, and 146 neutrons. To calculate the number of neutrons, subtract the atomic number from the atomic mass.

QUICK FACT

People have known about the element iron since ancient times. As a result, it became identified by its Latin name *ferrum*. Latin was the international language of scientists as they grew in their understanding of the atomic nature of matter. Since *ferrum* begins with the letters *Fe*, this became the symbol for an atom of iron.

Are atoms solid or mostly nothing?

Element and symbol
Atomic Number = number of protons
Atomic Mass = number of protons + number of neutrons

^{3} Li
7
lithium

In this image, there is a red marble for every blue marble. In the atom there is an electron for every proton. Depending on the element, the number of neutrons can be less, the same, or more than the number of protons.

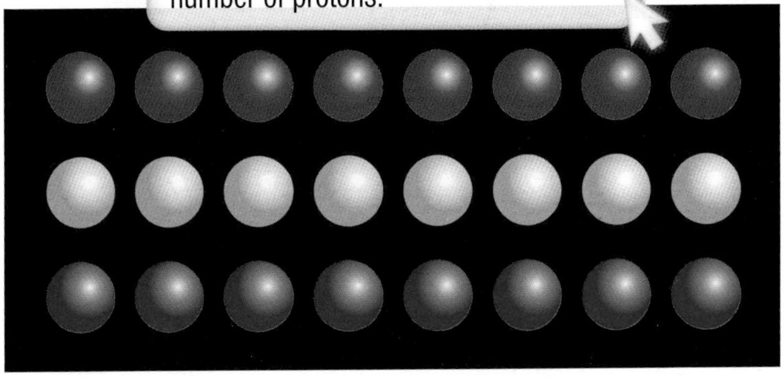

VOCABULARY

electron energy level (i-ˈlek-trän ˈe-nər-jē ˈle-vəl) a location of electrons surrounding the nucleus in the atom

period (ˈpir-ē-əd) a horizontal row of the periodic table

IN THE FIELD

Copper is useful in plumbing because of its properties. Copper's physical properties include hardness and strength, easy formation into pipes, and a high melting point. The chemical property that makes it useful in plumbing is that it will not easily react or corrode with materials normally in water. Plastic pipe is becoming more frequently used today because copper is expensive and possibly reactive with water that is too acidic. Polyvinyl chloride, or PVC, is used and, more recently, cross-linked polyethylene, or PEX. Their advantages include lower cost, lighter weight, flexibility, and lower reactivity.

Every element has its own set of properties. Physical properties describe characteristics like color, shape, size, hardness, mass, and melting point. Chemical properties describe how a substance reacts with other types of matter. For example, a chemical property of oxygen is that it fuels combustion. A chemical property of helium is that it will rarely react with anything. Hydrogen, however, easily reacts with other substances.

Why do elements have these chemical properties? It is because of the arrangement of their electrons, which have negative charges. The nucleus has a positive charge. Electrons move around and outside of the nucleus. The electrons repel each other because they have the same charge, yet they each spin in a way that one electron will attract another electron. This leads to pairing of electrons.

Oxygen is the essential element in combustion processes. A fire requires oxygen, fuel, and high temperature to burn.

Many tops can spin clockwise or counterclockwise. Similarly, if two electrons are in the same energy level, they must spin in different directions. This creates a force that counteracts natural repulsion.

Electrons are in electron energy levels, or shells, that surround the nucleus. The first level closest to the nucleus holds up to two electrons before it is full. Elements with one energy level are located in the first horizontal row across the top of the periodic table. These horizontal rows are called periods. All the elements in a period have the same number of electron energy levels, from one energy level in period one to seven levels in the seventh period across the bottom of the periodic table. The first period on the periodic table has only two elements—hydrogen, H, with 1 electron, and helium, He, with 2 electrons.

Eight electrons is the limit for the second level. Lithium, Li, has 3 electrons. Its first 2 electrons go in the first level, just like helium's 2 electrons. But its third electron has to go in the second level from the nucleus. Lithium is in the second period. Its placement there means that lithium has two energy levels in the atomic model. Nitrogen, N, has 7 electrons, 2 in the first level and 5 in the second. Sodium, Na, has 11 electrons, with 2 in the first, 8 in the second, and 1 in the third level. Notice that sodium, with three energy levels, begins the third row, or period, on the table.

QUICK FACT

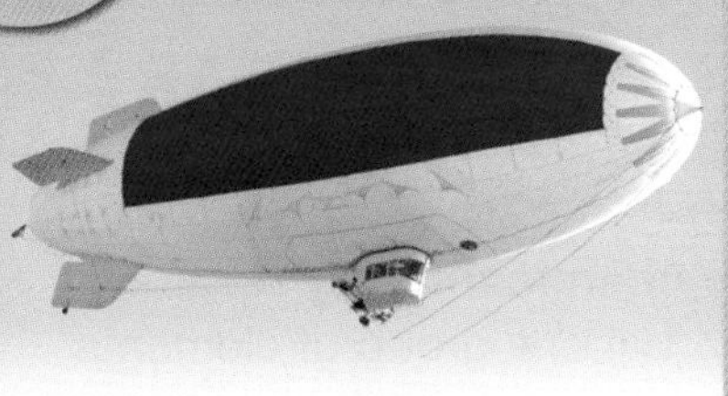

Helium, He, is lighter than the elements nitrogen and oxygen, which are the major components of air. It is less dense than air and is the reason blimps and balloons can float in the sky. Hydrogen would make them float even better. However, hydrogen is flammable, extremely reactive, and escapes containers easily. Helium's two electrons in the first energy level make it very nonreactive. In fact, helium is the least reactive element.

Atomic Model of a Nitrogen Atom

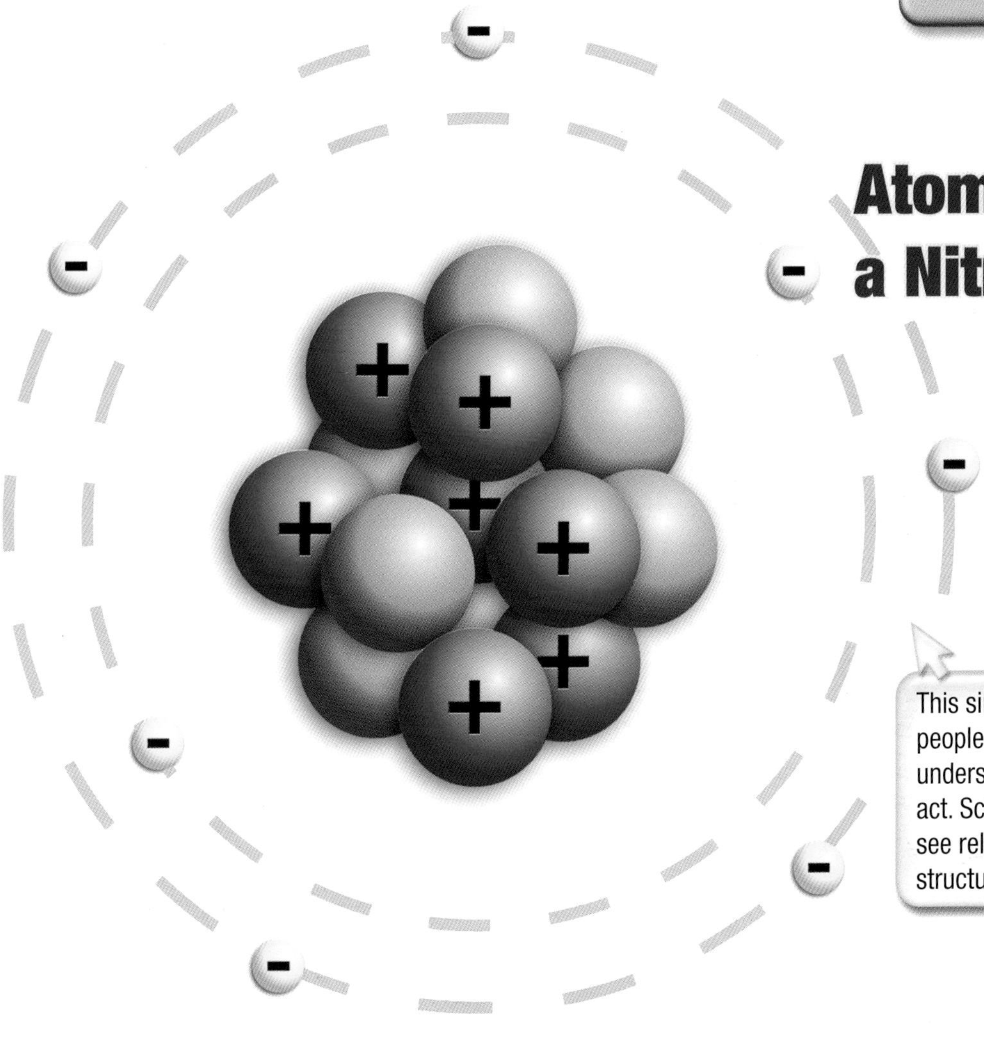

This simple model helps people predict and understand the way atoms act. Science uses models to see relationships between structures and properties.

CHEMICAL FAMILIES

VOCABULARY

chemical family ('ke·mi·kəl 'fam·lē) a group of elements that have similar properties

valence electron ('vā·ləns i·'lek·trän) an electron in the outermost energy level of an atom

metal ('me·təl) an element that is typically shiny and hard and a good conductor of heat and electricity

nonmetal ('nän·me·təl) an element that is typically dull and brittle and a poor conductor of heat and electricity

The periodic table organizes elements into vertical columns called *groups*, or chemical families. The elements in each of these families have similar properties. Carbon is in the fourteenth column of the periodic table of elements. That means it is in Group 14. It has 6 electrons. Two are in the first energy level. The other 4 electrons fit in the second energy level. The atomic model is a helpful tool to use in visualizing this. The second energy level is farther from the nucleus than the first energy level. In this element the second level is the outermost energy level. Electrons in this outermost level are called valence electrons. Carbon has 4 valence electrons. All elements in a chemical family have the same number of valence electrons.

Silicon is in the same chemical family as carbon. It has 14 electrons. The first 2 are in the first energy level, and 8 more electrons fit in the second energy level. The last 4 electrons go in the third level. Since its valence electrons are in the third level, silicon is located in the third period. Silicon and carbon both have 4 valence electrons, which means they have similar properties.

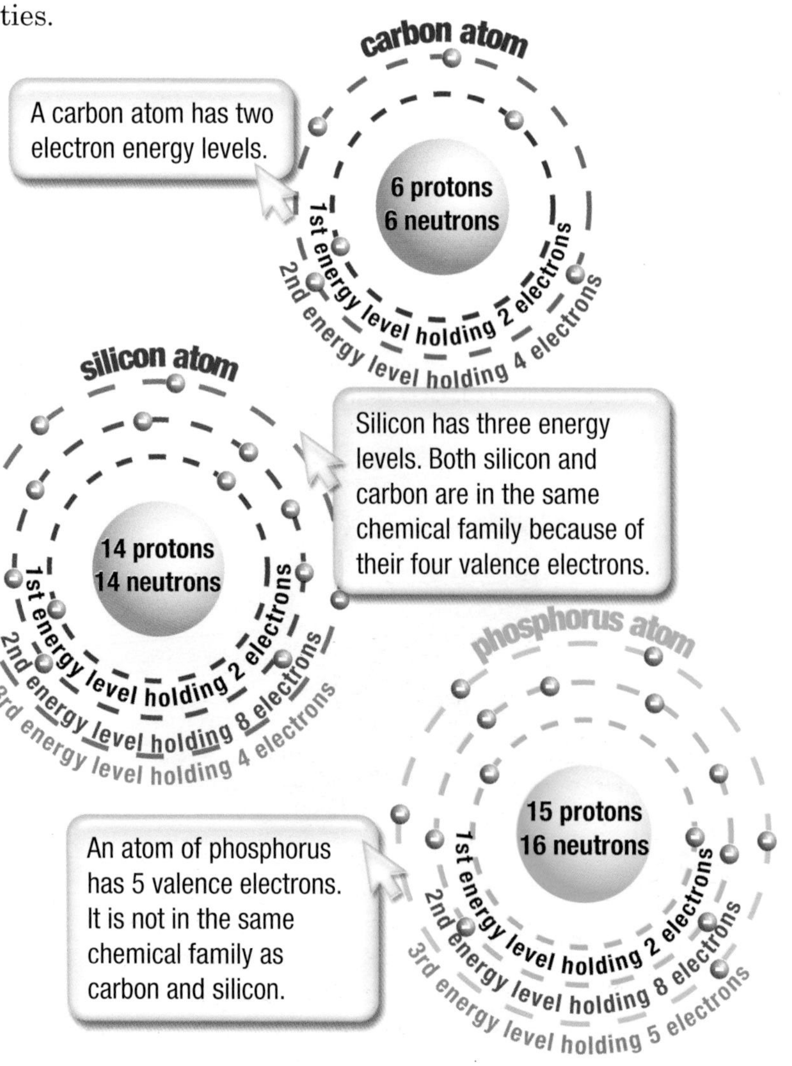

Most black diamonds are microscopic crystal clusters known as *carbonados*. Found near meteor craters, they have different amounts of fused carbon atoms than brilliant diamonds and are cemented with other elements like iron or xenon.

Atoms chemically react with other atoms because of the interactions between their valence electrons. All elements within the same chemical family react in similar ways because they have the same number of valence electrons.

The elements are organized on the periodic table not only by periods and groups, but by color codes. On the periodic table at the beginning of this chapter, most of the elements are colored orange. Each of these elements has 1, 2, or 3 valence electrons. These elements are known as metals, which react by losing electrons. Metals are usually shiny, hard, good conductors.

The elements coded with green are nonmetals. They usually have 5, 6, or 7 valence electrons. Nonmetals are dull, brittle, poor conductors. Nonmetals react by gaining or sharing electrons. The elements colored blue on the periodic table are between the metals and nonmetals and are called *metalloids*. Sometimes these elements act like metals. Other times they act like nonmetals.

IN THE FIELD

Organic chemistry is the field of science that studies carbon and its compounds. A compound contains more than one element. Carbon compounds are used, among other things, to manufacture all of these cleaning supplies and equipment. Carbon can bond with other carbon atoms. It also easily combines with many other nonmetals, such as hydrogen and oxygen.

Wedding rings are not solid gold. A mixture of the metals gold, silver, copper, and zinc create an alloy more durable than solid gold. Alloys can also have exotic colors.

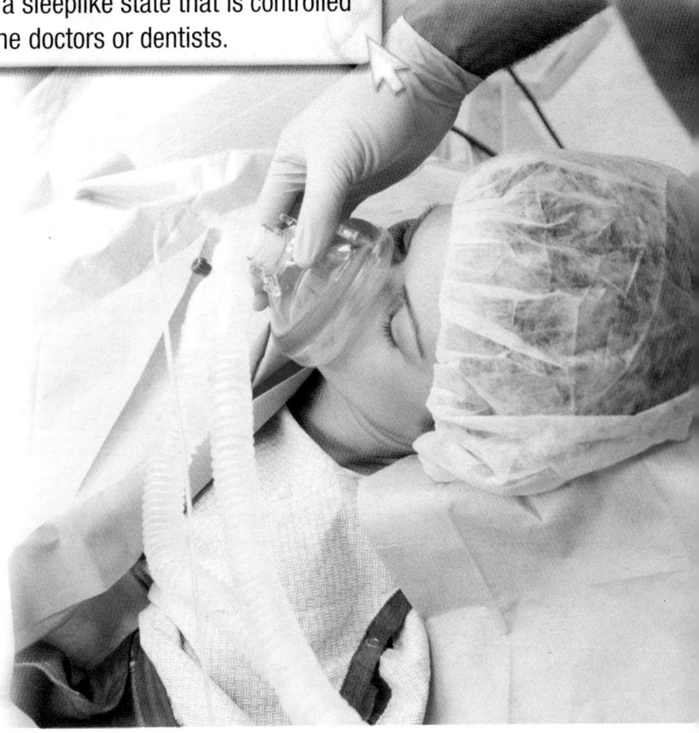

Painless surgery is possible because of molecules formed from nonmetals like nitrogen and oxygen. Breathing in nitrous oxide (N_2O) puts the patient into a sleeplike state that is controlled by the doctors or dentists.

Some wedding rings are made of titanium because of its properties, such as hardness, shininess, and nonreactivity with other materials.

BUILDING MOLECULES

VOCABULARY

electron dot diagram
(i-ˈlek-trän ˈdät ˈdī-ə-gram) a figure in which dots around an element's symbol represent valence electrons

QUICK FACT

This sand sculpture of a monkey is made of molecules of SiO_2. The electron dot diagram for SiO_2 is

:Ö::Si::Ö:

The number of valence electrons in an atom determines how an element will react. The structure of molecules can be predicted from an electron dot diagram. It is a figure in which each dot around an element's symbol represents a valence electron. Hydrogen has one dot, oxygen has six dots, and neon has eight dots. Most atoms need eight electrons to complete the electron level when forming stable molecules. They often accomplish this by combining with other atoms. Neon, however, does not usually combine with other atoms. This is because neon already has eight electrons.

An oxygen atom has 6 valence electrons. One hydrogen atom has only 1 electron. If two hydrogen atoms combine with one oxygen atom, oxygen will then have 8 valence electrons. The resulting molecule—two or more atoms joined—consists of one atom of oxygen and two atoms of hydrogen. This makes the compound water, or H_2O, by combining two or more different elements.

Water (H_2O)

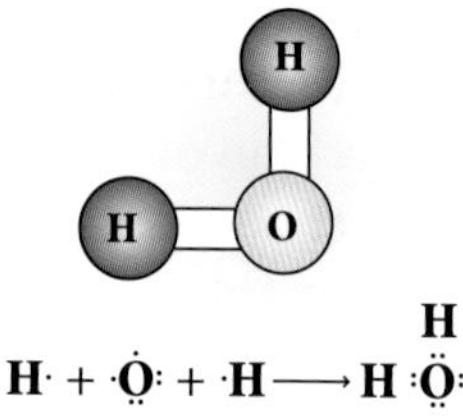

When nitrogen and hydrogen combine, the resulting molecule consists of one atom of nitrogen and three atoms of hydrogen. This makes a compound known as *ammonia*, or NH_3. It is used as a fertilizer and a cleaner.

Ammonia (NH_3)

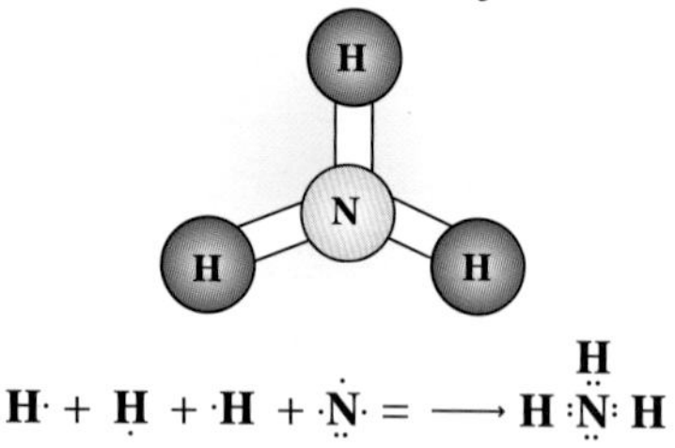

What is wrong with this electron dot diagram?

:C:

These are the electron dot diagrams for the elements in the second period of the periodic table. Each dot represents a valence electron.

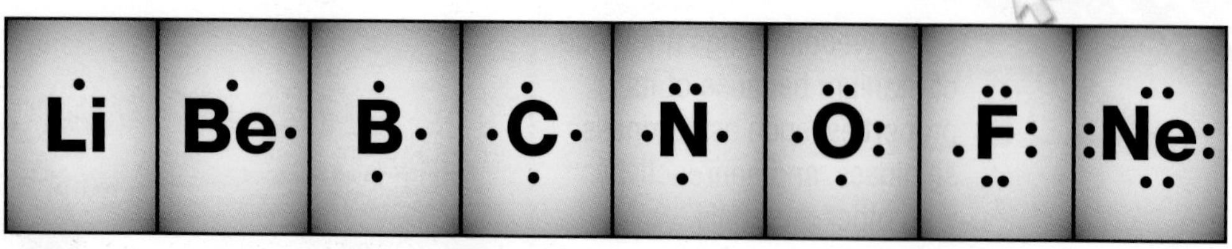

Carbon is called *the element of life* because it is a component of many molecules in your body, including proteins, sugars, and DNA. Scientists use electron dot diagrams to predict the structure of molecules containing carbon. The molecule on the right contains four hydrogen atoms and one carbon atom. This compound is methane, or CH_4. It is a gas used to heat homes and cook food.

Methane (CH_4)

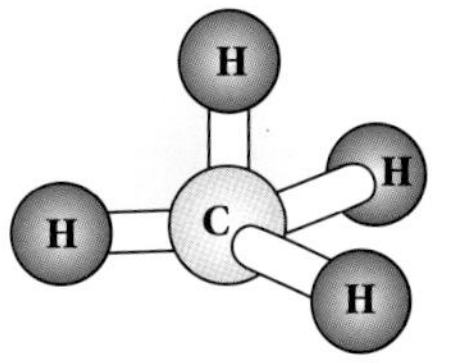

$4H\cdot + \cdot\dot{C}\cdot \longrightarrow H:\ddot{C}:H$ (with H above and below C)

Silicon is another element in the same chemical family as carbon. Silicon also has four valence electrons like carbon. This means it will react with four hydrogen atoms. The chemical formula for this compound is SiH_4. Note that silicon now has 8 electrons around it. This compound is silicon hydride, which is used in contact lenses.

Silicon Hydride (SiH_4)

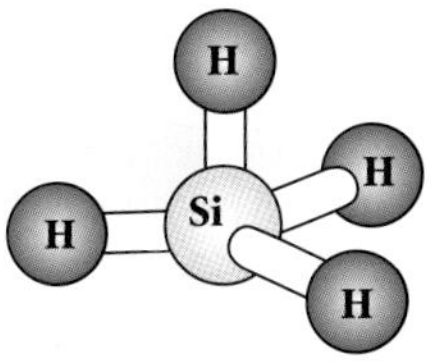

$4H\cdot + \cdot\dot{Si}\cdot \longrightarrow H:\ddot{Si}:H$ (with H above and below Si)

Chlorine has 7 valence electrons. It can join with a hydrogen atom to form hydrogen chloride, HCl. When HCl is dissolved in water, it makes an acid that is present in the stomach. Hydrochloric acid reacts with food molecules to help digest food in the stomach.

Hydrogen Chloride(HCl)

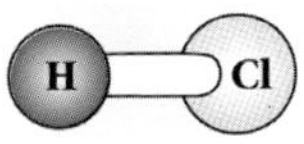

$H\cdot + \cdot\ddot{Cl}: \longrightarrow H:\ddot{Cl}:$

What parts of the atom does the symbol represent? $:\ddot{\underset{\cdot\cdot}{Ar}}:$

The sugar in this cotton candy is made of many molecules containing the elements carbon, hydrogen, and oxygen.

STRUCTURES AND PROPERTIES

QUICK FACT

This is an image of the element potassium, K, reacting with water. The chemical change immediately produces a violet-colored flame. This is evidence of how reactive potassium is. However, when potassium is a part of a compound, as in a banana, it is very stable.

The closer two magnets are to each other, the stronger the force of attraction. Conversely, the greater the distance between the magnets, the less attraction there is. This is quite similar to what happens in an atom. Electrons in the first energy level are pulled close to the nucleus. Electrons in the second, third, or higher energy levels are held more loosely. This means that outer valence electrons are more easily lost or gained than inner level electrons.

Lithium, sodium, and potassium are in the far left chemical family on the periodic table. Lithium has one valence electron in the second energy level. Sodium has its lone valence electron in the third level. Potassium has its 1 valence electron in the fourth level. Lithium holds its valence electron the tightest of the three. Potassium's valence electron is farthest from the nucleus. This means potassium holds its valence electron more loosely than lithium or sodium. Therefore, potassium will lose its valence electron more easily than either lithium or sodium. Potassium will react more readily with other elements.

Which planet in the solar system is held most loosely?

Sodium is a soft, silver-colored metal. It is highly reactive but not as reactive as potassium.

Lithium is the least reactive of the metals pictured on this page.

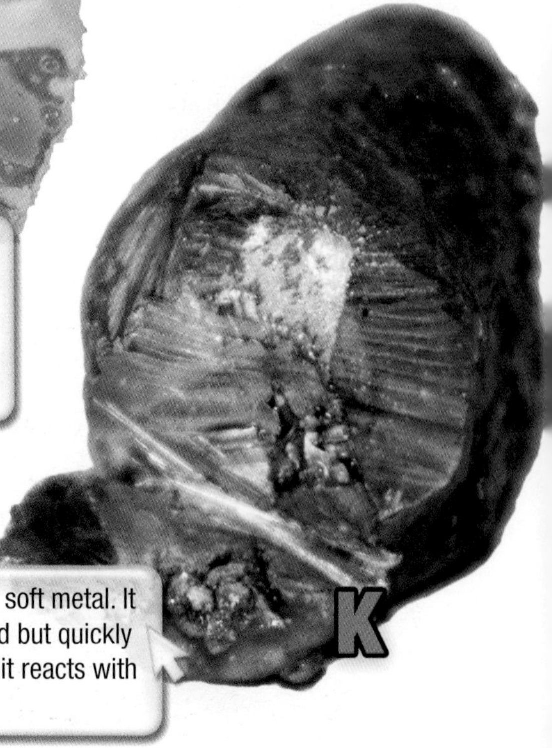

Potassium is a soft metal. It is silver colored but quickly turns black as it reacts with oxygen.

Metals, such as potassium and lithium, are very reactive. This is because their valence electrons are far from the nucleus. Nonmetals react in the opposite way. A nonmetal, such as fluorine, has 7 valence electrons. Since it needs 8 outer electrons to become stable, fluorine gains 1 electron when it reacts. Chlorine also has 7 valence electrons, but chlorine's valence electrons are not held as tightly as fluorine's since they are farther from the nucleus. Thus, fluorine will gain an electron more easily than chlorine will. This means fluorine will react with other elements more easily than other nonmetals.

Conversely, the element argon has 18 electrons in one atom, 8 of which are valence electrons. This means that argon is nonreactive. Two of the 18 electrons are in the first energy level, 8 in the second level, and 8 in the third level. An argon atom does not need to gain or lose any electrons since it is already stable. The distance between the valence level and the nucleus, as well as the number of valence electrons, are two structures of the atom that affect its properties.

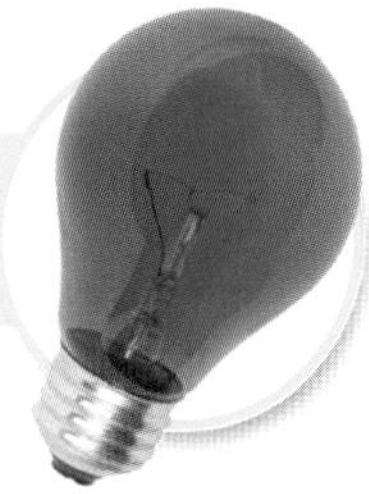

Is a reactive or nonreactive gas needed inside a lightbulb?

Signs like this use nonreactive gases like neon and argon. No chemical change is occurring inside these tubes.

The green chlorine gas inside this clear glass ball does not react with the glass.

This green frosted Christmas ornament is made by etching the glass using a highly reactive compound containing fluorine.

LINKS

Music Link
Talk to a music instructor about the theory behind scales. Focus on the topic of octaves. Write a short report relating what you have learned about the periodic table and the structure of music.

History Link
Use the Internet to research how World War II led to the rearrangement of the periodic table. Some key terms to aid your search are *the Manhattan Project*, *atomic bomb*, and *Glenn Seaborg*. Prepare an oral report in order to present what you learned.

Technology Link
Visit a business that employs welders, and interview a welder during one of his or her breaks. Call ahead to arrange details of your visit. Prepare questions that will help you understand how chemical properties are involved in industrial use, especially in welding. Design a poster illustrating what you learn.

CHAPTER 6

STATES OF MATTER

KEY IDEAS

- Four observable states of matter are solid, liquid, gas, and plasma.
- Energy interactions among atoms and molecules account for changes in state.
- Water possesses unique properties which enable it to support life on Earth.
- Temperature affects states of matter, pH, and viscosity.

Most substances on Earth are in one of three states of matter—solid, liquid, or gas. Solid items have a definite structure. The atoms and molecules that make up a solid are unable to move freely within the object. They have the ability to vibrate, but the structure prevents the atoms and molecules from sliding past one another. Liquids allow flow and movement of particles because they have a higher amount of energy than solids. As a result, the atoms and molecules are able to slide past one another to change positions within the substance. Gases have even more energy than either solids or liquids. This means that gas atoms and molecules are usually very spread out. Particles in a gas state do not have a set position and actually spread out as far from one another as is physically possible. Often, all that will limit the distance a gas will spread is the boundary of its container. Since there are almost no boundaries in space, gas particles there are very far apart from one another.

Atoms and molecules in a solid are tightly packed together like these balloons. The only movement that occurs is a vibration, but the particles remain in place.

These balloons represent a gas because they are spread out. There is a great deal of energy, movement, and distance between the particles.

Atoms and molecules are still close together in a liquid, but there is more energy. This allows more movement and gives a liquid the ability to flow.

Strange but True

What does lightning have to do with the states of matter?

STATE CHANGES

VOCABULARY

deposition (de·pə·ˈzi·shən) the change from a gas to a solid without passing through the liquid state

sublimation (sə·blə·ˈmā·shən) the change from a solid to a gas without passing through the liquid state

plasma (ˈplaz·mə) a superheated gas composed of electrically charged particles

ion (ˈī·ən) an atom that has gained or lost one or more electrons

A substance's state of matter is determined by the amount of energy it contains. Water gives clues about the relationship between energy and three state changes. Each state of water—solid, liquid, and gas—contains specific properties. These properties are graphed on a cooling or heating curve. Each curve shows what happens to water when heat energy is removed or added. They also include data about changes in state. Scientists also create cooling and heating curves for other substances besides water.

Between state changes there are time periods where the temperature remains constant and unchanging. If the substance is cooling, it is either condensing or freezing. If the substance is warming, it is either melting or boiling. Sometimes, however, if enough energy is removed or added, the substance skips a state. When a gas skips the liquid state and becomes a solid, it is called deposition. When a solid becomes a gas without passing through the liquid state, it is called sublimation.

Why does the temperature remain temporarily constant when a substance is changing states?

This heating curve for water shows how the states change as energy is added. Each horizontal line represents a place where water is in the process of changing to the next state.

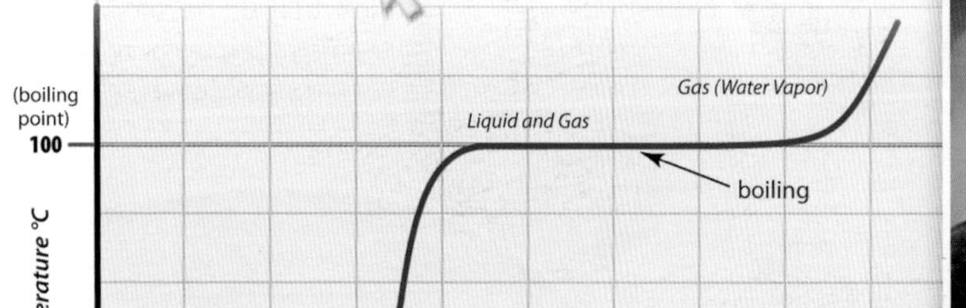

Dry ice is solid carbon dioxide (CO_2)—a common atmospheric gas. As sublimation occurs, the cold temperatures affect the surrounding gases. This causes them to condense just enough to create a mist. The CO_2 skips the liquid state.

Surprisingly, there are more than just three states of matter, although not all of them occur naturally on Earth. The fourth state of matter is plasma. This state of matter is a superheated gas that has been stripped of electrons. When atoms lose electrons, as in plasma, they become known as *ions*. Atoms are also considered ions if they gain electrons.

An excellent example of plasma is lightning. Other examples include fire, welding arcs, fluorescent lamps, and neon signs. Plasma can also be found in space. Stars, including the sun; solar winds; interstellar gas clouds; comet tails; the auroras; and the ionosphere are all plasma. Scientists believe that about 99% of the matter in the universe exists in the plasma state.

Plasma has properties quite unlike the other states of matter. While it does not have a definite shape or volume, plasma carries electric currents. Plasma usually takes the form of neutral gaslike clouds, although it can form threads and beams.

IN THE FIELD

Two scientists, Satyendra Nath Bose and Albert Einstein, worked together in 1925. Since that time, scientists have been working with their ideas to confirm or disprove them. It was not until 1995 that a Bose-Einstein condensate was actually produced in a lab and declared to be the fifth state of matter. Sometimes science takes decades to catch up with someone's hypotheses and research.

Welders must wear protective gear to protect their skin and eyes because of the heat and brightness of the plasma. It can actually cause blindness if someone looks directly at the arc without the mask shielding him or her.

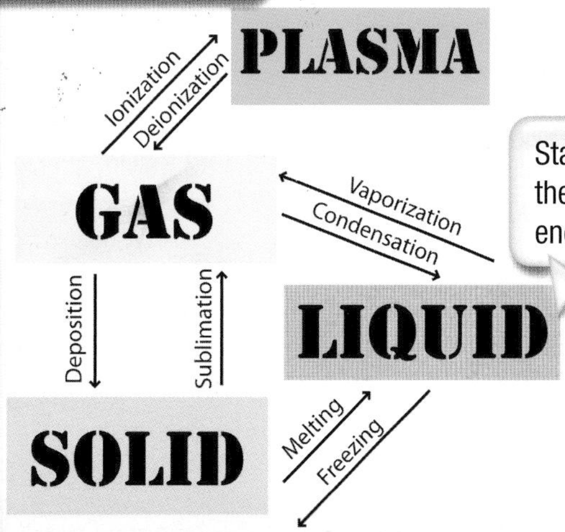

State changes require the addition or removal of energy in order to occur.

Strange but True

Lightning is an example of plasma, the fourth state of matter, discovered in 1879 and named in 1929. It exists on and near Earth, but more plentifully in outer space.

TEMPERATURE SCALES

VOCABULARY

absolute zero
('ab·sə·lo͞ot 'zē·rō) the lowest possible temperature at which matter has no remaining thermal or heat energy

Kelvin scale ('Kel·vən 'skāl) a temperature scale that begins at absolute zero

heat capacity
('hēt kə·'pa·sə·tē) the ability to store and release heat energy

Measuring heat is important in science because it allows scientists to accurately compare and identify changes that occur in matter. One early device that showed changes in temperature was the thermoscope, invented by Galileo Galilei in 1597. Temperature changes in this device were detected by the rising and falling of a liquid inside a tube. In 1714, Daniel Fahrenheit created a mercury thermometer. Using mercury enclosed in a tube, this device was more accurate than other thermometers at that time. Fahrenheit also devised the first working temperature scale, in which water froze at 32° and boiled at 212°.

In 1742, Anders Celsius developed a new temperature scale. On the Celsius scale, water freezes at 0° and boils at 100°. Each unit of measurement was called *a degree Celsius*. Sir William Thomson, also known as *Lord Kelvin*, designed an absolute scale in 1848 that identified the lowest possible temperature. He called this temperature absolute zero because there was a complete absence of heat and motion at the atomic and molecular level. He based the intervals of his scale on the centigrade scale, and it is now known as the Kelvin scale.

A Galileo thermometer, different from the thermoscope, uses buoyancy to display temperature. The colored bulbs are made with varying densities to respond to temperature changes. This was only reliable once temperature scales had been developed.

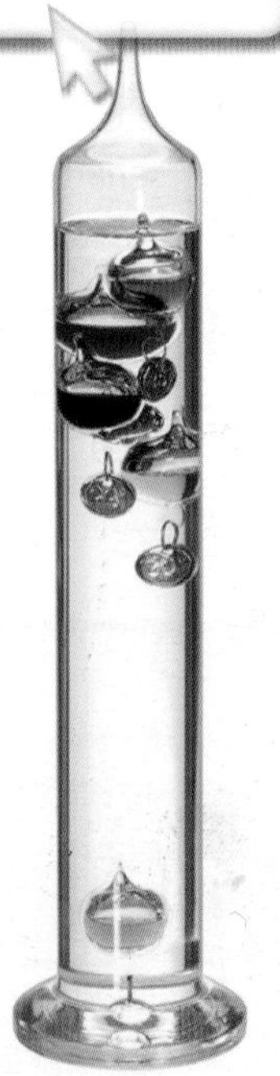

How can conversions be made between °F and °C without using thermometers?

Space is very cold. The average temperature that most scientists agree on for all of space is below 3 Kelvin, almost absolute zero.

Scientists will often use an absolute scale because the temperature values are positive numbers. This helps avoid calculation errors that can occur when working with negative numbers. One of the properties that scientists calculate is the heat capacity of a substance. Some substances can absorb, store, and release large amounts of heat energy. Uniquely, water is one material that has a high heat capacity. When heat is added to water, the water diffuses, or spreads, heat throughout the entire body of water. The larger the amount of water, the longer it takes to heat up. This also means that the water will not cool very quickly. Water's higher heat capacity than rock or soil helps keep islands and coastlines from experiencing extreme changes in weather and temperature. Not all substances have the same heat capacity. Some substances do not diffuse heat well. This causes most of the heat to be focused where the source of heat is applied. Other substances diffuse heat equally, but quickly. Those substances have a low heat capacity.

IN THE FIELD

Scientists still research temperature today. Cryologists are scientists who study regions that are controlled or affected by low temperatures. These can be places on Earth or on other planets. Areas of study on Earth include glaciers, snow, ice sheets, and frozen ground. Scientists observe and investigate the relationship these cold creations share with the earth as a whole.

When liquid water changes state and evaporates into water vapor, it can be lifted over land masses like mountains. This often results in cooling, condensation, and precipitation. This process continues the water cycle, and the water eventually returns to the oceans. The energy trapped in the different states of water is transferred to the environment around it, even causing weather changes.

Metals absorb and release heat more quickly than water. This makes them ideal for cooking and baking. The glowing metal in the oven has less heat capacity than water, despite the difference in melting points.

UNIQUENESS OF WATER

VOCABULARY

polarity (pō·ˈlâr·ə·tē) the quality of having opposite charges for different points of a molecule

hydrogen bond (ˈhī·drə·jən ˈbänd) a weak bond that connects hydrogen-containing molecules at polar areas

surface tension (ˈsər·fəs ˈten·shən) the elastic property of liquids that allows drops to form and creates the smallest area possible at the surface of a liquid

solubility (ˌsäl·yə·ˈbi·lə·tē) the ability of one substance to dissolve in another

viscosity (vis·ˈkä·sə·tē) the resistance of a liquid to flow

Water is unique for other reasons besides its heat capacity. One of water's most noticeable properties is that its molecules have opposite charges. This is referred to as polarity. The molecules in water become slightly positive or slightly negative because electrons are not evenly distributed. Since water molecules have polarity, they are called *polar molecules*. Slight attractions between polar molecules permit hydrogen bonds to form. These bonds allow polar molecules to attract one another and stay connected. These attractions cause water to have a great deal of surface tension. Surface tension can be observed when water remains in a glass, even when the water level is slightly higher than the top edge of the glass. Surface tension is also visible in a graduated cylinder. When observed closely, the water is slightly higher at the sides of the container than in the middle. Neither of these would occur without the polarity of water and the related surface tension.

Surface tension caused by the polarity of water molecules keeps this globe of water together in zero gravity on the space shuttle *Discovery*.

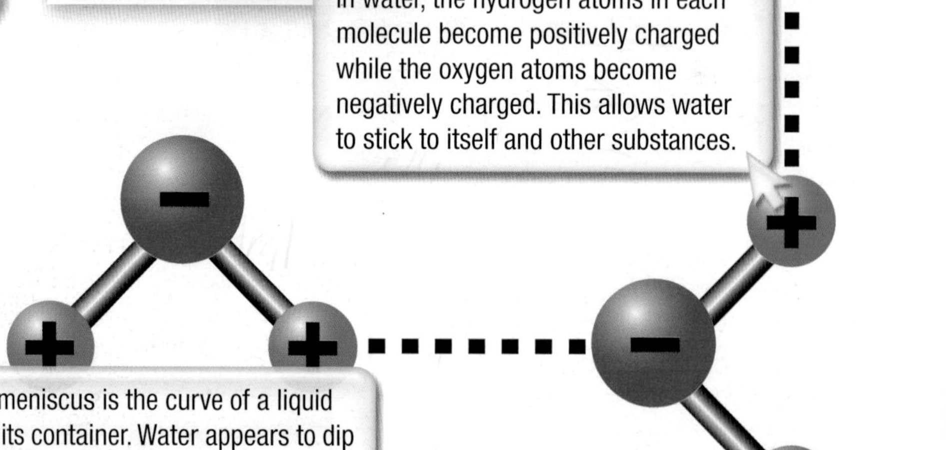

In water, the hydrogen atoms in each molecule become positively charged while the oxygen atoms become negatively charged. This allows water to stick to itself and other substances.

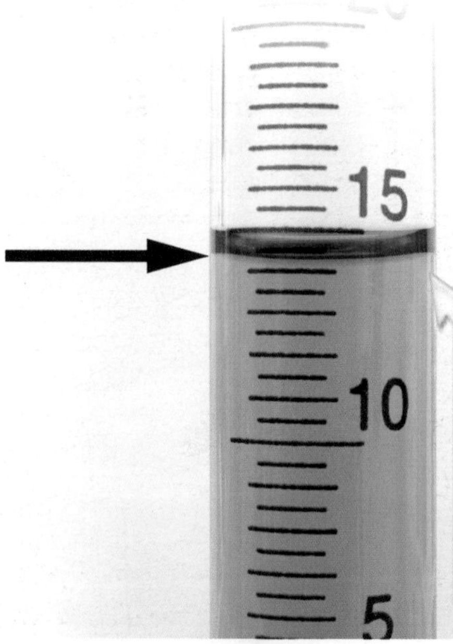

A meniscus is the curve of a liquid in its container. Water appears to dip down at the center. This center point is the meniscus, which is the point measurements should be taken from. The raised portion is the result of the polarity of the substance and exhibits surface tension.

Polarity and hydrogen bonding give water the ability to dissolve many substances. Water can dissolve solids, such as minerals and salts, or gases, such as oxygen and carbon dioxide. Many of these materials have a high solubility in water. Solubility is the ability to dissolve. Because water is able to dissolve so many substances, it is known as *the universal solvent*.

God designed water with another unusual property that is critical to life on Earth. Unlike most substances, it becomes less dense upon freezing. This allows ice to rise to the surface rather than sink. If ice sank, any living things trapped under it would be crushed or frozen.

All liquids have a viscosity, or resistance to flow. Water has a lower viscosity than honey or glue, for example. Temperature and chemical composition affect a substance's viscosity. Warm maple syrup is less viscous than cold maple syrup; it pours more easily.

QUICK FACT

Surfaces like this leaf of a lotus plant have inspired a variety of self-cleaning and antibacterial technologies. Tiny particles on the leaves provide a bumpy texture that repels dirt. The attraction of water and dirt molecules to one another is greater than their attraction to the surface. This results in the water droplets combining with the dirt and rolling off to leave a clean surface. Inventors have used this concept to keep dirt away from flags, canopies, windows, and surfaces in hospitals.

What substance besides water is less dense as a solid than as a liquid?

The lava that formed this tall, angular volcano had high viscosity, causing the lava to flow slowly. As it cooled, the lava piled upward. Low viscosity lava, on the other hand, forms flatter volcanoes.

Most matter contracts as it cools and expands slightly as it heats. Expansion joints in windows, siding, sidewalks, roads, and bridges allow for movement as temperatures change.

pH SCALE

VOCABULARY

pH scale ('pē-'āch 'skāl) a range of values from 0 to 14 that indicates the concentration of hydrogen ions in a solution

acid ('a-səd) a substance with a pH less than 7.0

base ('bās) a substance with a pH greater than 7.0

Since water is the universal solvent, many substances dissolve in it. Ions are produced during this process. Some molecules break apart and produce hydrogen ions (H^+). Others produce hydroxide ions (OH^-), which are made from hydrogen and oxygen atoms. The pH scale is used to determine the concentration of hydrogen ions in a substance. This scale ranges from 0 to 14. The neutral point is pH 7. Pure water has a pH of 7. This means that pure water is neither an acid nor a base.

If a substance has a pH below 7, it is an acid, indicating more hydrogen ions. Some acids are very strong, like battery acid at pH 1.0. Others are weak, like milk at pH 6.4. A substance with a pH above 7 is a base, indicating very few hydrogen ions and the presence of hydroxide ions. Drain cleaners, at pH 12, are strong bases. Baking soda is a weak base at pH 8.4. Table salt (NaCl) is neutral with a pH of 7.

Acids range from 0 to 6.9, with 0 being the most acidic. Bases range from 7.1 to 14, with 14 being the most basic. The symbol pH is an abbreviation for *power of hydrogen* in French.

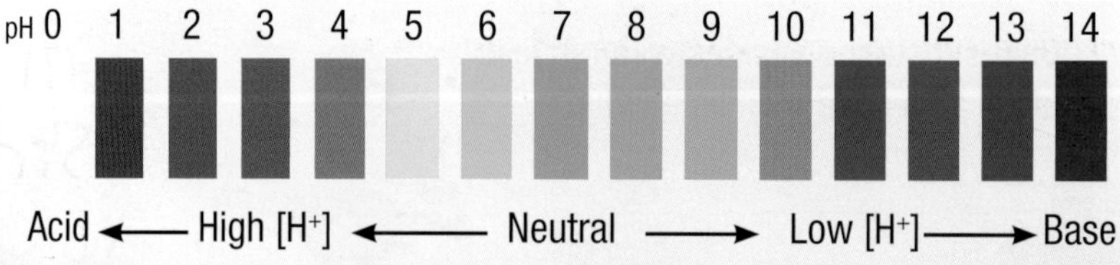

pH Scale

Soaps and other cleaning agents have a high, or basic, pH. One of the properties of bases is a soapy feel.

Citrus fruits have a low, or acidic, pH. This is partly why certain fruits taste so sour.

Acids and bases can greatly influence chemical reactions. Some reactions require a stable pH, so scientists seek out substances that will allow only small changes in pH. These substances are called *buffers*. When a buffer is used, the number of hydrogen ions remains constant, or close to it. This prevents the pH from changing much, if at all.

Buffers are important for people as well. The human body is designed to maintain pH equilibrium. Water plays an important role in this process. Body fluids, such as blood and saliva, contain water and dissolved buffers. When the pH of a fluid becomes too high or low, diffusion takes place between the cells and the external fluids around them, balancing out the pH. As a result, the body is able to ensure that its pH stays within the appropriate range. It even corrects pH changes caused by exercise or diet.

Saliva acts as a buffer in the mouth. Each day a person's body can produce somewhere between $\frac{3}{4}$ to 2 L (3 to 8 cups) of saliva. This is one reason why it is so important to stay hydrated.

Items like dairy products and meats contain bacteria. As bacteria reproduce, the pH of the food is altered. Since bacteria take longer to multiply at cooler temperatures, these foods last longer when refrigerated.

Heat and changes of state can be used for many purposes. One of them is to perform work. Heat, or thermal energy, can be converted into mechanical energy by using a machine known as *a heat engine*. Two common types of heat engines are the external and internal combustion engines. External combustion engines burn fuel outside of the engine. A steam engine, for example, uses fire as a heat source to turn water into steam. The steam is then forced into a cylinder and moves a piston back and forth. The piston is attached to a rod that moves a flywheel, or propeller.

The internal combustion engine burns fuel, such as gasoline or diesel, inside the engine. The pistons move up and down in the cylinder and turn a crankshaft. Each complete cycle by the piston is called *a stroke*. The entire process occurs in either two or four strokes. Most diesel and gasoline engines have four, six, or eight cylinders and use the four-stroke process—intake, compression, power, and exhaust. These four strokes take place in each cylinder and are repeated many times every second.

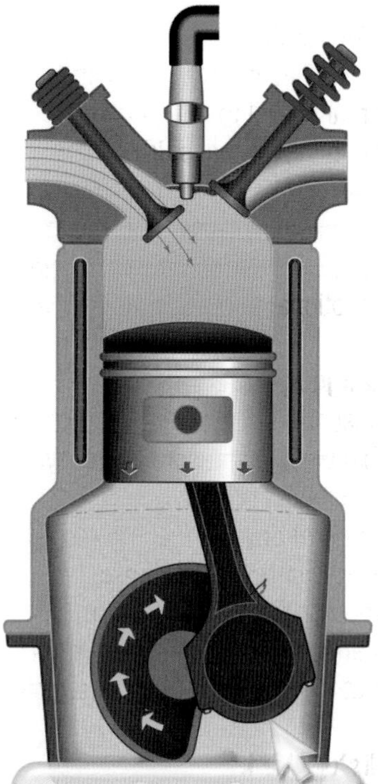

Air enters through the valve opening as the piston travels downward.

Internal Combustion Engine

The valves are closed as the piston travels upward. The air becomes compressed and heat increases.

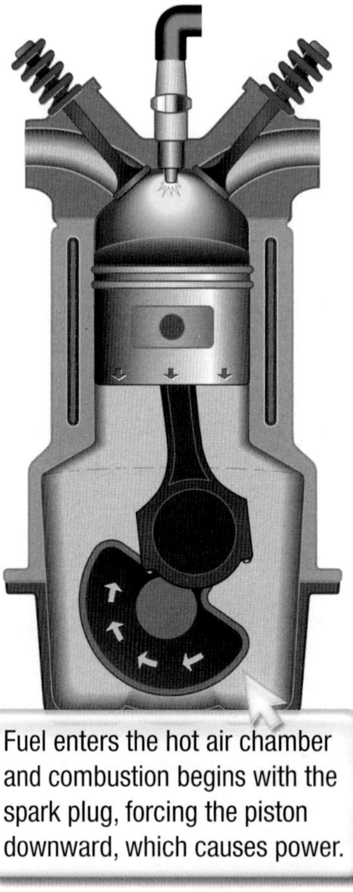

Fuel enters the hot air chamber and combustion begins with the spark plug, forcing the piston downward, which causes power.

Exhaust and any unused fuel exit through the exhaust valve as the piston rises.

Sometimes it is necessary to transfer thermal energy from one area to another in order to keep a certain area cool. Heat naturally moves from warmer temperatures to colder temperatures. Therefore, transferring thermal energy to warmer locations requires work to be done. Cooling systems, such as air conditioners and refrigerators, perform this task.

An air conditioner transfers heat from the inside of a room or a car to the outdoors. A refrigerator works in a similar way, using a liquid called *a refrigerant* and a system of tubes and coils. The refrigerant goes through a series of changes—high pressure, low pressure, evaporation, and condensation all play a part. When the refrigerant becomes very cold, the heat inside the refrigerator is attracted to the cold. The heat moves from the inside of the refrigerator to the refrigerant in the tubes. The tubes then move the heat outside of the refrigerator where the heat is released into the room by way of the coils on the back. A thermostat controls the temperature inside the refrigerator.

How can the earth be used for a home's heating and cooling system?

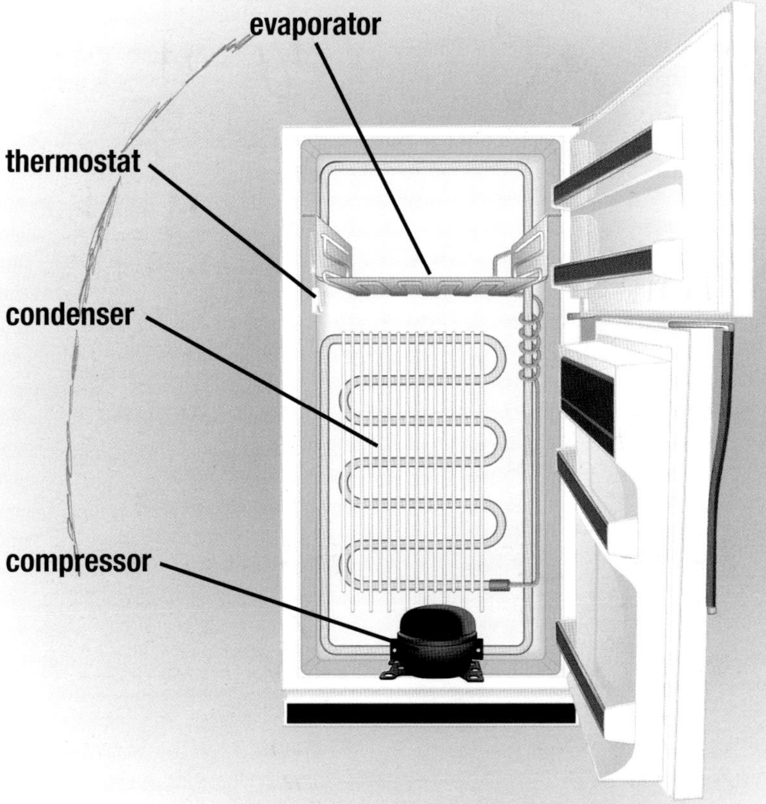

LINKS

Bible Link
Use a concordance, website, or other tool to note a few of the things Jesus said and did involving water. Include what you have learned in this chapter about water, and prepare a brief devotional to present to the class.

Language Arts Link
Observe and record all the ways that water is present around you throughout an entire day. On a different day, use your examples to explain why water is so important on Earth. Be sure to mention the properties of water that are present in each example.

History Link
Create a time line describing the progress of temperature measurement. Write a brief description of the people involved and why their contribution was notable.

Technology Link
Research what scientists have discovered about plasma or Bose-Einstein condensate. Write a summary paper describing its uses and how people have benefited from these discoveries.

CHAPTER 7

FLUIDS

KEY IDEAS

- States of matter are determined by temperature and the strength of attractive forces.
- Archimedes' principle explains why objects sink, float, or rise in fluids.
- Pascal's principle describes how hydraulic systems work.
- Bernoulli's principle helps explain how lift works.
- Flight involves four forces: weight, lift, thrust, and drag.

Earth consists mostly of solids, such as rocks or trees, and fluids, which are liquids or gases. Tiny atoms make up the individual elements. Atoms can often combine to form molecules. Stronger forces between these small particles tend to make solids. Weaker forces tend to make fluids. Diamonds, for example, are held together by strong forces. Milk, however, is held together by weaker forces.

Temperature also affects the state of matter. As the temperature drops, liquids freeze into solids. This happens because the molecule vibrations slow down and get close together—except for water, which expands as it freezes and then floats as ice. If heat energy is added to the solid, it melts and forms a liquid. This forces most liquid molecules to move farther apart and to vibrate faster. If the liquid is heated to its boiling point, it changes into a vapor or gas. The vapor molecules move as far apart as possible and accelerate to very high speeds.

The flight of this hang glider and the surging of the waves can both be explained by the properties of fluids.

QUICK FACT

Water is the only substance on Earth that occurs naturally in all three common states of matter: solid ice, liquid water, and gaseous vapor. Water is able to do this because of the unique way God designed water molecules. If water did not have its particular structure and properties, it would only be found in one natural state instead of three.

Strange but True

What does this image have to do with fluids?

SHAPE AND VOLUME

VOCABULARY

pressure (ˈpre·shər) the amount of force exerted on a certain area

OUTLOOK

How did the solids, liquids, and gases that make up the world get started? Many people used to think that all matter has always existed. However, evidence continues to grow that disproves this idea and supports what the Bible says in Hebrews 11:3: "By faith we understand that the universe was formed at God's command, so that what is seen was not made out of what was visible."

An easy way to contrast the states of matter is to look at their shape and volume. A golf ball is solid, so its shape remains spherical no matter what container it is in. Calculating the volume would be difficult to do with a ruler, but it is possible to determine by placing the ball in a measured amount of water. The golf ball displaces the same amount of water as its volume, and the water in the container rises accordingly. If the golf ball is moved into another container, its volume does not change. Therefore, solids are described as having both definite shapes and definite volumes.

Although liquids have a definite volume, they do not have a definite shape. When lemonade is poured from a tall, square glass into a short, round glass, the volume of the liquid will still be the same. It does not change. However, the lemonade will take the shape of whatever container it is in. Therefore, liquids have a definite volume even though they do not have a constant shape.

Has the volume or shape of the milk stayed the same after the spill?

As the golf ball enters the water, the water is pushed aside. Since the container prevents the water from moving down or to the side, the water is displaced upward. Once the splashes fall back, the level of the liquid will be higher than before.

Gases have neither definite shape nor definite volume. Since the gas particles are held together by very weak forces, the particles will diffuse, or spread out evenly, and completely fill any container they are in. When a person inhales, he or she brings air into the lungs. The air then takes the shape and volume of the lungs. If that same person then exhales into a balloon, the air will adjust to fit inside the balloon. If the person adds more air, the air will continue to adjust to the new volume and shape of the balloon as long as the balloon holds the air inside. Once the balloon pops, however, the air is no longer in the same container. The gases disperse to share the shape and volume of their new environment.

When air goes into a rigid, sealed container, the pressure of the air increases. As it increases, there is less room for free movement of the atoms or molecules. This makes the particles more likely to collide and bond with one another. Condensation then occurs.

IN THE FIELD

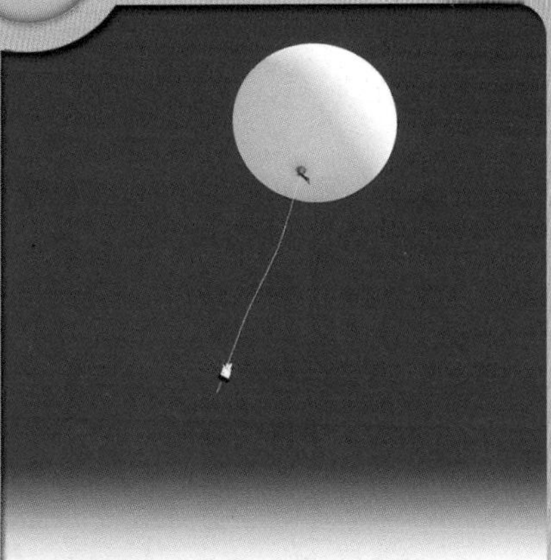

Scientists use weather balloons like this one to collect data from the upper atmosphere. The balloon is filled with a gas that rises in air. As the balloon goes up, it grows larger and larger because the outside air pressure continues to decrease. Eventually, the balloon becomes so large that it bursts. At this point, the instrument connected to the balloon falls back to Earth. Tracking devices allow the scientists to recover the instruments for further study.

Can the volume of the hot air inside this balloon change?

The gases in this bottle have taken on the shape and volume of the bottle.

Fluids flow because the forces between their molecules are weak enough to allow the molecules to slip past each other. However, the forces are strong enough that the liquid molecules stay together as they flow.

PROPERTIES OF FLUIDS

VOCABULARY

Archimedes' principle (är·kə·ˈmē·dēz ˈprin·sə·pəl) a submerged object is pushed upward by a force equal to the weight of the fluid it displaces

buoyant force (ˈboi·ənt ˈfôrs) the upward force exerted by a fluid

Pascal's principle (pas·ˈkalz ˈprin·sə·pəl) pressure is transferred equally throughout a fluid in all directions

hydraulic system (hī·ˈdrȯ·lik ˈsis·təm) a system that uses fluids to increase or transfer forces

Rock inside a volcano has melted because of very high temperatures within the earth. The lava flow is the fluid product of this volcano's eruption. The lava travels down the mountain, either melting or burning everything in its path—including the road, vegetation, and homes.

Strange but True

A fluid's ability to flow produces several useful properties. Archimedes, an ancient Greek scientist, discovered that a submerged object is pushed up by a force equal to the weight of the fluid it displaces. This fact is called Archimedes' principle. Buoyant force, or *buoyancy,* is the upward force caused by the fluid. When the weight of the object is greater than its buoyancy, the object sinks. When the weight of the object is less than its buoyancy, the object rises in the fluid. When weight and buoyancy are equal, the object floats.

Archimedes' principle explains why boats float in water and why blimps float in air. Boats, for example, are intentionally designed to displace their weight in water so that they can remain afloat. A ship displaces the water with its weight. The water then pushes back on the ship with an equal but opposite force. Blimps perform similarly when they navigate through the air, which then responds with a buoyant force.

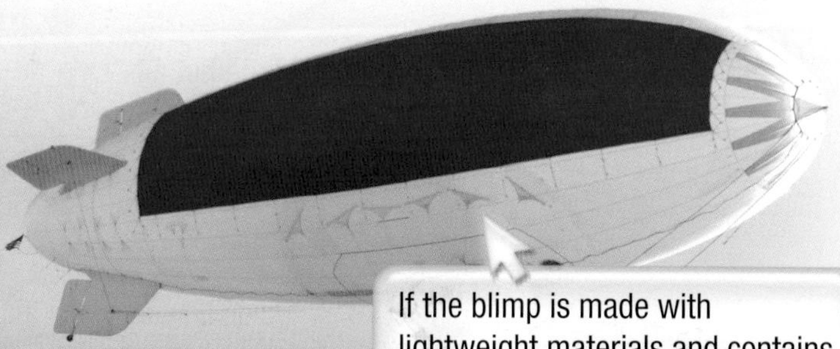

If the blimp is made with lightweight materials and contains a lightweight gas like helium, the buoyant force can equal or exceed the weight of the blimp.

Enormous aircraft carriers are floating airports. They weigh a tremendous amount yet float on the ocean because they displace a large amount of water.

Some objects, like this sponge, contain large amounts of air, which make it easier for buoyancy to overcome its weight.

Pascal's principle states that the pressure applied to a fluid is transferred equally throughout the fluid in all directions. Pascal's principle can be observed when someone squeezes a bottle of water. The water will change its shape to fit the shape of the bottle. If you poke a hole in the bottle and squeeze the sides, the contents would come out of the bottle as long as you apply pressure.

Pascal's principle explains how hydraulic systems work. Hydraulic systems are designed to increase or transfer a force through fluids. The brake system on an older car is a good example. The driver exerts a small downward force on the brake pedal. This creates pressure, which is then transferred to the brake fluid in the brake lines. The increase in pressure exerts a force at the brake pad that stops or slows the car. The brake lines themselves are small, meaning they have a small area. However, when the brakes are pushed, the force is constant at the brake pedal and at the pad, which has a larger area. This allows one foot to stop a car.

How does this fire truck's boom work?

IN THE FIELD

An auto mechanic is trained to diagnose problems and perform repairs on multiple systems for many different automobiles. Some older vehicles have more simplified systems, while some newer cars are almost entirely computerized. Both new and old vehicles take advantage of hydraulic systems. Mechanics can have a broad knowledge base and know about many cars or they can be more selective and specialize in certain kinds of cars.

This car's brake lines extend long distances. Any pressure applied remains constant all the way to the pistons that push on the brake pads.

Large machines use hydraulic systems to enable one farmer to cultivate and harvest huge fields alone.

Manufacturing, patient care, and the military all use robotics, which are powered by hydraulic systems.

BERNOULLI'S PRINCIPLE

VOCABULARY

air pressure ('âr 'pre·shər) the force exerted by air

Bernoulli's principle (bər·'nōō·lēz 'prin·sə·pəl) pressure decreases as a fluid speeds up

QUICK FACT

Scientists prove Bernoulli's principle by using the law of conservation of energy. This law is based on the fact that energy cannot be created or destroyed, but it can change in form. In other words, the total amount of energy stays the same. For example, when a pipe containing water narrows, the water speeds up. If the kinetic energy of a fluid is increased by moving faster, some other form of energy must decrease. This is what causes the drop in water pressure.

Hydraulics work by transferring pressure through liquids. Gases can also be pressurized. The force of gravity on the atmosphere produces air pressure. It is similar to the increased pressure a swimmer feels, especially on the eardrums, when he or she dives to the bottom of a deep pool. More water above the diver means there is more pressure. The water molecules are constantly moving and colliding. Conversely, when someone climbs a mountain, there are fewer air molecules above him or her than at sea level. Therefore, there is less air pressure.

Daniel Bernoulli, a scientist in the eighteenth century, studied the pressure of moving fluids. He discovered that the pressure drops as the fluid moves faster. This fact is known as Bernoulli's principle. This principle is used by home builders every day. Waterlines in a house direct the flow of water from a lower level to an upper level. When the water comes into a house at or below ground level, it must go up in order to reach the faucets. To do this, the builder can either add a pump or use progressively smaller pipes to speed the water up as it travels through the pipes.

How does air pressure keep the liquid from leaving this glass?

As a diver goes deeper underwater, the weight of the water above the diver increases. This increases the pressure on the diver's body.

Hiking at high altitudes is difficult because there are fewer air molecules in each breath. The body becomes dehydrated faster. This makes the body work harder.

Bernoulli's principle explains what happens as a fluid flows. It also explains how lower pressure is caused by greater speed, or greater speed is caused by decreased pressure. The opposite of each is true as well, in that higher pressure and decreased speed share a similar relationship.

This relationship is shown in a venturi, which is a tube with a smaller diameter in the middle. Because the tube narrows, the air moving through must speed up. This causes a drop in pressure in the narrow portion of the tube. The somewhat U-shaped connecting tube acts as a meter to demonstrate the effect of the change in pressure. The liquid is higher in the vertical tube connected to the area of lower pressure in the venturi. The higher pressure from the larger portion of the venturi pushes down into the other vertical tube. The difference in pressure between both vertical tubes is known as the *pressure differential*.

OUTLOOK

The law of conservation of energy is a fact supported by much scientific evidence. It also matches with biblical teaching. Everything in the universe was created by God. The Bible says in Ecclesiastes 3:14, "I know that everything God does will endure forever; nothing can be added to it and nothing taken from it. God does it so that men will revere Him."

VENTURI

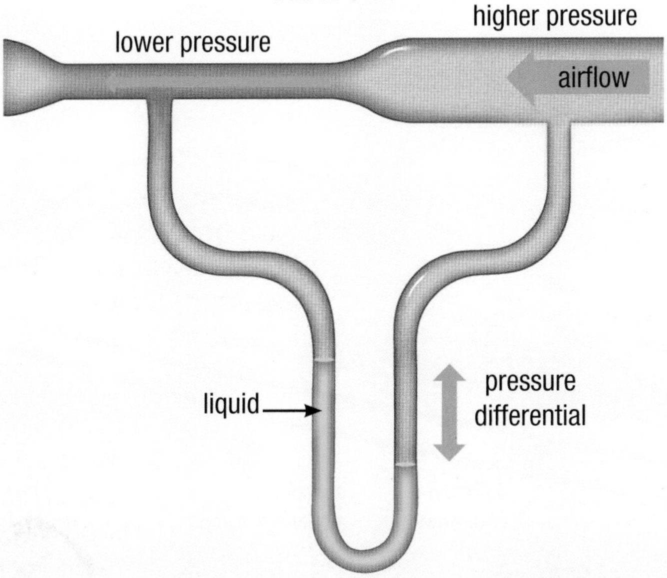

When the shower is running, the curtain pulls inward. The falling water inside the curtain creates low pressure because of its movement. The air pressure outside the curtain helps push the curtain inward.

FLIGHT

VOCABULARY

airfoil ('âr·foi·əl) an object whose shape contributes to lift

lift ('lift) the force that pushes an aircraft up

weight ('wāt) the downward force on an object caused by gravity

thrust ('thrəst) the force that pushes an aircraft forward

drag ('drag) the backward force on an aircraft caused by friction

Bernoulli's principle is demonstrated in the way air moves over an airfoil. A wing is an airfoil that is curved and slightly thicker at the front and sharp and narrow at the back. As air moves over the top of a wing, it is forced to move faster than the air below the wing because of the wing's unique shape. Bernoulli's principle states that the faster air on top exerts a lower pressure on the top of the wing. This also means that the slower air under the airfoil exerts a greater pressure on the bottom of the wing. This forces the airplane up. This force, called lift, makes the airplane rise. An aircraft's airfoil affects lift because of its shape and the direction that the front of the wing is angled.

When a pilot is flying a plane, he or she is able to control the wings to produce lift. The plane accelerating down the runway causes the air to move past the wings more quickly. This produces lift due to the wing's shape. The lift can be further increased by the up and down tilt of the wing.

Why can airplanes fly upside down?

IN THE FIELD

Flight requires fast-moving air. Outer space has so little matter that there is not enough air to generate lift. Yet, space shuttles were made with wings. The wings were not used for flying in space but for returning to Earth. Once the mission of this type of space shuttle was completed, it re-entered Earth's atmosphere and flew to the ground, using lift and drag to slow it down enough for a safe landing.

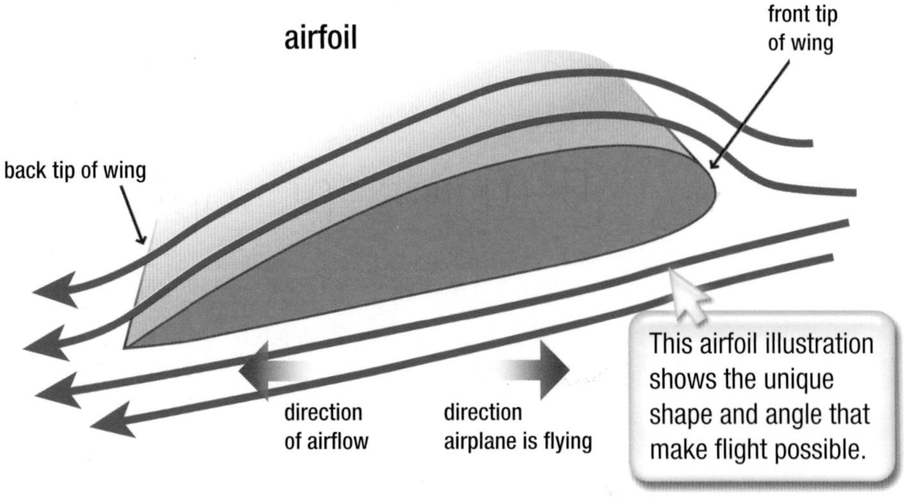

This airfoil illustration shows the unique shape and angle that make flight possible.

Three other forces act on an airplane in flight—weight, drag, and thrust. Weight pushes down and is caused by the pull of Earth's gravity. It works against lift. If the weight is greater than lift, the airborne plane descends. When weight equals lift, the airplane flies level. If the weight is less than lift, the aircraft rises.

Propellers and various types of engines create thrust, which pushes an airplane forward. As the airplane moves, air pushes against the plane and causes drag. This force resists thrust. When thrust equals drag during level flight, the airplane moves at a constant speed. If thrust is greater than drag, the airplane speeds up. If it is less than drag, the aircraft slows down.

The pilot maintains the tilt of the wings and speeds up to rise. Eventually, the pilot will adjust the wings and the speed to maintain a constant altitude until it is time to descend and land.

Why are the blades of this propeller in the shape of an airfoil?

QUICK FACT

Gliders are lightweight aircraft that usually have no source of thrust. A powered airplane tows the glider high in the sky and then releases it. Pilots are often trained in gliders because the absence of thrust simplifies the process of piloting a plane. Pilots use hot air rising from the ground, called *thermals*, or other geographical features to find lift for their gliders. Gliders have been known to travel a thousand miles and reach heights of 10.5 km (6.5 mi) using these methods.

The B-2 Stealth Bomber is sometimes called the *flying wing*. Its unusual shape causes the entire plane to help generate lift.

APPLICATIONS OF LIFT

IN THE FIELD

Hobby enthusiasts design, build, and compete in contests with model airplanes like this one. Thorough understandings of the associated scientific principles like Bernoulli's principle and Newton's third law of motion help make them successful. Others do the same with model cars, trucks, and speedboats. Each is controlled with radio waves transmitted from a controller to a receiver in the vehicle.

Bernoulli's principle is demonstrated in many other applications. Race cars use upside-down airfoils called *spoilers* to produce downward forces. This helps these fast cars stick to the road. More friction is created between the tires and the road, allowing them to corner faster. Airfoils are used both on the front and rear of the cars for stability and improved cornering. However, spoilers can create too much friction and increase drag, which reduces the top speed of a car, especially on straightaways. Properly placed spoilers can produce both wanted traction and streamlined speed for a faster car.

Helicopters also generate lift using airfoils. The airfoils are the blades that rotate above the helicopter. When these blades spin fast enough, the lift generated overcomes the weight of the helicopter. These blades work much like the propellers on airplanes. In fact, all propellers are airfoils and produce lift. However, the propellers on an airplane are oriented so that they help create the thrust that pushes the airplane forward.

Why does this Formula One race car have both front and back spoilers?

The pilot can control the direction of the helicopter by adjusting the position of the rotors.

Boomerangs utilize the shape of an airfoil to fly. Throughout history, boomerangs have been used as toys and hunting tools.

Newton's third law of motion—action and reaction—also explains curving balls. For instance, a table tennis player can change the way the ball travels by the way he or she hits the ball. Topspin can be produced by hitting slightly up while returning a shot. This causes the back of the ball to force air upward. As a reaction to this, the air forces the ball down. Once topspin is mastered, players can hit the ball harder and yet it will curve down and hit the table. Golf balls are often hit with backspin. This causes the back of the ball to force air downward. As a result, the air lifts up on the ball. Since this helps the ball stay in the air longer, it can travel almost 50% farther than a shot without backspin. In baseball, pitchers can throw a pitch so that the back of the ball is moving from left to right. This pushes the air to the right. The reaction forces the ball to curve to the left, making it more difficult to hit.

LINKS

Sports Link
Play a game with a plastic perforated ball on a windy day with some friends. Demonstrate the different ways the ball can curve. This should include both throwing and hitting the ball. Experiment with the differences between the ball moving against the wind, with the wind, and perpendicular to the wind.

Technology Link
Research the different uses of airfoils in technology and make a poster displaying six various types. Write a brief description about each one.

Creative Writing Link
Write a short story about your experiences as a molecule of air when an airplane passes by. Include the different things that happen to your neighboring molecules that help produce lift for the airplane.

Why are there seams on a baseball?

The table tennis player changes the ball's direction by creating different types of spin.

Soccer players use spin on the ball to direct their shots and passes.

CHAPTER 8

WHY THINGS MOVE

KEY IDEAS

- Newton's laws of motion describe why motion occurs.
- Speed, velocity, acceleration, and momentum are measurements of motion.
- Friction is a resistance to motion.

The Greek philosopher Aristotle was born about 2,400 years ago. He thought that all objects contained something within that gave them the potential to move. When that potential was active, the object moved. When that potential was inactive, the object remained still. He believed that potential for motion existed because the elements within objects tended to seek their natural place in the order of things. For example, he thought that a stone placed on the surface of the ocean would fall through the water because the stone's natural place was on the ground beneath the water.

Most people accepted many of Aristotle's ideas as fact for over 2,000 years. During the sixteenth century, Galileo Galilei of Italy challenged these ideas. For another century, scientists performed experiments to gain understanding about motion, although they could not yet explain why motion occurred. It was not until the late 1600s that Aristotle's ideas were replaced by Sir Isaac Newton's laws of motion.

How does this animal move from one place to another?

NEWTON'S LAWS OF MOTION

VOCABULARY

force ('fôrs) a push or a pull on an object

inertia (i·'nûr·shə) the resistance to a change in motion

Aristotle, Galileo, and Newton saw the laws of motion as unchanging principles. Aristotle observed that pushing or pulling directly on an object caused it to move. Sir Isaac Newton realized that the earth's gravity could pull on an object from a distance without touching it. He concluded that each planet was held in orbit by the gravitational pull of the sun. Newton inferred from this that unless an external force occurred, an object's motion would remain constant, whether still or moving.

Newton determined that an object at rest remains at rest unless another force pushes or pulls the object. Similarly, an object in motion will continue to move at a constant rate unless acted upon by another external force. This conclusion became known as *Newton's first law of motion*. Newton used the term inertia to describe an object's resistance to a change in motion. The inertia of an object depends on its mass, or the amount of matter in it. For example, it takes more force to move a bowling ball at rest than a balloon, and a moving bowling ball requires more force to stop than a balloon.

These images illustrate Newton's first law of motion.

Strange but True

The pangolin, known as the *scaly anteater*, lives in Asia and Africa. When it curls up in a ball for self-defense, its hard scales point outward. The pangolin does not move by rolling. Instead, it uses its back two legs for walking and the front two to dig for food and to keep its balance.

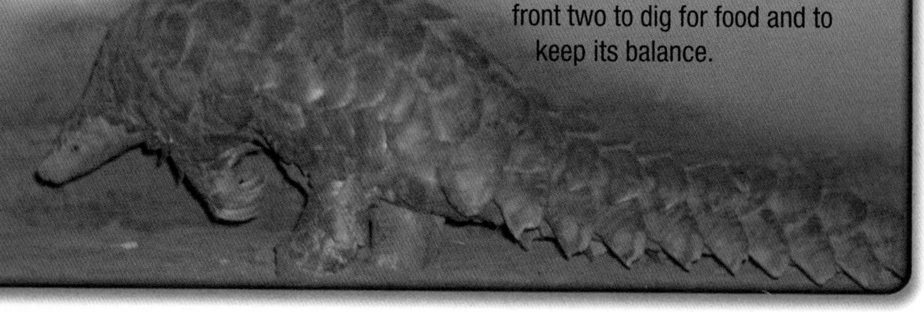

All objects change motion only when forced to change. An object's ability to speed up or slow down is affected by its mass and the amount of force exerted on it. This concept is known as *Newton's second law of motion*. The more mass an object has, the more force it takes to change its speed and direction. The more force that is applied to an object, the greater the change. For example, it takes a bulldozer less force to push a small rock than a boulder because of the boulder's larger mass.

Forces are always paired and opposite. For every action, there is an equal and opposite reaction. This is called *Newton's third law of motion*. For example, once a spacecraft's rockets are ignited, fiery gases are pushed out. When the rocket engines push the gases out, an opposite and equal reaction occurs. The gases push the rocket and its attached spacecraft forward. When the rocket engines are shut off, the gases stop pushing. The vehicle continues to move at a constant speed through space. It would coast at this speed forever, according to Newton's first law, unless another force were applied to it.

Newton's Laws of Motion	Description
first	An object at rest tends to stay at rest and an object in motion tends to stay in motion unless acted upon by an outside force.
second	Force is the mass of the object multiplied by its acceleration. ($f = m \times a$)
third	For every action there is an equal and opposite reaction.

IN THE FIELD

Deep Space 1 was a spacecraft designed and launched by NASA in 1998. Its engines, which were fueled by xenon, thrust the spacecraft forward using ion propulsion. This type of propulsion provided about 10 times more thrust than chemical rocket engines. The xenon gas was put into an electron engine and converted into ions that were accelerated to high speeds. They were then pushed out of the engine to move the spacecraft. This backward thrust propelled *Deep Space 1* farther through space than any other spacecraft of that time and demonstrated Newton's third law.

The reason football players wear so much gear is that it helps protect their bodies from being injured during forceful tackles and collisions on the field. It does this by absorbing some of the force from the contact with the other player.

SPEED AND VELOCITY

VOCABULARY

average speed (ˈa·və·rij ˈspēd) the total distance traveled divided by the total travel time

velocity (və·ˈlä·sə·tē) the measure of an object's speed and direction

Newton proved that motion occurs when an unbalanced force is exerted on an object. Speed and velocity are two ways to describe the movement of an object. Speed is the distance covered in a certain amount of time. It relates how fast an object is moving. The distance represents how far the object travels. The time describes how long it takes the object to move that distance. The mathematical formula to calculate speed is:

speed = distance ÷ time

Most objects do not move at a constant speed while traveling. For example, a race car driver changes speed numerous times throughout a race based on how he or she drives around the other cars and the different sections of track. Yet, the average speed is calculated by using the total distance of the race and the total time it took the driver to complete it. The driver exceeds the average speed many times during the race, but drives more slowly or even stops during parts of it as well.

What is the speed of light?

Some bowlers can roll the ball at 40 kph (25 mph).

The average large aircraft takes off at 290 kph (180 mph).

An object's position changes when it moves. The object not only travels at a speed, but also in a direction. Velocity is the measurement that is used to note both the speed and the direction that an object travels. For example, if a girl tosses a ball straight up into the air and watches it fall, she could make several observations. As the ball travels in the upward direction, the speed slows down until finally it stops just for a split second. The speed decreases, yet the direction remains the same. Once the ball starts to fall because of gravity, the ball begins to speed up in the opposite direction. If at some point she notes that the speed going up is the same as the speed coming down, she would need to point out that the ball is traveling in opposite directions. In doing so, she would be referring to the ball's velocity.

QUICK FACT

How fast does a skydiver fall? As fast as a race car! A skydiver must pull the cord on his or her parachute early enough that a safe landing can be made. The speed of a skydiver can reach up to 200 kph (124 mph).

If these snails are traveling at the same speed, their velocities are not the same because they are moving in different directions.

These two boats are moving in the same direction, yet their speeds are different. Therefore, they have different velocities.

ACCELERATION AND MOMENTUM

VOCABULARY

acceleration (ik·ˌse·lə·ˈrā·shən) the change in an object's velocity over a period of time

newton (ˈnōō·tən) the standard metric unit for the measurement of force

momentum (mō·ˈmen·təm) the property of a moving object that causes it to tend to keep moving

Acceleration occurs when an object's speed changes from one rate to another over a certain period of time. If a toy car speeds up as it moves in a straight line, its acceleration could be calculated by using the following formula:

$$\text{acceleration} = \frac{\text{ending speed} - \text{beginning speed}}{\text{time}}$$

If the speed were measured in meters per second, or m/sec, and the time of travel in seconds, the resulting unit of acceleration would be meters per second per second, or m/sec^2.

Another way to think about acceleration involves the force that moves an object and the object's mass. Every object resists a change in motion, and the amount of resistance depends on the object's mass. Newton's second law states that larger forces and smaller masses result in greater accelerations. Similarly, smaller forces and greater masses cause smaller accelerations. This concept is expressed in the following mathematical formula:

$$\text{acceleration} = \text{force} \div \text{mass}$$

The metric unit of measuring force is called a newton and is abbreviated as *N*. A newton is the force that causes an object with a mass of 1 kg to accelerate at 1 m/sec^2. Its mathematical formula is kg × m/sec^2. One newton of force is about the weight of an apple. A newton spring scale is often used to measure the amount of force exerted by an object.

If this toy car were traveling at 2 m/sec when you began timing it and then ended 2 sec later at 6 m/sec, its acceleration during that time would be 2 m/sec^2.

If the force to move a 25-kg object is 100 N, then the object's acceleration is 4 m/sec^2.

An object in motion will continue to move at a constant velocity unless acted upon by another force. This tendency to keep moving is called momentum; it includes the object's mass, speed, and direction. The mathematical formula to calculate momentum is:

momentum = mass × velocity

Since mass is typically measured in kilograms and velocity in meters per second, the standard unit of measurement for momentum is kilogram-meters per second. It is abbreviated kg×m/s.

The study of momentum is important even outside of science. For example, a coach who wants a softball player to hit the ball so that it will be more difficult to stop could have the player use a heavier bat. When the player swings the heavier bat at the same speed as before, more momentum is released into the ball and causes it to travel farther and for a longer period of time. When two objects like the ball and the bat collide, momentum is not lost as long as there is no friction involved. This transfer of momentum occurs according to the law of conservation of momentum.

QUICK FACT

The word *conservation* means *keeping* or *not changing*. The law of conservation of momentum refers to the keeping, or preservation, of momentum. A way to understand this is to consider what happens in the game of pool. When the pool stick strikes the cue ball, the momentum of the pool stick is transferred to the cue ball. When the cue ball hits a stationary pool ball head-on, all the momentum of the cue ball shifts to the stationary ball. This causes the stationary ball to move and the cue ball to stop. If the cue ball hits the stationary ball at an angle, some of the momentum remains with the cue ball and some transfers to the stationary ball.

LAW OF CONSERVATION OF MOMENTUM

Momentum is not created or destroyed. Without other outside forces involved, when two objects collide, the total momentum is the same before and after the collision.

Newton's cradle demonstrates the law of conservation of momentum. Momentum is transferred from the first ball, through the center balls, and then pushes the last ball away. In theory, this should continue forever, but because of gravity, friction, and air resistance, the motion eventually slows to a stop.

FRICTION

VOCABULARY

friction ('frik·shən) the force that resists motion between two surfaces in contact with each other

static friction ('sta·tik 'frik·shən) the force that resists movement of an object at rest

kinetic friction (kə·'ne·tik 'frik·shən) the force that resists the motion of a moving object

air resistance ('âr ri·'zis·tənts) the action of friction caused by air

Gravity and friction are two forces on Earth that push against moving objects. Many everyday tasks depend on the properties of friction. If there were no friction, people would not be able to walk, bicycles would not gain traction, and even holding a pencil would be difficult.

Friction not only relates to objects in motion, it also relates to objects at rest. When two surfaces in contact with each other are not moving, static friction is present. A good example of this is a large boulder on top of the ground. Once the boulder is put into motion, kinetic friction resists its movement, eventually causing it to stop if no additional force is applied. Newton's first law of motion states that an object in motion tends to stay in motion unless acted on by another force. Friction is an example of one of the additional forces that resists the object's movement. Friction is caused by the rough surfaces on objects or by the electrical attractions between the atomic particles in the surfaces and acts in a direction opposite to the motion.

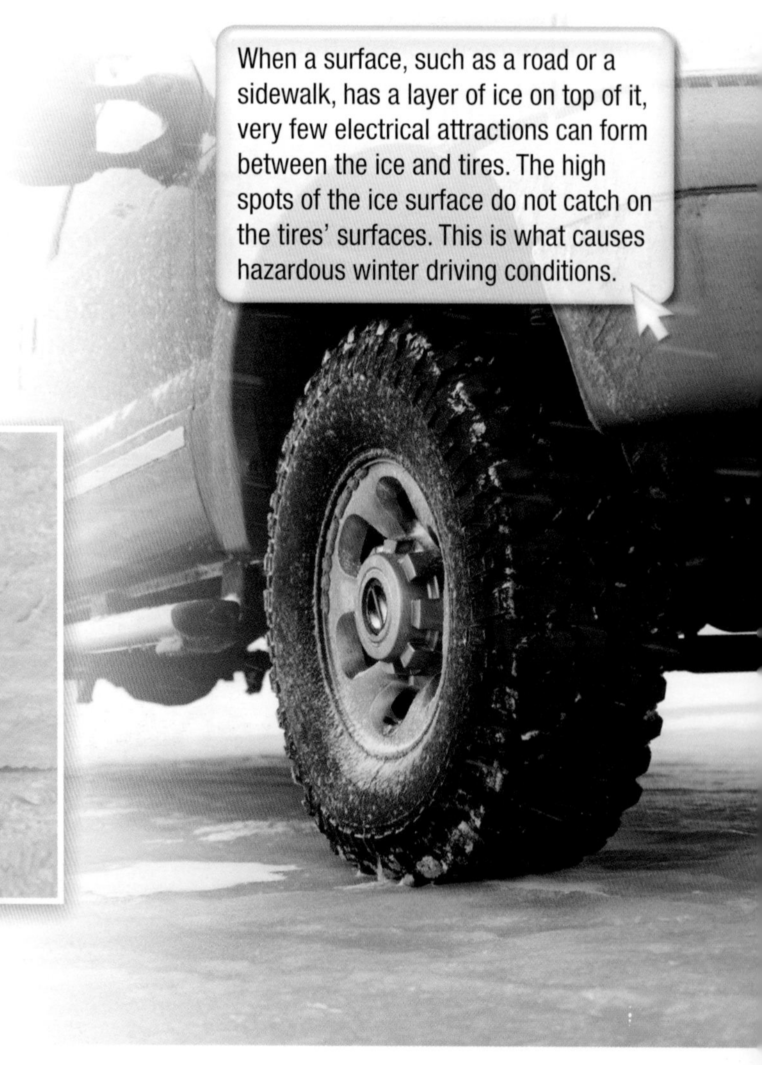

When a surface, such as a road or a sidewalk, has a layer of ice on top of it, very few electrical attractions can form between the ice and tires. The high spots of the ice surface do not catch on the tires' surfaces. This is what causes hazardous winter driving conditions.

Static friction keeps this boy from sliding down the hill until he pushes off.

Another example of friction is seen when a runner's feet push backward against the ground. If the ground is slippery, the feet just slide backward. If the surface has enough friction, the push of the runner's feet against the ground enables forward motion.

Not all friction takes place between solid surfaces. It can also happen when a solid surface comes in contact with a fluid. A motorboat is a good example. An outboard engine mounted on the back of the boat pushes water backward from the boat with its propeller. This causes the boat to move forward. The friction between the propeller and the water as well as between the boat and the water helps the movement occur. Oars may also be used in the action of pushing against the water. In reaction, the friction from the contact with the water moves the boat forward. Another example of friction between a solid surface and a fluid is that of a plane pushing through the air. The force of the air pushing against the plane is known as *drag*, or air resistance.

Why are machine parts coated in oil?

IN THE FIELD

Ball bearings are used in machines to reduce friction between the moving parts. They are small metal balls that are typically coated with oil and also help bear the load of the machine. They function by fitting into a groove and move within it. They are inexpensive mechanisms designed to decrease friction by allowing objects to roll instead of slide.

Carpet increases friction. It explains why it is more difficult to push some furniture on a carpeted floor than on a smooth floor.

Air resistance allows these skydivers more control of their rate of descent.

PERPETUAL MOTION

VOCABULARY

perpetual motion
(pûr·ˈpe·chə·wəl ˈmō·shən) motion that continues endlessly

thermodynamics
(ˌthûr·mō·dī·ˈna·miks) the scientific study of how energy transfers from one place to another and from one form to another

IN THE FIELD

Each year Carnegie Mellon University hosts a high school science competition. Students from all over the country compete to win a $100,000 scholarship prize sponsored by Siemens Westinghouse. Previous winners of this prestigious competition researched areas such as technology, genetics, and ecology.

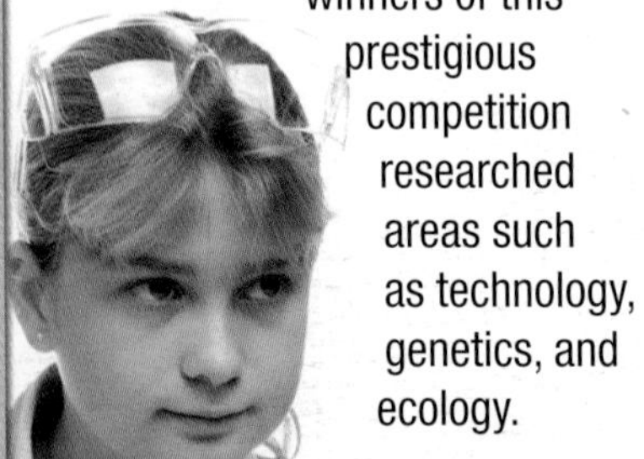

For hundreds of years people have attempted to create a machine that, once started, would run forever. A machine with perpetual motion would provide an unending source of power at little to no cost. It would create its own energy to fuel itself and overcome the effects of gravity, friction, and loss of energy.

No one has ever succeeded in building a perpetual motion machine and most scientists believe it to be impossible. The reason for this is that the machine must overcome two basic laws of thermodynamics. The first law states that energy cannot be created or destroyed but is converted or transferred from one type to another. The second law involves *entropy*, which means that things slow down and wear out. For example, heat always flows from a hotter area or object to a colder one. When a machine is on, most of the heat energy is converted into work, but some of the heat energy transfers to colder materials within and around the machine. Since some of the energy is transferred, the machine requires additional energy to continue to perform its tasks. If no additional energy is available, the machine slows down and stops. Scientists who have attempted to make a perpetual motion machine were not successful in overcoming these two laws of thermodynamics.

Recorded history identifies many who have tried to create a perpetual motion machine. A common design was an overbalanced wheel onto which movable weights were firmly attached. Each was placed on its own axle and attached to the wheel. As the wheel rotated, the weights at the bottom would begin to shift outward from the wheel, while those on the top would move close to the wheel. Villard de Honnecourt, a thirteenth-century Frenchman, was one of the first to build such a device. The thought was that the weights moving outward would create enough momentum for the wheel to continue rotating. However, this did not prove true.

In the 1880s, British professor John Gamgee tried to invent a perpetual motion machine. He replaced the water in a steam engine with ammonia, since ammonia's boiling point is much lower than that of water. His thought was that the boiled ammonia would produce ammonia gas, which in turn would condense back into liquid form and be reheated by the high temperature remaining in the engine. What he failed to consider was that the heat of the engine had to decrease for the condensation to occur.

LINKS

Art Link
Create a poster that illustrates your version of a perpetual motion machine.

Bible Link
Research the biblical account of Creation. Compare this information to the laws of thermodynamics. Write a thoughtful response to the question of whether or not God is bound to the laws of thermodynamics.

Technology Link
Research how industries reduce the amount of energy lost in their machines. Include the usage of lubricants and machine components. Write a report on your findings.

Why is a windmill not a perpetual motion machine?

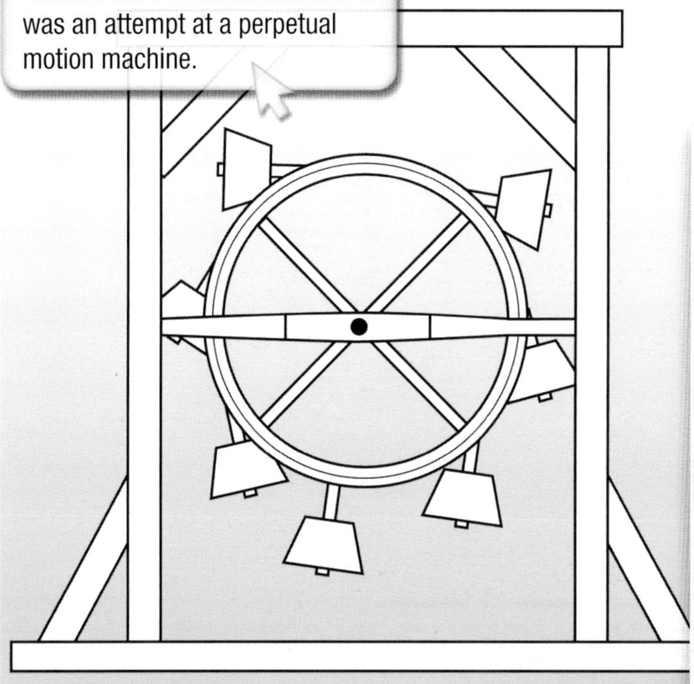

Honnecourt's overbalanced wheel was an attempt at a perpetual motion machine.

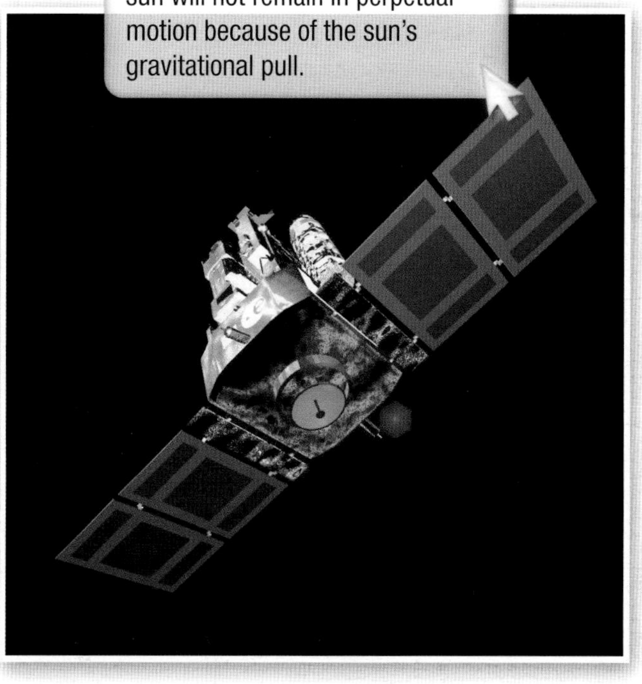

Scientists believe that even the *SOHO* spacecraft that orbits the sun will not remain in perpetual motion because of the sun's gravitational pull.

UNIT 1 LIFE SCIENCE: DIVERSITY

UNIT 2 PHYSICAL SCIENCE: STRUCTURE

UNIT 3 EARTH AND SPACE SCIENCE: PATTERNS

– the study of oceans, rocks, weather, and celestial bodies

UNIT 4 HUMAN BODY: DECISIONS

CHAPTER 9

OCEANS IN MOTION

The presence of liquid water allows life to exist on Earth. The vast majority of this water is found in the world's oceans. It is distributed across Earth's entire surface and into the atmosphere through the hydrologic cycle. Water has a high heat capacity and plays a key role in moderating the planet's temperatures.

Water molecules move through the oceans because of density differences in the same way that air molecules circulate throughout the atmosphere. In the atmosphere, temperature is a key indicator of density. In water, density is often determined by both the temperature and the salinity of the mass of water. Ocean water movements can be seen in tides, waves, and currents.

KEY IDEAS

- Ocean water is constantly in motion.
- Ocean water moves in predictable patterns based on its characteristics.
- Marine organisms are uniquely suited to live in their habitat.

All living things on Earth depend on water. The movement of water in the atmosphere and oceans is one key feature that makes Earth uniquely suited to sustain life.

OUTLOOK

While the earth's surface has a ratio of almost three parts water to one part land, this may have changed throughout the earth's history. Surface features that exist now have not always existed. For instance, new volcanic islands continue to form to this day.
In addition, catastrophes have occurred in the earth's past that have drastically changed the shape of its surface. This makes it difficult for scientists to predict what things looked like before present-day observations were made and records were kept.

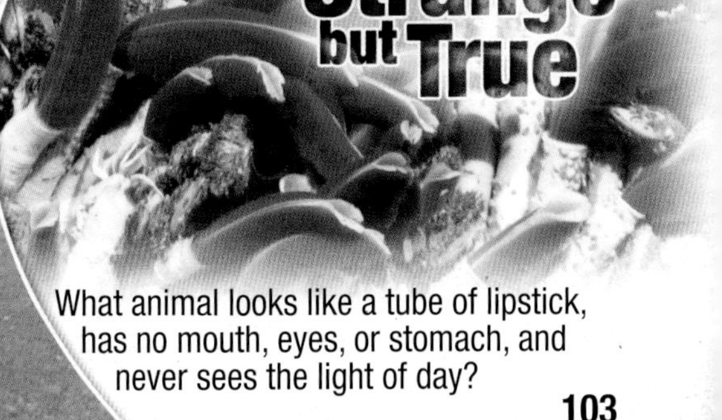

What animal looks like a tube of lipstick, has no mouth, eyes, or stomach, and never sees the light of day?

WATER MOVEMENT

VOCABULARY

wave ('wāv) a movement that transfers energy from point to point through matter

current ('kûr·ənt) the continuous flow of ocean water in a certain direction

IN THE FIELD

Knowing the water level in a given location is very important for many purposes, such as predicting tsunamis and storm surges, navigating ships through the water, coastal engineering, and charting the seafloor. Water level data is observed in the United States by the National Ocean Service (NOS) and is passed on to shipmasters. This allows them to determine the best time to enter or leave a port and to prevent large ships from running aground or having collisions.

The earth is a dynamic, moving planet. Many factors interact with its oceans to produce expected patterns of water movement. Tides are the vertical movement of water and are caused mainly by the pull of gravity from the moon and the sun. The gravitational pull from other solar bodies also contributes to tides, but to a much smaller degree. The combined gravitational pull creates repeated cycles of changing water levels in the ocean as well as other large bodies of water around the world. Tides alternate between low and high levels twice daily. Fishing and other water activities are often dependent on the tides.

Waves are another type of motion that occurs in oceans. An ocean wave is the movement of energy through a body of water. It begins in the open sea and occurs for different reasons. Most waves form when wind energy is transferred to the ocean's surface. Certain waves are due to seismic activity that has moved a large amount of water. These are called *seismic sea waves* or *tsunamis*.

What is a tidal stream?

The changing of the ocean's water level because of tides in specific areas has been measured by mariners for hundreds of years.

While the energy of a wave in the open sea moves toward shore, the water itself stays mostly in the same place. Near the shoreline the seafloor slopes upward. As the waves approach the shoreline, the water becomes more shallow. The bottom of the wave hits the ocean floor. Friction between the floor and the wave causes the wave to slow down and change in shape. The water forms a peak and breaks onto the shore. It is at this point that the wave and the water both move forward.

A current results from the difference in the properties of water masses. The different properties include temperature, density, and salinity. In addition, wind affects surface currents. All currents are affected to some degree by both gravity and the Coriolis effect. The Coriolis effect is a result of Earth's rotation, which causes ocean and wind currents to swirl in specific patterns from the poles to the equator. In the Northern Hemisphere, most currents rotate in a clockwise direction. In the Southern Hemisphere, they rotate counterclockwise. Currents are generally the horizontal movements of water. However, some vertical currents do exist.

What is the reference point for the moving water on Earth?

QUICK FACT

Oceans affect weather and climate. The upper 3 m (10 ft) of the ocean retains more heat than is in the entire atmosphere. Ocean temperatures keep coastal temperatures from fluctuating between extremely hot and cold. Seas also store and transport carbon dioxide (CO_2), an important factor in the global warming theory. It has been estimated that half of the CO_2 that has been added to the atmosphere in the last hundred years—mostly due to the burning of fossil fuels—has been absorbed by the ocean. In fact, most of the CO_2 emitted into the atmosphere will be absorbed by the ocean over several decades and centuries.

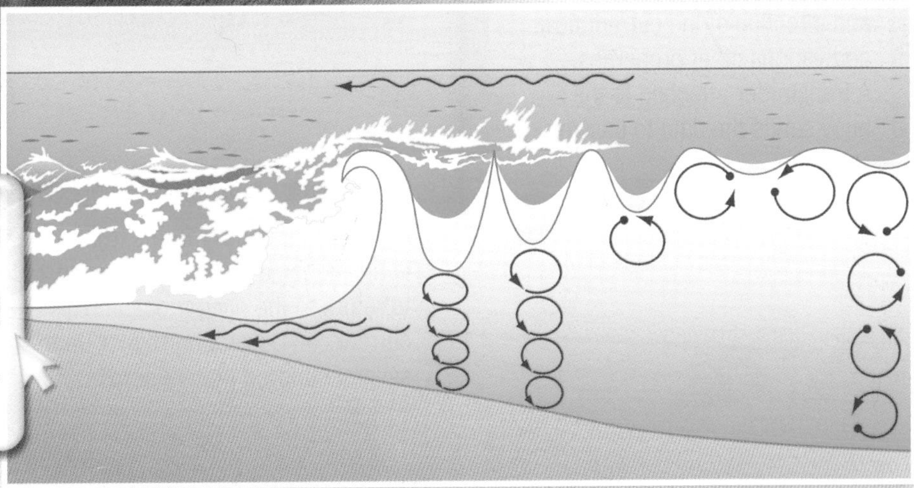

As the wave approaches the shore, friction between the ocean floor and the wave causes the wave to slow down and the wave height to increase. When the water reaches a certain height, the crest falls over or breaks, and becomes the surf.

VOCABULARY

longshore current ('lông·shôr 'kûr·ənt) a movement of water caused by waves that strike the shore at an angle

rip current ('rip 'kûr·ənt) a strong flow of water that returns seaward perpendicular to the shore

There are two main types of ocean currents—surface and deep. A surface current is driven by the wind and flows horizontally. Global winds are responsible for the major surface currents of the world. These winds cause the currents to flow in giant circular paths called *gyres*. Surface currents also occur on a smaller scale. A longshore current is caused by waves that move at an angle toward the shore. Water erodes some of the sand and then deposits it farther down the coast. This can cause large amounts of erosion to develop along shorelines.

A rip current is an effect of a longshore current. It takes place when water returns to the sea. When a sandbar forms and water breaks through it, a rush of water is created that moves outward much more quickly than the surrounding water. Although this normally occurs in a very narrow area, it can be extremely dangerous for swimmers. To escape a rip current, a person should not panic but swim parallel to the beach and then back to shore.

IN THE FIELD

Surface currents can now be studied by the modern drifter, a high-tech version of a message in a bottle. This device consists of a surface buoy and a sea anchor attached to a long tether. Drifters measure temperature, speed and direction of the current flow, and various other properties. A transmitter attached to the buoy sends the data to passing satellites.

Waves approach the shoreline at an angle and produce a longshore current. Sandbars often form in areas of longshore currents.

A rip current usually forms from a break in a sandbar, causing fast-moving water to return to the deeper ocean. This current can be very narrow or up to several hundred meters across.

Deep currents are caused by differences in density. Warm or less salty water is less dense and rises. Water that is salty or cold is denser and sinks. Therefore, water in the polar regions sinks and is replaced by warm tropical water. As the cold water flows toward the equator, it warms and rises. These deep sea currents are connected and are often called *the great ocean conveyor belt*.

Many organisms depend on ocean currents in order to obtain the nutrients they need to survive. Upwelling occurs when cold, nutrient-rich water from the bottom of the ocean moves up toward the surface. Plankton feed on the nutrients. Downwelling occurs along the coast when water is forced downward and is replaced by surface water, which is not as nutrient-rich as deep water.

When the easterly trade winds become stronger and cold upwellings intensify as a result, La Niña may take place. This naturally occurring climate cycle takes place along the equator and the South American west coast. The water, which is colder than usual, affects the surrounding air and brings colder temperatures to the neighboring regions.

How does the boiling water inside of a pan show the fluid-like movements of currents?

Deep currents circulate around the world in a conveyor belt fashion. It is hypothesized that one complete cycle takes about 1,000 years.

QUICK FACT

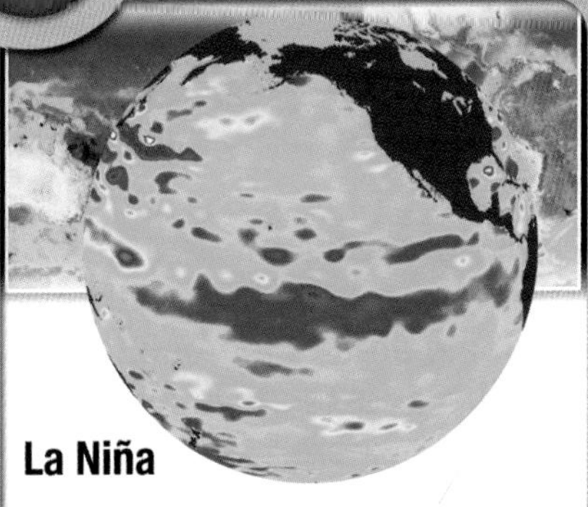

La Niña

La Niña is characterized by unusually cold ocean temperatures. Conversely, El Niño brings about warmer than usual water temperatures and weather conditions. El Niño prevents upwelling from occurring and causes the water to have limited nutrients. This phenomenon was originally recognized by fishermen off the coast of South America when the water appeared to be unusually warm. Both events occur every two to seven years and have significant impact on global climates.

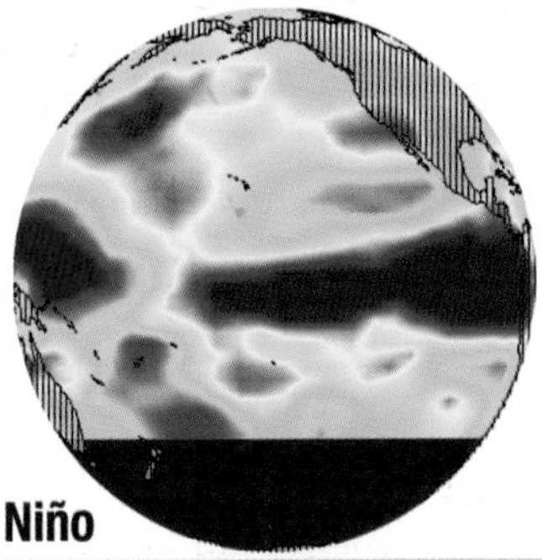

El Niño

OCEAN ZONES

VOCABULARY

continental shelf (kän·tə·ˈnen·təl ˈshelf) a gently sloping area of the ocean floor that extends outward from the shoreline

intertidal (in·tər·ˈtī·dəl) relating to an ocean zone located between high- and low-tide lines

neritic (nə·ˈri·tik) relating to the area of the ocean that extends from the low-tide line out to the edge of the continental shelf

oceanic (ō·shē·ˈa·nik) relating to the zone that extends from the edge of the continental shelf and covers the entire open ocean

The ocean is divided into various areas with different characteristics. The water column is a vertical section of the ocean and is divided according to temperature. The surface layer of this column extends from the surface to an average depth of 200 m (656 ft). Sunlight penetrates this layer, producing an average worldwide temperature of 17°C (63°F). Extending from the bottom of the surface layer to about 1 km (3,280 ft) is the transition layer, or thermocline. Here, temperatures decrease rapidly to about 4°C (39°F). The deep layer starts at the base of the transition layer and extends to the ocean floor. The temperature in this area is just above the freezing point of water. When descending through the water column, temperature decreases and pressure increases.

The ocean floor is divided into specific areas. The continental margin reaches from the edge of the continents to the abyssal plain. It includes the continental shelf, which is the shallow edge of a continent that is submerged in water; the continental slope; and the continental rise.

Scuba divers are able to stay underwater to study plants and animals by using special equipment to breathe. Scuba is actually an acronym, which stands for *self-contained underwater breathing apparatus.*

Ocean water can have a lower freezing point because of its salinity level.

The ocean is also divided into horizontal regions. The intertidal zone is located along the shoreline between the high- and low-tide lines. This area is subject to the wind, waves, alternating periods of submersion under the water and sand, and exposure to air and sunlight. Marine organisms that live here must be suited to survive the constant pounding of the surf.

The neritic zone is the area of water directly over the continental shelf. This region usually reaches to about 200 m (600 ft) below the surface. The water is warmed by sunlight and receives a steady supply of nutrients. The neritic zone is similar to the rainforest in that there is also a high productivity and a great diversity of species here. Coral reefs and kelp forests are found in the neritic zone.

The oceanic zone begins at the edge of the continental shelf. It is the largest marine environment, but it supports fewer known organisms than the neritic zone. This is because sunlight only penetrates a relatively short distance into the water and fewer nutrients are available.

In what zone would this animal likely be found?

OUTLOOK

An ice cap is a mass of ice and snow that permanently covers a large area. Much of the freshwater that exists on the earth's surface is frozen in the form of polar ice caps and glaciers. As they melt, there is concern that the additional water might change ocean currents and create land-usage issues for future generations. According to Psalm 104, the waters are gathered to where God has chosen for them to be. Even if the ice caps melt, this is not a calamity in God's eyes. He continues to work out His plan on the earth that He created.

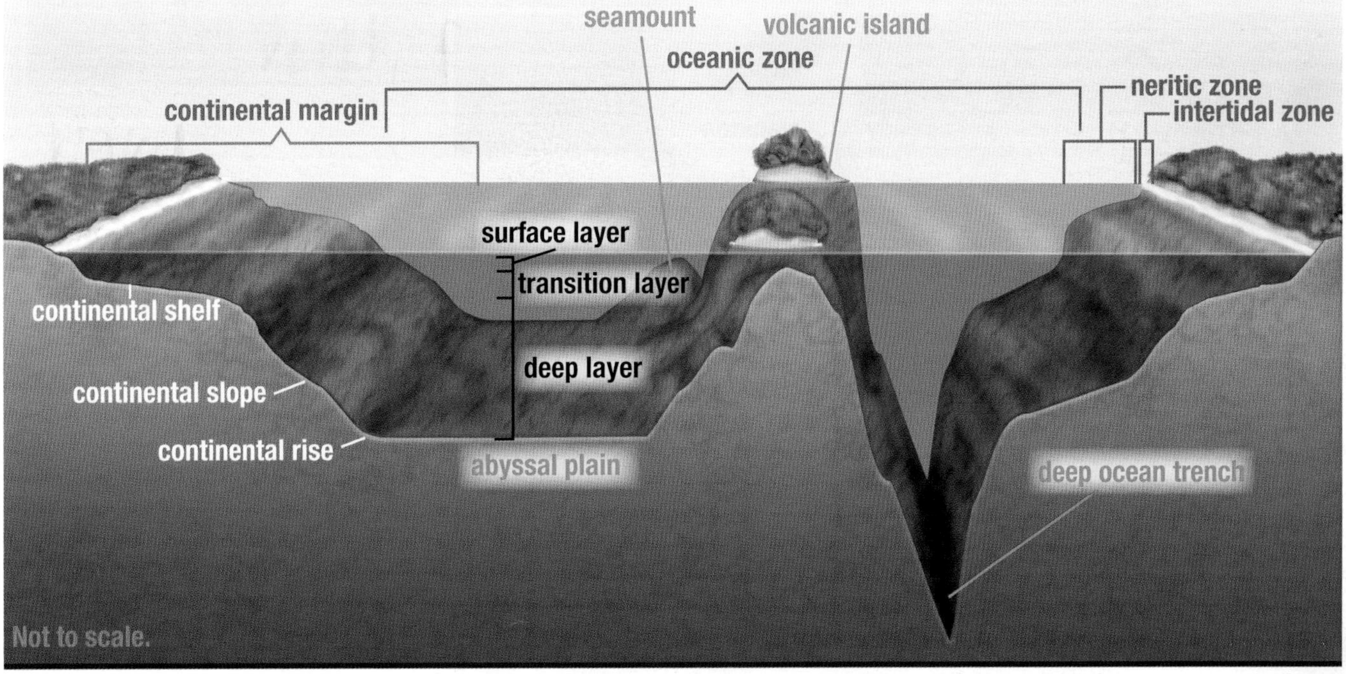

MARINE LIFE

VOCABULARY

plankton ('plank·tən) the tiny algae and animals that float in the surface zone

nekton ('nek·tən) the free-swimming organisms

benthos ('ben·thäs) the organisms that inhabit the ocean floor

bioluminescence (bī·ō·,lo͞o·mə·'ne·səns) the production of light by living organisms

Many types of organisms inhabit the various ocean zones. Marine organisms are divided into three main groups according to where they live and how they move. Floating in the surface layer are plankton. These tiny organisms play extremely important roles as primary producers of food and oxygen. They are the basis of the ocean food webs. Nekton are those animals that swim freely through the ocean. Sharks, whales, squid, and most fish are nekton. Some mollusks are included as well. Organisms that live on or near the ocean floor belong to the benthos group. Some benthos, such as sponges, sea anemones, and plants, stay in one location. Other benthos, such as clams, crabs, lobsters, and octopi, move from place to place.

The intertidal zone is inhabited mostly by benthos. Tide pools form when the tide retreats and water fills depressions in the ground. Organisms living in these areas must be able to withstand changes in temperature, salinity, and wet and dry conditions. This group is primarily made up of invertebrates, such as barnacles, sea urchins, mussels, starfish, snails, and crabs.

Organisms that can survive the unique conditions of tide pools are often very beautiful and fun to watch.

Plant and animal plankton live near the surface of the ocean and are at the base of the food web. The free-swimming animals, from small to large size, are nekton. Benthos are found on the ocean floor.

Coral reefs and kelp forests are frequently found along the continental shelf in the neritic zone. Coral reefs are made by tiny coral animals that secrete a substance that becomes a hard structure. The empty skeleton is left behind when the animal dies. Over years, coral reefs form and are home to thousands of different species. Kelp forests grow in the cold waters of the neritic zone worldwide. Kelp are large, heavy algae and require rocky ground to anchor their root-like structures. Various nekton, such as sea otters, live in these underwater forests.

In the depths of the oceanic zone where there is no sunlight, bioluminescence is particularly important. Certain undersea creatures have the ability to produce their own light in order to attract a mate or prey or to escape a predator. Hydrothermal vents are located deep on the ocean floor near diverging oceanic plates. Although dark and cold, this harsh environment is home to hundreds of species which thrive on chemicals and minerals that escape from the mantle through these vents.

OUTLOOK

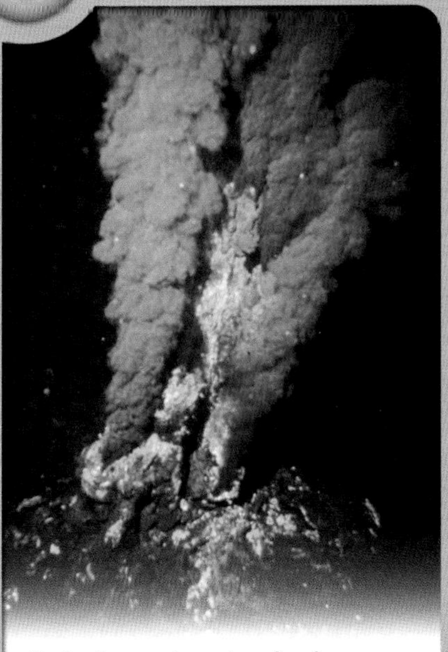

Hydrothermal vents, also known as *black smokers*, spew boiling hot, mineral-rich water. They can be several stories tall. These vents were first discovered on the ocean floor in 1977 off the coast of South America. Since then, many have been found in locations along plate boundaries throughout the world's oceans. Even without sunlight many organisms survive this extreme environment.

Coral reefs form in shallow, sunlit tropical waters. Many types of organisms have habitats in and around the reefs.

Strange but True

Tubeworms live near vents in the ocean floor. They live in a symbiotic relationship with bacteria that produce food from chemicals. Tubeworms can grow to be 1 m (3 ft) long and often become food for other deep-sea dwelling animals!

BRINE POOLS

VOCABULARY

brine pool ('brīn 'po͞ol) an area of water on the ocean floor that has high salinity

IN THE FIELD

Famous oceanographer Jacques Cousteau (1910–1997) contributed greatly to the field of underwater exploration. He developed the very first type of scuba gear, providing alternatives to large and expensive underwater suits that had previously been in use. He traveled the oceans in a converted minesweeper called *Calypso* to explore the mysteries that had long existed underwater. In order to help fund his travels, Cousteau wrote books and made films of his discoveries. His legacy continues through *The Cousteau Society*, which works to help protect the valuable natural resources of the oceans.

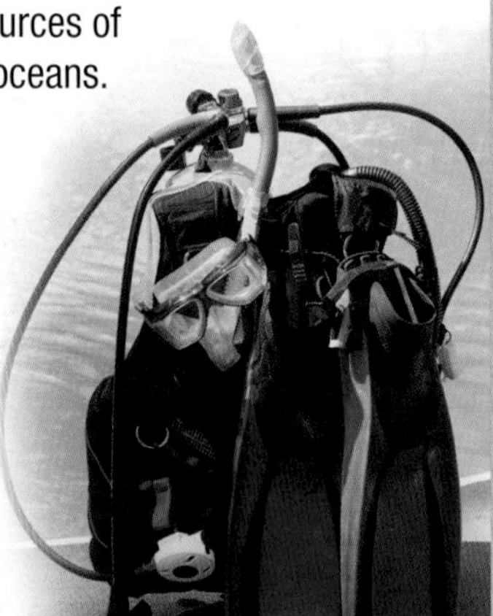

On Earth, most organisms are suited to thrive in very specific environments. One unique environment located on the ocean floor is the brine pool. With a much higher salinity than the surrounding waters, brine pools mark the location of salt deposits. These pools of very salty water range from 1 m to 20 km (1 yd to 12 mi) across. The salinity of the water causes them to be very dense, forming salt lakes within the ocean.

Brine pools develop as the salt deposits beneath the ocean floor come into contact with seawater and dissolve. Exploration of large pools is difficult because submersibles tend to float on top of them and are not able to dive down into them. The high salt concentration makes even very heavy things float. Although the environment is extremely salty, brine pools have their own uniquely adapted benthic community.

Why does the food coloring diffuse throughout the water?

A variety of mussels are able to survive in the extremely salty water of a brine pool.

This man is very buoyant because of the density of the surrounding saltwater.

Extremophiles are organisms that thrive in extreme conditions that many other living things would not be able to survive. Most extremophiles are microscopic. Halophiles are extremophiles that need high concentrations of salt to grow. They often color the water a pinkish-orange. Hyperthermophiles are extremophiles that thrive in temperatures higher than 60°C (140°F). These include organisms that live near hydrothermal vents, hot springs, and volcanoes.

Some organisms can adjust to changes in their environment. Lake Nicaragua, which drains into the Caribbean Sea, is an example of an area where certain organisms can move freely from freshwater into the saltwater of the sea. Adult bull sharks have the ability to swim in both types of water by controlling their own internal salt and water levels as needed. They move out to sea to mate and produce offspring. This gives their young a chance to grow and develop in the most favorable environment possible for bull sharks, which is saltwater.

LINKS

Language Arts Link
Write a story about life in the ocean as if you were plankton, nekton, or benthos. Describe what kind of organism you are, where you live, and what kind of other marine life share your habitat.

Technology Link
Use the Internet to research how technological advances have made undersea exploration more accessible. Document three different kinds of equipment, and describe how they have helped increase knowledge of the ocean. Present the information to the class.

History Link
Research the development and uses of the diving craft *Alvin*. Why was it developed? What has it been used for? What are its capabilities? Prepare a short report on your findings.

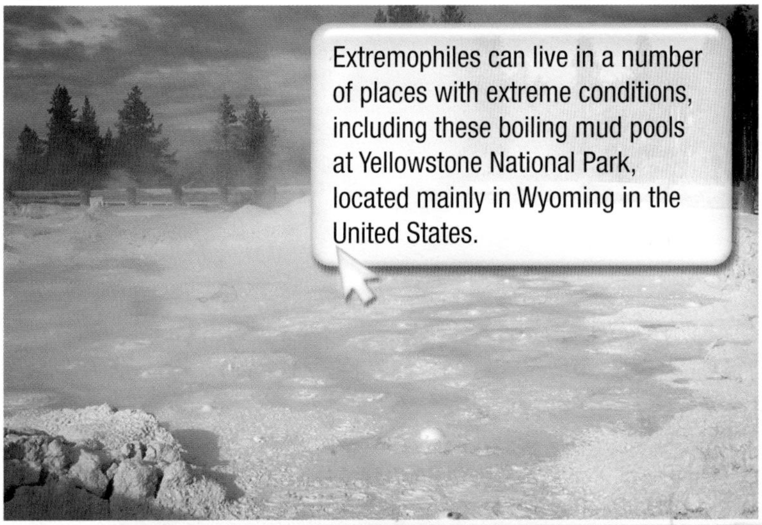

Extremophiles can live in a number of places with extreme conditions, including these boiling mud pools at Yellowstone National Park, located mainly in Wyoming in the United States.

Lake Nicaragua is the second largest lake in Central America. A dormant volcanic chain runs right through the lake, resulting in many beautiful islands.

CHAPTER 10

ROCK RECORDS

KEY IDEAS

- Rocks are constantly being transformed in a natural cycle.
- Both gradual and catastrophic processes erode, break down, and deposit rock.
- Fossils form in a variety of ways.
- The geologic column is used to describe major rock layers. There are three major interpretations of the layering.

The earth's crust contains minerals in the form of elements and compounds. Minerals have a definite chemical composition and crystal structure. They come in many colors, shapes, and textures. Rocks are made mostly of inorganic, or nonliving, materials such as minerals. Some rocks are also made of organic matter, or once-living things. The rock cycle, a natural process, constantly transforms rocks into one of three types—igneous, sedimentary, and metamorphic. The theory of plate tectonics explains how rocks recycle from one form to another. Oceanic crust, or the layer of solid material found under the ocean water, consists of the youngest, or newest, rock. This is because magma seeps up through the mid-ocean ridge and hardens, forming a new layer of igneous rock. Continental crust is the thickest and found below the continents. It is older than oceanic crust and is composed of all three types of rocks.

This is rock salt, or halite. It consists of sodium chloride, which at one time was in solution. Since water is constantly in motion, the many particles that make up one sample of halite most likely came from many different locations.

Rock features such as these buttes at Lake Powell, Utah, in the United States show that materials have been deposited in layers and that portions have since eroded away.

Strange but True

For what purposes can people use this dirt?

> **VOCABULARY**
>
> **grain** ('grān) the mineral or rock particles that give rock its texture
>
> **foliated** ('fō·lē·ā·təd) a layered appearance caused by the parallel arrangement of grains

Geologists classify rock into three main types—igneous, metamorphic, and sedimentary. Igneous rock forms when magma cools and hardens. If rock becomes very hot without melting, is put under great pressure, or both, it becomes metamorphic rock. Pre-existing rocks that undergo weathering and erosion break down into smaller pieces. Sedimentary rock forms when minerals and these pieces of other rocks combine into a solid.

Many different materials can make up the three types of rock. Most rocks contain grains, which are mineral particles or other tiny rocks. Grains take time to form and can cause different patterns within rocks. Additionally, coarse-grained rocks are those that have grains that are large and easy to see. Slow-cooling magma far below the earth's surface produces coarse-grained rock. The cooling process takes so long that larger crystals develop. This type of rock is known as *intrusive rock*. Fine-grained rocks have small, microscopic grains. Quick-cooling igneous rock forms small grains. This type of rock cools rapidly and is known as *extrusive rock*.

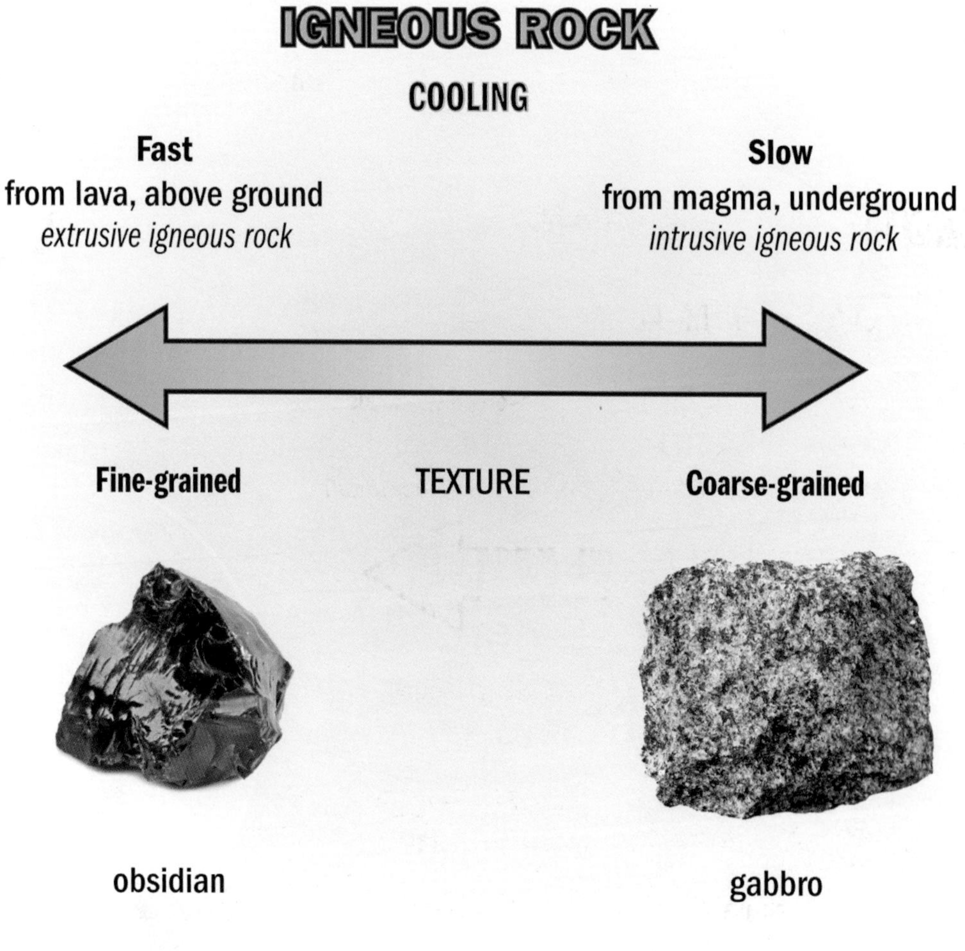

Heat, pressure, or the combination of both help to form metamorphic rock. Foliated rock occurs when pressure squeezes the minerals flat, stretching them to appear as layers or stripes within the rock. Metamorphic rock that is formed strictly by heat tends to be non-foliated.

Sedimentary rock makes up only a small portion of the earth's crust. However, it is the most visible rock on the earth's surface. The size of sediment affects the way a sedimentary rock is formed. Some sedimentary rocks are formed by sediments that are deposited, pressed, and cemented together. Other sedimentary rocks are formed when dissolved minerals crystallize from an evaporating solution.

All rock begins with a variety of materials and is transformed according to a range of factors. This results in a great diversity of rock types, about which even geologists disagree.

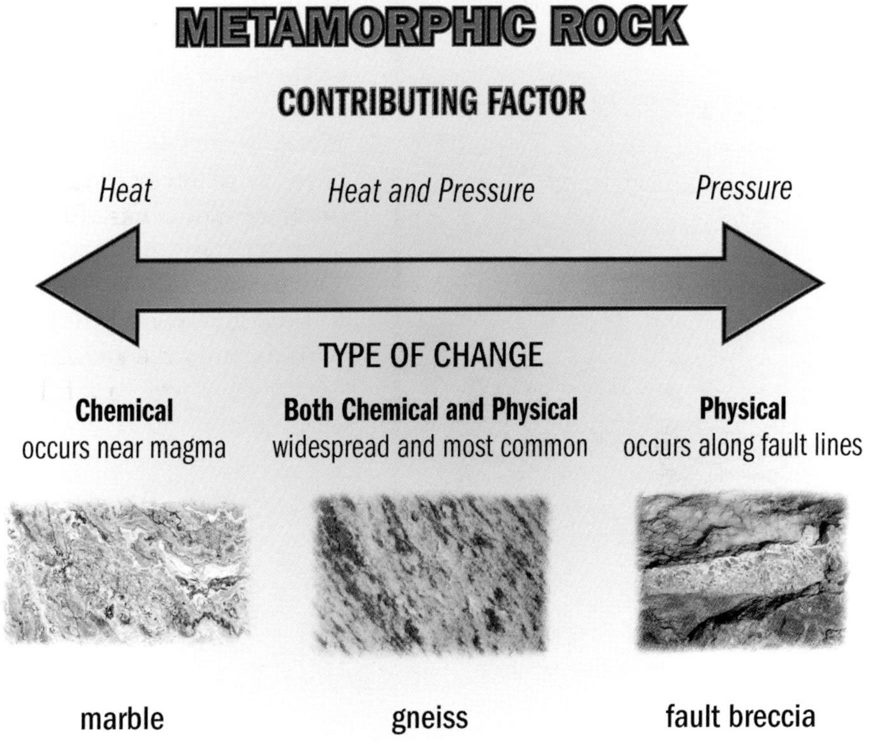

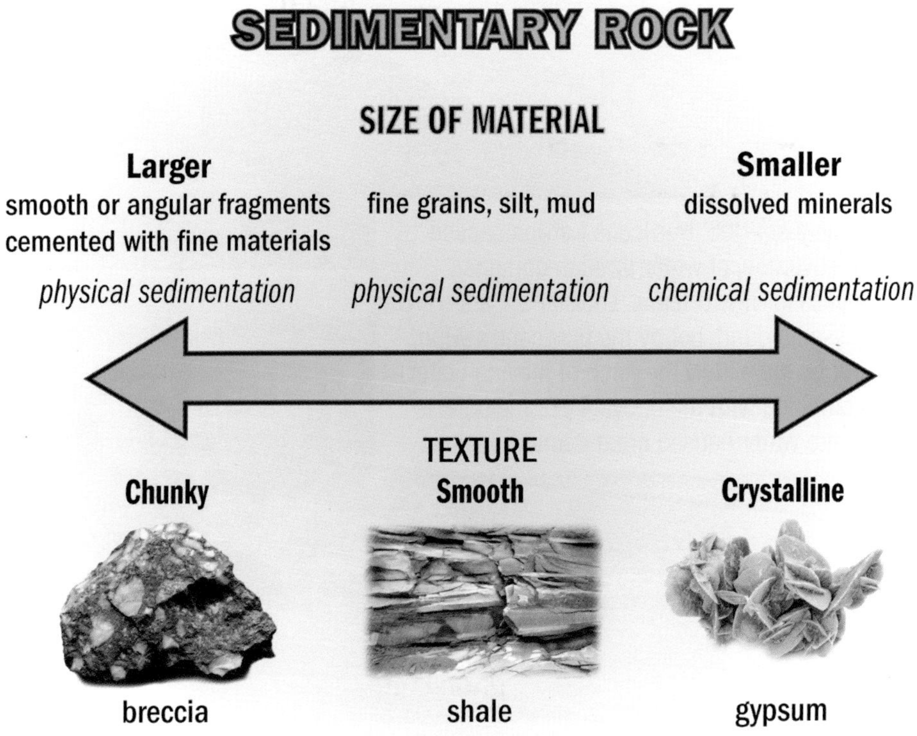

BREAKDOWN

VOCABULARY

load ('lōd) the dissolved or suspended matter in a body of water

QUICK FACT

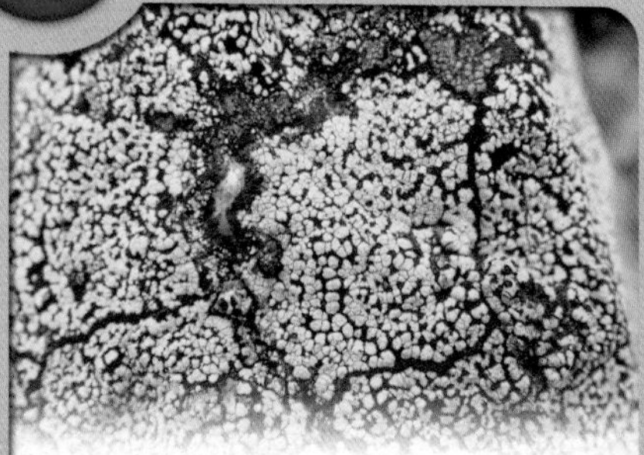

A rock with lichen living on it breaks down faster than a bare rock. This is due to the symbiotic relationship of the algae and fungi that make up the lichen. The algae capture sunlight for energy and growth, and the fungi help capture water and small particles. Accumulated water freezes and thaws within the rock crevices. Sometimes, even the acidity of the water breaks the rock down. The two processes remove minerals, some of which are used by the lichen. Eventually, enough soil collects in the cracks of the rock for plants to begin to grow there. When the plant seeds germinate, the growth of the roots causes further breakdown.

Breakdown is the process by which something becomes divided into smaller and smaller pieces. Weathering causes the breakdown of rock by the actions of water, wind, and changes in temperature. Rock can also be broken down more rapidly through movements of the earth's crust, explosive volcanic eruptions, and flooding. After rock fragments have been broken down, erosion often carries them away. Water, wind, and weight, or the force of gravity, cause most erosion.

Water succeeds at breaking down and eroding rock material because of several reasons. First, water can dissolve many minerals that make up rock. Second, water can penetrate into small cracks and apply pressure, or expand rock by freezing. Third, water flows easily, moving rock fragments and even large boulders. While flowing, water also carries with it a load, which is any dissolved or suspended matter.

Peyto Lake in Banff National Park, Canada, is a striking turquoise color because of the mineral particles in its load. These particles reflect the blue-green sector of the light spectrum.

In August 2005, Hurricane Katrina caused the overflow of water through damaged levees in New Orleans, Louisiana. Cars were tossed around, not by the hurricane's wind, but by the water. The force of moving water combined with the buoyancy of the objects in the water caused great damage.

Wind also breaks down and erodes rock. When wind blows over the top of sand, it moves the grains of sand vertically and horizontally. This process is called *deflation*. These small pieces may then blast against larger rock formations, chipping more bits loose because of the friction. This is called *abrasion*. As the particles move along, they collide with other material, such as soil, causing more tiny fragments to move. Abrasion is so effective that a man-made form of it, known as *sandblasting*, is used to remove graffiti from concrete walls and take away painted lines from roadways.

Weight, or the force of gravity, is extremely effective at eroding rock fragments because it acts on all matter, regardless of the weather or location. Soil and rock may shift downhill slowly, fall in small amounts, or move rapidly as in a landslide. In fact, the force of gravity contributes to water's erosive ability by causing the water to flow downhill. The moon's gravitational pull also influences the tides that wash in and out along coastlines.

What time of year are travelers most likely to encounter rockfalls?

IN THE FIELD

Weathering and erosion are common processes in nature, yet often they occur in places we do not want! Scenic beachfront properties come with a high risk of damage due to ocean tides and waves. Seepage of underground water can create sinkholes that swallow up the ground above.

Weathering and erosion changed a rock into this shape. Sand particles, picked up by the wind, have blasted against the rock and chipped it away. The height of the vertical column indicates the maximum height that most of the sand particles reached.

Water formed these hoodoos in Bryce Canyon, Utah, by breaking down and carrying away much of the rock material.

DEPOSITION

VOCABULARY

deposition (de·pə·'zi·shən) the process in which sediment is laid down

Water and wind can only carry eroded material so far. Eventually, the material settles in a process known as deposition. Water and wind tend to sort material by density, size, and shape. Water deposits material in layers called *strata*. An individual layer may be hundreds of feet thick or as thin as a coin. Most strata are horizontal but may also be sloped, rippled, or overlapped. This is due to crossbedding, which is an unusual effect of wind and water that causes tilted layers within the main strata. Sediments caught in glaciers are also deposited, yet much differently. A glacier deposits its load randomly.

Since scientists observe erosion and deposition, a number of scientists believe that these same processes, acting over long periods of time, explain past geologic changes as well. This is known as *uniformitarianism* and usually assumes spans of time in the millions and billions of years. Scientists also apply this theory to the entire universe.

Deposition by water or wind can result in ripples and distinct lines. The lines occur because of the action of the water or wind, as well as the different densities, sizes, and shapes of the particles moved.

This glacier shows layers of annual winter precipitation alternating with layers of dust deposited during each dry season. Geologists drill core samples to determine the rates of formation. When this ice melts, years of dust deposition will be re-deposited.

Suppose a uniformitarian geologist believes that material in a certain region is deposited at a rate of 2 cm ($\frac{3}{4}$ in.) per 100 years. According to his or her calculations, it would have taken 30,000 years for 6 m ($6\frac{1}{2}$ yd) of material to be deposited.

Another belief related to deposition is *catastrophism*. It was proposed by French geologist Georges Cuvier in the early nineteenth century. Catastrophists believe that geologic changes were the result of random catastrophes. Some geologists conclude that the Creation event and the Great Flood of Noah's time involved massive forces and large amounts of moving water, causing tremendous erosion and rapid deposition. In this view, ongoing erosion and deposition occur on a smaller scale over longer periods of time compared to these major events. Catastrophists believe Earth's changes and geologic features occurred in thousands of years versus millions and billions of years.

Some geologists who do not believe in the biblical account of Creation have begun to reconsider the widespread evidence for catastrophes. They join in theory with other geologists who have agreed with the long time spans of uniformitarianism but want to recognize the Creation and the Flood. This new belief, called *neo-catastrophism,* has emerged, in which small processes over long periods of time and rapid, large-scale devastations are considered equally important in geologic formation.

OUTLOOK

Many scientists maintain a uniformitarian emphasis despite evidences of rapid catastrophic flooding and mountain and glacier formation. In keeping with the truth of God's Word, how does uniformitarianism compare to the biblical account?

Annual layers in sedimentary rock are known as *varves*. This photo shows varves distorted from their horizontal position. Since water would not deposit sediment in such chaotic and vertical ways, geologists conclude that powerful forces have acted on the rock and soil since it was deposited.

This sandstone formation shows crossbedding. The original deposition likely occurred catastrophically.

FOSSIL FORMATION

VOCABULARY

mold fossil (ˈmōld ˈfä·səl) the shape of a previously living organism preserved in sediment

trace fossil (ˈtrās ˈfä·səl) the preserved remains of footprints, eggs, burrows, or droppings

resin fossil (ˈre·zən ˈfä·səl) a small organism preserved in fossilized tree sap

petrifaction (pe·trə·ˈfak·shən) the process by which an organism is completely replaced by minerals

Deposition can trap organisms in the sediment. The theory of catastrophism is one explanation of how an event can kill, bury, and preserve trapped organisms as fossils. There are three ways to categorize fossils: by the time period in which the organism is believed to have lived, by the type of organism, or by how the fossil was formed.

There are four basic fossil formations. Mold fossils occur when an organism's shape is preserved. Material moves around or fills the organism and hardens before the organism itself breaks down. When a mold fossil is later filled in by mud or minerals and then hardens, a cast fossil forms. This creates a solid copy of the organism's original shape.

Trace fossils are preserved evidences of behaviors, such as nests, burrows, eggs, and prints from walking or crawling. Droppings, known as *coprolites*, are also trace fossils. They provide scientists with information on the feeding behavior of animals.

Why are so many shells preserved as fossils?

Though most fossils appear as varieties of organisms that are still alive today, some may give us a glimpse of unique, extinct creatures and plants. Whether dinosaurs lived along with humans or long before humans, they are exciting discoveries.

Trace fossils, such as this dinosaur coprolite, give evidence of the existence of organisms.

Fossilization often shows evidence that deposition was the cause of death. Fossil graveyards have been documented around the world.

The most complete fossils are resin fossils. These occur when small organisms, usually insects, are well preserved in amber, or fossilized tree sap. Biologists value resin fossils because they can study the organism itself. Freezing has preserved even larger organisms. The frozen remains of woolly mammoths, including hair and skin, have been found in the Russian region of Siberia and in Alaska in the United States.

Dissolved minerals can also work their way into the spaces of a dead organism. These minerals harden into crystals, and replace all or part of the organism. This is the process of petrifaction. When wood gets covered by sediment and is preserved in this manner, it becomes petrified wood.

Catastrophic burial produces the best fossils. Most fossils are of marine invertebrates. Almost all of the remaining fossils come from algae and plants. Fossils are usually found in sedimentary rock. Scientists think that the relatively few mammal fossils were deposited through special Ice Age circumstances.

IN THE FIELD

Geologists often use radiocarbon dating to determine the age of organic materials within rocks. This method detects the amount of remaining carbon-14 in the rock samples. Based on this amount, geologists then assign ages to minerals and igneous and metamorphic rocks. Though the process is logical, it relies heavily on assumptions, including the initial amount of carbon. More commonly, rock ages are first assigned based on the assumed ages of the fossils they contain.

What is this machine pumping?

Petrified wood may appear much like wood itself, but closer examination reveals hardened minerals where air spaces once were.

Small organisms can become preserved in amber. The animal is first trapped on sticky resin, dies, and is then covered with more resin.

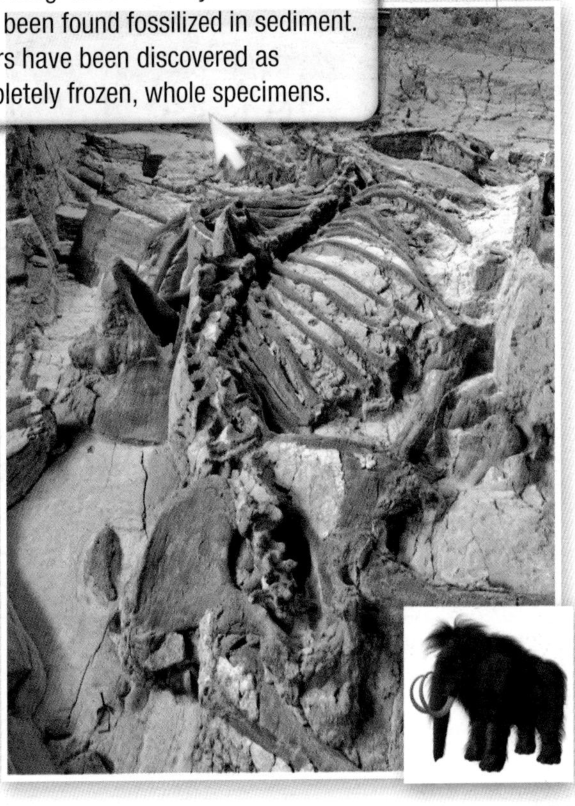

Some long-extinct woolly mammoths have been found fossilized in sediment. Others have been discovered as completely frozen, whole specimens.

CREATION AND EVOLUTION

VOCABULARY

creationist (krē-ˈā-shə-nist) one who believes in the biblical account of Creation

evolutionist (ˌe-və-ˈlü-shə-nist) one who believes in the theory of evolution

Civilizations worldwide have long addressed the basic desire to understand the origin of Earth and humankind. Scientists have played a large part in searching for the answer. One key point that some people disagree on is the involvement, and even the existence, of God.

In Genesis, the account of Creation is given. Simply stated, God created the heavens and the earth. Within six days He made day and night; the heavens and the earth; vegetation; the sun, moon, and stars; all the living creatures in the waters, the sky, and on land; and human beings—male and female. God created the vegetation and all living creatures to be fruitful and multiply after their own kind. Humankind was told to subdue the earth and rule over it. On the seventh day, God rested after having designed intricate and complex forms of life.

Many who believe this record of origin state that the first seven days of Creation were literal days of 24 hours each and that God finished His work and rested all within one week. Others who believe the account of Creation consider the first days to be seven periods of time that were significantly longer. Regardless, all creationists believe that God created the heavens and the earth and everything within them.

CREATION

DAY 1

Genesis 1:3–5
- Light
- Day and night

DAY 2

Genesis 1:6–8
- Sky
- The expanse separated the waters.

DAY 3

Genesis 1:9–13
- Earth (dry land)
- Seas (gathering of the waters)
- Vegetation with seeds

DAY 4

Genesis 1:14–19
- Lights in the sky to separate day and night, for signs to mark seasons, days and years, and to give light on Earth
- Greater light to govern the day
- Lesser light to govern the night
- Stars

DAY 5

Genesis 1:20–23
- Living creatures to fill the water
- Birds to fly in the sky
- Marine reptiles
- Every living creature that moves in the water

DAY 6

Genesis 1:24–31
- Living creatures on the earth (livestock, everything that moves on the ground, and wild animals)
- Humankind

DAY 7

Genesis 2:1–2
- God rested from all His work which He had done.

A number of people do not think that Earth came into existence by design or that people were uniquely created apart from the animals. Rather, these individuals believe that Earth and the solar bodies evolved by a natural process from existing matter and energy. Evolutionists also hold that animals developed at different rates—from simple cells to more complex species. Key factors involved in the theory of evolution are random chance and vast amounts of time.

Evolutionists believe that the genetic code within simple organisms mutated, or changed, from generation to generation, over millions and billions of years. They believe that the beneficial genetic mutations, which increased the odds of an organism's survival, were passed on to their offspring. Over time, these mutations lead to the development of more complex descendants. This idea became known as the process of *natural selection*. Evolutionists have theorized that as more and more of the positive mutations were passed along, different organisms, distinct from their ancestors, evolved as totally new species.

Both creationists and evolutionists agree that the universe as we know it has not always existed. The ongoing dispute about the origin of life is often referred to as *the Great Debate*.

QUICK FACT

The Scopes trial was a highly publicized legal case in the United States about the right to teach the theory of evolution. It took place in Dayton, Tennessee, in 1925 and was centered on John Thomas Scopes, a high school teacher who taught the theory of evolution in his classroom. At the time, it was illegal for Tennessee public school teachers to teach concepts that went against the biblical account of Creation. The Scopes trial is often referred to as *the Monkey Trial* because some scientists believe that orangutans, chimps, and humans have common ancestors.

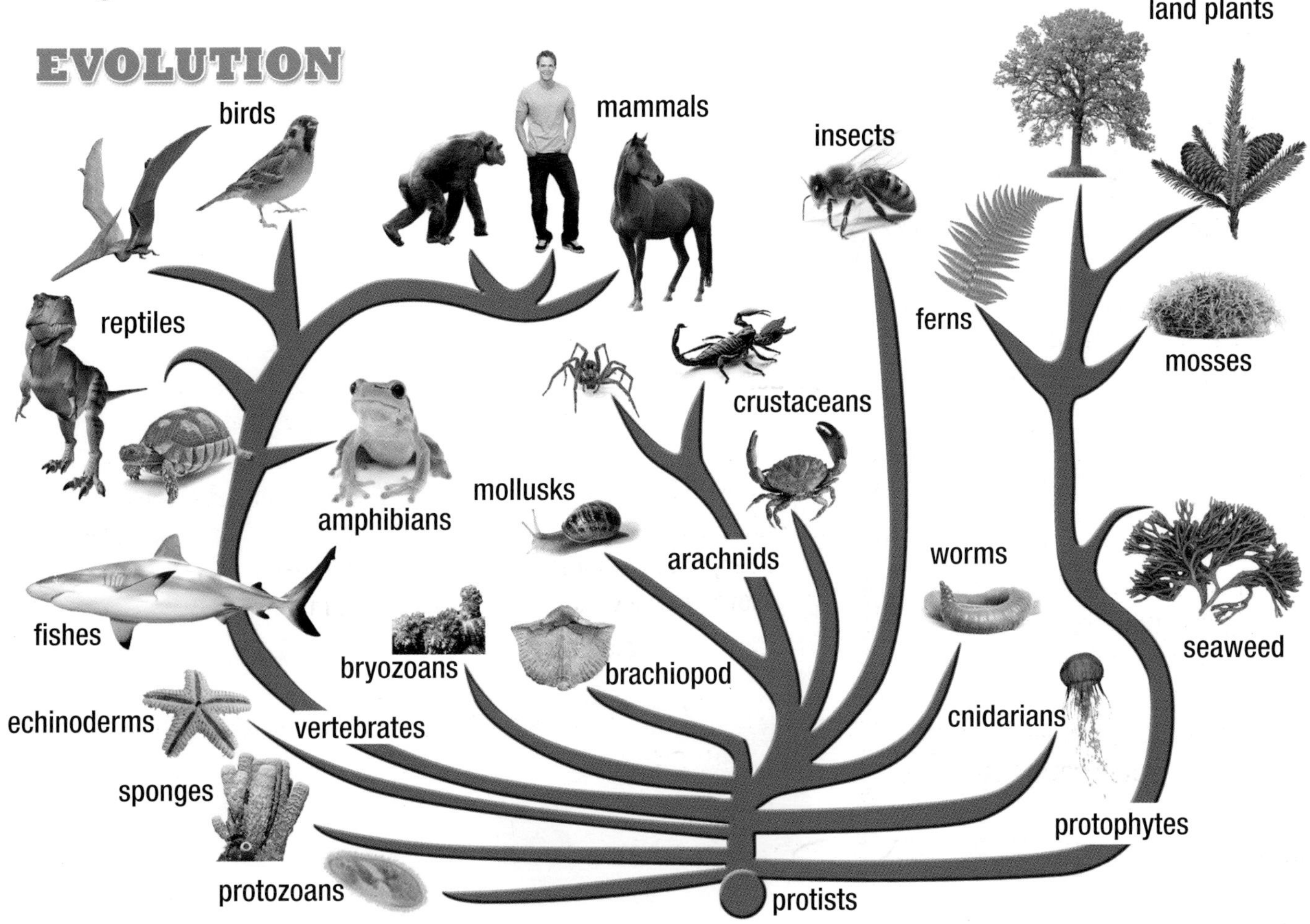

GEOLOGIC LAYERS

VOCABULARY

geologic time scale (jē·ə·ˈlä·jik ˈtīm ˈskāl) a chart or diagram that describes the events of Earth's history in chronological order

geologic column (jē·ə·ˈlä·jik ˈkä·ləm) a vertical sequence of strata that provides a historical record of Earth's eras and periods

OUTLOOK

British scientist Sir Richard Owen coined the term *dinosaur* in the early 1840s. From the discovery of dinosaur tracks to their bones and coprolites, evidence is overwhelming that these huge creatures once existed. While the word *dinosaur* is not found in Scripture, there are references to large animals that Bible scholars believe are dinosaurs. Job 40:15–41:34 describes two creatures—the behemoth, a remarkably large animal, and the leviathan, a fearless animal with great strength. It is important to keep in mind that while everything may not be accounted for in the Scriptures, the truths uncovered by science never contradict the Bible.

Deposition in one particular location may produce many fine layers every year; however, geologists are interested in strata on a larger scale in order to study their relation to the age and history of the earth. Scientists today typically use four major divisions of time to describe rock layers. The Precambrian era is considered the oldest and longest span of time. This is followed, in order, by the Paleozoic, Mesozoic, and Cenozoic eras. These four eras are further subdivided into periods.

Scientists have different interpretations of the presence of fossils within the earth's strata. The deepest strata containing large fossils are found within the Cambrian period, which is the first period within the Paleozoic era. Some of these fossils are from complex creatures. Many Creation geologists state that the fossils noted as being within the Cambrian period point to rapid burial that took place during the first stages of the Great Flood. These geologists also believe the fossils identified within the Cretaceous period, which is within the Mesozoic era, began during the final stage of the Flood. The Cretaceous period includes fossils of larger vertebrates, including extinct dinosaurs. Therefore, for creationists, the Cambrian through Cretaceous periods represent one extinction event.

Other scientists state that fossils were formed in the Cambrian and Cretaceous periods millions of years ago. Most of these geologists believe a rapid period of evolution occurred during the Cambrian period. They call it *the Cambrian explosion*. Some describe the Cretaceous period as the time when the last of five extinction events happened. They calculate that it was about 400 million years after the Cambrian period and call it *the late-Cretaceous mass extinction*.

This paleontologist carefully works on a dinosaur fossil. Scientists often use the layer the fossil was found in and carbon dating to determine the age of the animal. A scientist who holds a creationist view may come to a much different conclusion about the age of the fossil than a scientist who holds an evolutionist perspective.

The geologic time scale is a diagram created by scientists to display the different groupings of time. It includes geologic events and changes in life forms. This time scale has become a tool for describing a geologic time line, which is a theory that is not commonly agreed upon.

A complete sequence of strata as presented on the geologic time scale is rarely found in any one location. However, geologists compare various layers from around the world and arrive at a combined description. This is known as the geologic column.

Sometimes geologists will speak of the geologic column as the total sequence of strata found in one location. A local geologic column is based on direct observation and only includes a portion of the whole geologic column. Its layers may also be inverted in different order because of catastrophic events.

LINKS

Art Link
Design a poster that depicts your interpretation of Creation.

Language Arts Link
Write a critique of the theory of evolution. Distinguish between claims that are supported by facts and those that are not. Expound on why evolution takes just as much faith as the belief in Creation.

History Link
Create a time line that illustrates the literal 24-hour days of Creation. Then create a time line that represents the origin of humankind according to evolutionists. Decorate the time lines with illustrations or pictures.

Trilobites are fossils of marine arthropods that are commonly found in the geologic column. They flourished during the Cambrian explosion and became extinct toward the end of the Permian period. For this reason, the Cambrian period is also called *the Age of the Trilobites*.

Strange but True

The pigments in these ochre pits were used by the aborigines of Australia for body paint and native art.

CHAPTER 11

VIOLENT MOTIONS

Sometimes the temperature in a home becomes too warm or too cool. If the home has a thermostat, its function is to regulate the air inside the home to stay within a certain temperature range. Often, the temperature is not exactly what the dial or display reads, but it is within a comfortable range close to that setting. In a similar way, the earth operates within a certain range that allows life to exist.

The earth is a planet designed for motion and balance. It is constantly moving toward a state of equilibrium. Motion does not stop once equilibrium is achieved, but it is balanced within a specific range. This concept includes all areas on and in the earth, including air and water, as well as the movement of the lithospheric plates. As forces act on the earth, they continually cycle between imbalance and equilibrium. Simply because forces are equal does not mean that they are nonexistent.

KEY IDEAS

- Forces on Earth cycle between imbalance and equilibrium.
- The earth's constant motion directly affects its surface and atmosphere.
- Severe weather and major surface events are often the result of the earth moving toward a state of balance.

In living and nonliving things alike, a state of balance, or equilibrium, occurs everywhere on Earth. Without it, life could not exist. This concept reflects God's character and glory.

OUTLOOK

Although weather patterns may change as the earth adjusts to a state of balance, God has promised that He will never again destroy all living things by flood. He gave the rainbow as a sign of His covenant. When you are concerned about what is happening around you, remember the rainbow and trust His promise that "as long as the earth endures, seedtime and harvest...will never cease." Trust that God will take care of you, just as He takes care of the earth.

Strange but True

What four main environmental clues indicate a tornado?

EARTHQUAKES

VOCABULARY

focus ('fō·kəs) the point beneath the earth's surface where rock breaks and causes an earthquake

epicenter ('e·pi·sen·tər) the point on the earth's surface directly above the focus

P wave ('pē·wāv) a type of seismic wave that compresses and expands

S wave ('es·wāv) a type of seismic wave that moves side to side and up and down

One example of equilibrium being restored on Earth as a result of opposing unbalanced forces is an earthquake. The motion of an earthquake is very similar to the action of a stretched rubber band. When two lithospheric plates are forced in different directions, it produces stress in the rock, and potential energy builds. The rock can only stretch so far before breaking. When it breaks, the plates snap back in an elastic motion, releasing the pressure that has built up. The elastic rebounding of the plates is called *an earthquake*. The energy that is released travels as seismic waves through the earth's interior and along its surface.

Most earthquakes actually begin underground. The location under the earth's surface where the movement occurs is called the focus. Directly above the focus on the earth's surface is the epicenter. The seismic waves carry energy and travel from the focus in all directions. The seismic waves that move out from the focus through the earth's interior are called *body waves*. There are two types of body waves—P waves and S waves. When these waves reach the epicenter on the earth's surface, they are called *surface waves*.

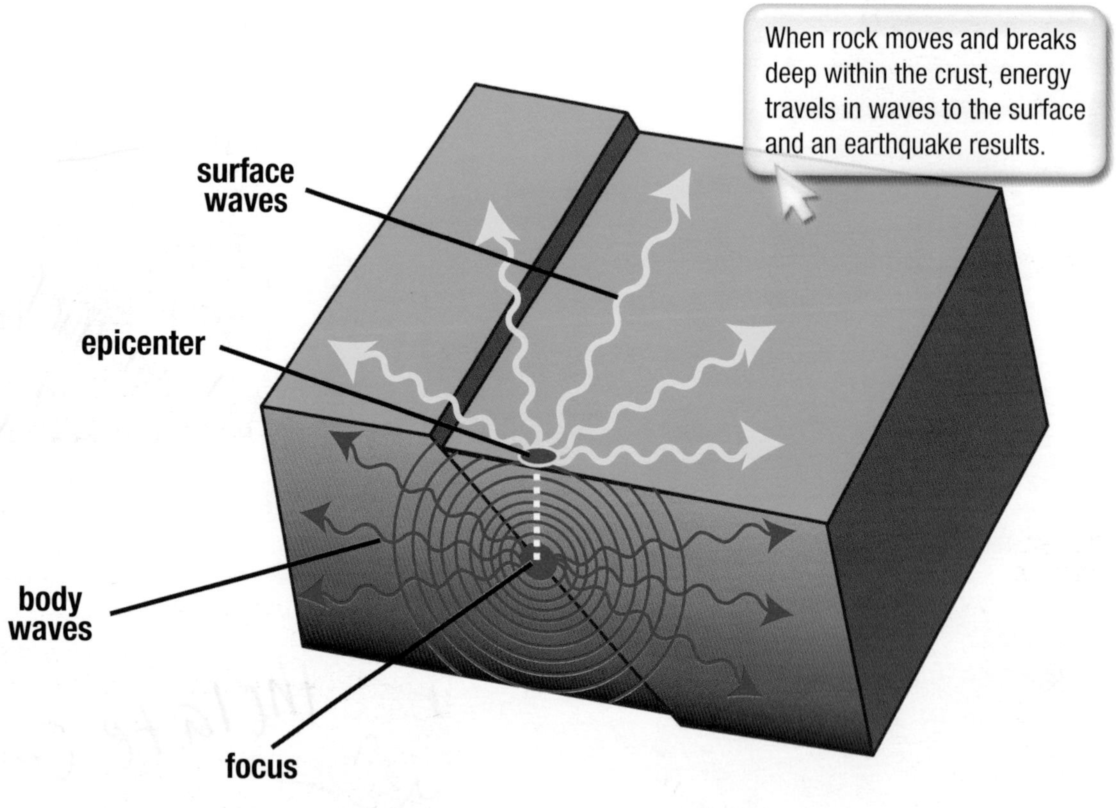

P waves, also known as *primary waves*, move the fastest. They are the first to be detected and can travel through solids, liquids, and gases. P waves compress and expand as they spread outward from the focus, causing rock particles to squeeze and stretch. S waves, or *secondary waves*, are the second-fastest waves. They shake the ground back and forth, causing the rock to stretch and change shape in a sideways direction. Unlike P waves, S waves cannot travel through liquids. While P waves can damage buildings, it is the S waves that shake structures violently. When P and S waves reach the surface, they become surface waves. Even though surface waves are the slowest, they can produce severe ground movements and are the most destructive type of wave.

Seismologists measure earthquakes with different types of scales. The Mercalli scale rates an earthquake's level of damage from 1 to 12. The Richter scale measures the strength, or magnitude, of an earthquake on a scale that ranges from 1 to 10. The Moment Magnitude scale estimates the total energy released by an earthquake, also on a scale from 1 to 10.

IN THE FIELD

Architects and engineers are required to be familiar with government-issued building codes. These codes specify how buildings must be constructed. They help ensure the safety and health of all who will be in the buildings. These codes are even more important in areas with significant earthquake activity. The structure and the construction materials must be strong, yet elastic, to withstand the stretching and shaking forces of an earthquake. Rubber and steel devices known as *laminated rubber bearings* not only support a building's weight, but allow its foundation to move with the ground. Buildings like these in Japan are designed with rubber bearings and other specialized equipment to minimize damage when an earthquake occurs.

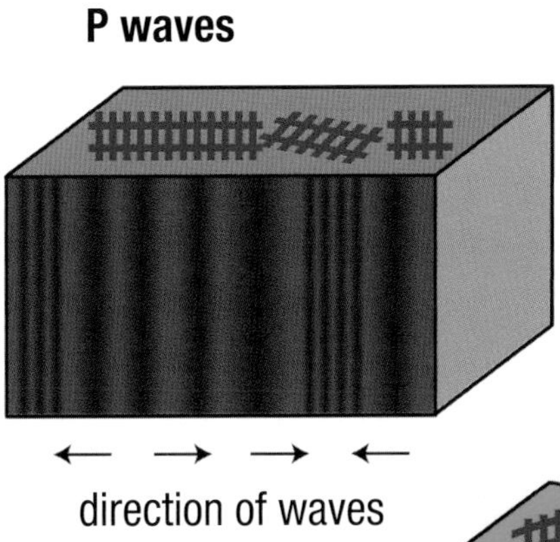

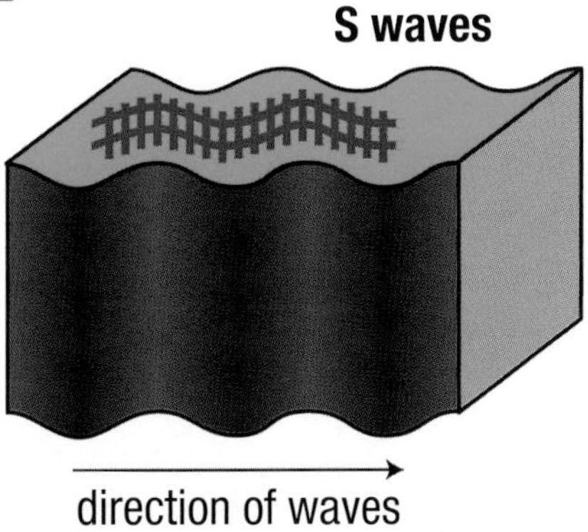

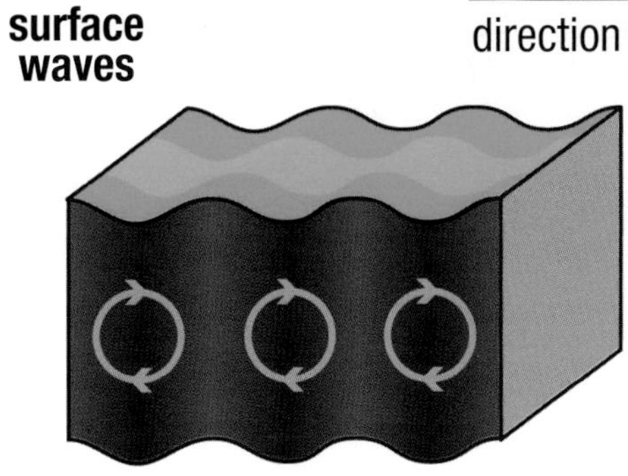

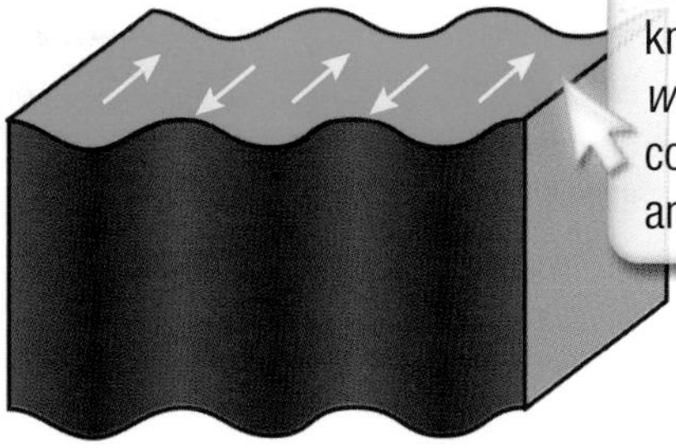

Once P waves and S waves reach Earth's surface, they become known as *surface waves* and will have a combination of P-wave and S-wave movements.

VOLCANOES

VOCABULARY

vent ('vent) the opening in a volcano through which magma and gases escape

shield volcano ('shēld väl·'kā·nō) a gently sloping mountain made of lava released from nonexplosive eruptions

cinder cone ('sin·dər 'kōn) a steeply sloped volcano made of pyroclastic material from explosive eruptions

composite volcano (kəm·'pä·zət väl·'kā·nō) a tall, cone-shaped mountain made of alternating layers of lava and pyroclastic material

QUICK FACT

The Hawaiian Islands are a chain of volcanoes formed over time as a result of plate movement with volcanic activity. These islands are believed to be located on a hot spot under the Pacific plate, which generates new volcanoes as the plate shifts.

Volcanic eruptions are another way in which pressure under the earth's surface is released. Volcanoes are fed by a magma chamber, which is a pool of molten rock located underground. The magma travels through a long channel, or pipe, up to the surface, where it escapes through a vent. Often there is a central vent at the top of the volcano. The bowl-shaped area around the central vent is called *a crater*. Volcanic eruptions can produce cinders, ash, gases, and either lava or fragmented rock known as *pyroclastic material*. Lava is liquid magma on the earth's surface. Pyroclastic material forms when magma is blasted into the air and solidifies.

There are three stages of volcanic activity. An active volcano is one that has recently erupted or shows the possibility of erupting soon. A dormant volcano is one that is not currently erupting, but shows signs that it may erupt again. If it erupts again, its status changes to active. A volcano is considered extinct if it has erupted in the distant past and shows no sign of erupting again.

A volcano forms when magma breaks through the crust and lava flows on the surface.

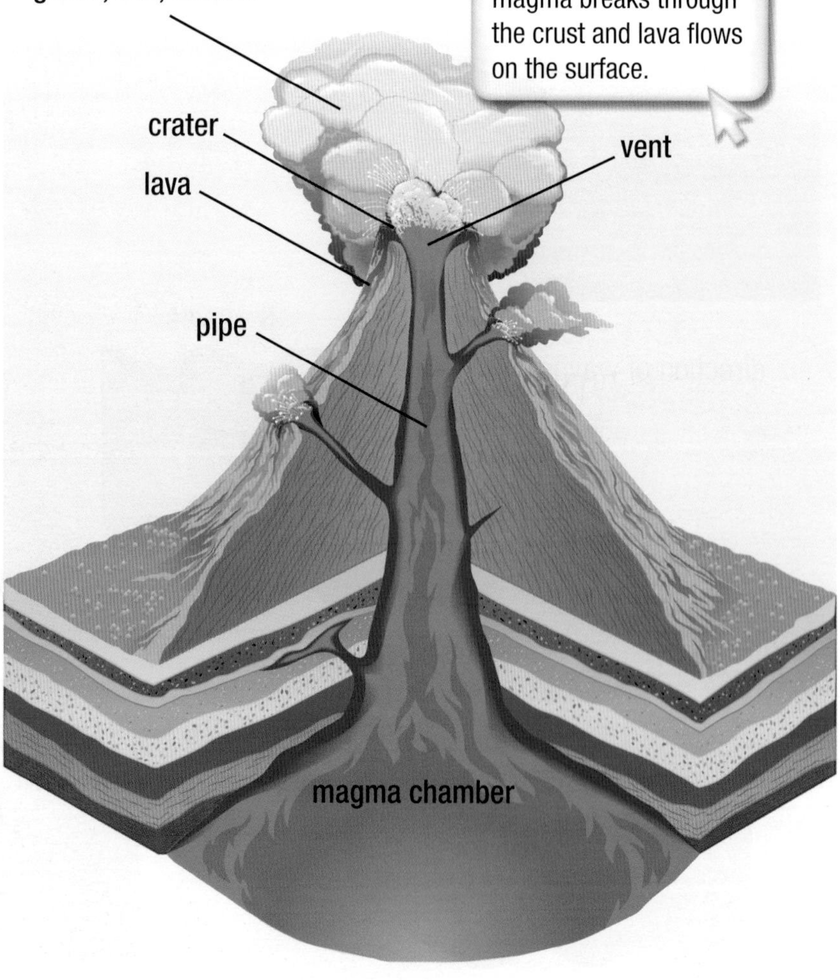

There are three basic types of volcanoes—shield volcanoes, cinder cones, and composite volcanoes. A shield volcano is similar in shape to that of a soldier's shield lying face up. This type of volcano forms when lava flows like a thin liquid down the sides. Shield volcanoes have quiet, nonexplosive eruptions and spread out over wide areas. These volcanoes can be enormous. For example, the Hawaiian Islands were formed from shield volcanoes.

A cinder cone is usually small and erupts only a short time. Its steep, cone-shaped hill is formed from pyroclastic material, which includes ashes, cinders, and hardened pieces of magma. Usually at the top of this type of volcano is a bowl-shaped crater.

A composite volcano, also known as a *stratovolcano*, usually has alternating layers of pyroclastic material and lava. It forms from explosive eruptions followed by quieter, nonexplosive flows of lava. This type of volcano is extremely dangerous because it can erupt without much warning and can destroy entire civilizations. Most composite volcanoes are located on the Ring of Fire, which edges the Pacific Ocean. Mount Vesuvius, Mount Saint Helens, and Mount Fuji are composite volcanoes.

IN THE FIELD

Scientists who study volcanoes are known as *volcanologists*. They often have the opportunity to visit exciting places and make a difference in the world! Many volcanologists in the United States are employed by the US Geological Survey. Some work in areas with significant levels of volcanic activity to help predict eruptions. These predictions allow the local residents to be warned in case they need to evacuate.

How is a geyser like a volcano?

Black Butte in Oregon is an extinct cinder cone volcano.

Mount Fuji, a composite volcano, is Japan's highest mountain. At this time it is classified as active although it has been dormant since 1707.

Mauna Kea, a shield volcano in Hawaii, is the tallest mountain in the world when measured from its base on the seafloor to the summit. It is over 10 km (6 mi) tall.

THUNDERSTORMS AND TORNADOES

VOCABULARY

squall line ('skwȯl 'līn) a row of severe thunderstorms

tornado (tôr·'nā·dō) a rapidly rotating column of air that extends from a cumulonimbus cloud and touches the ground

Fujita scale (fo͞o·'jē·tə 'skāl) a scale used to rate tornado intensity

QUICK FACT

Waterspouts, tornadoes, and dust devils have the same motion but form under different conditions. Most waterspouts form over coastal waters and exhibit winds of less than 108 kph (67 mph). They typically move slowly, if at all. However, some waterspouts can start as tornadoes over land and then move over a body of water. This type can be very destructive. Tornadoes threaten life and property and stem from a downward cloud formation associated with thunderstorms. Dust devils form from swirling winds under sunny conditions during fair weather and are usually harmless.

Thunderstorms and tornadoes re-establish atmospheric balance, even though they sometimes leave behind great damage. Thunderstorms are small, intense weather systems that bring strong winds, heavy precipitation, thunder, and lightning. They form when warm, humid air rises rapidly. As the rising air cools, dense cumulonimbus clouds known as *thunderheads* develop. The air pressure drops and a storm results. When several thunderstorms are aligned in a row, it is known as a squall line.

Lightning occurs as a result of the movement of air within a cloud, which produces opposing electrical charges. When the space between the positive and negative charges reaches a certain point, the charges are released as lightning. Thunder is the sound that results from the rapid expansion of superheated air through which the lightning travels. When severe thunderstorms form, the resulting cumulonimbus cloud will often take the shape of an anvil. It may even produce hail. These types of powerful thunderstorms are called *supercells*. Meteorologists begin looking for tornadoes once supercells are sighted.

Waterspouts are spinning columns of rising moist air over bodies of water. They can form in fair weather or be the result of a tornado that passes from land over water.

A cumulonimbus cloud forms this anvil shape when it expands to the top of the troposphere. The flat top indicates that it may produce strong storms and tornadoes.

Occasionally a tornado can develop along a squall line. A tornado is a rapidly rotating funnel cloud that develops from a thunderhead. Although a tornado is typically brief, scientists speculate that its wind speeds can reach up to 512 kph (318 mph). Most, however, are weaker, with winds less than 160 kph (100 mph). A tornado's intensity is rated on the Fujita scale, which ranges from F-0 to F-5. The intensity is based on wind speed and how much damage the tornado causes to structures and vegetation. Tornado safety plans are important to have in place. In the event of a tornado, people should stay away from windows, move to a basement or the middle of the ground floor, and never try to outrun a tornado.

Hail is often produced in severe storms along with tornadoes. The updraft and downdraft in a cumulonimbus cloud cause water drops to repeatedly move upward, freeze, and fall a short distance until they become large enough to fall to the ground.

Strange but True

Evidence of a wall cloud, large-sized hail, unusual sky color that is often dark green, and a loud roar similar to a freight train can indicate a tornado.

What color would a tornado over this area probably become?

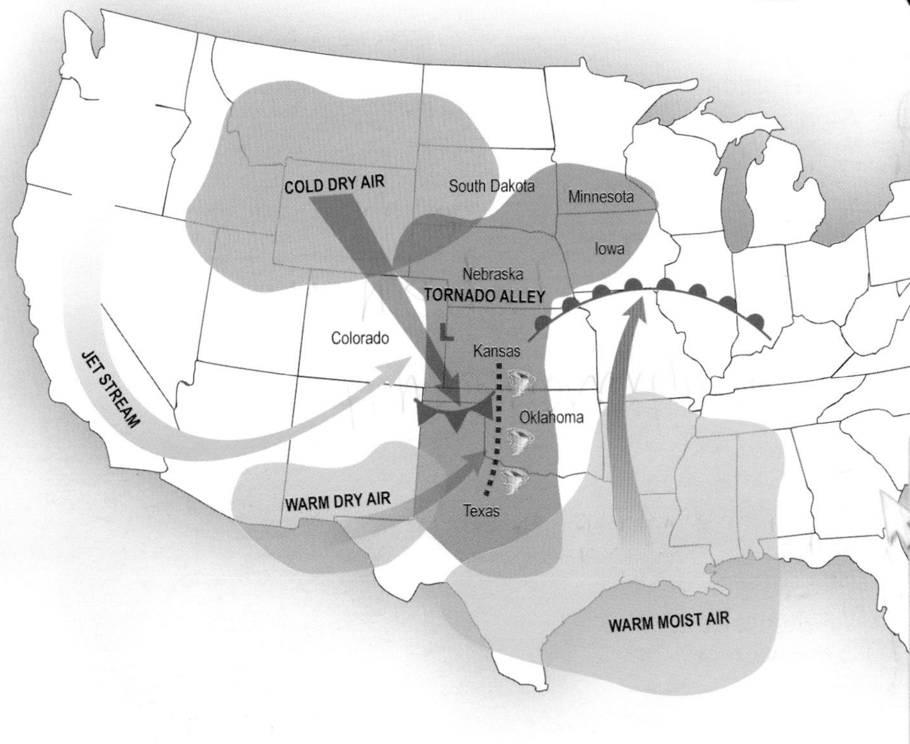

The majority of the world's tornadoes occur in the midwestern region of the United States, known as *Tornado Alley*. Cold, dry air masses from the north travel southward, where they meet with warm, moist air masses coming from the Gulf of Mexico. As the two collide, instability in the atmosphere results and storms form.

HURRICANES

VOCABULARY

tropical cyclone ('trä·pi·kəl 'sī·klōn) a rotating storm system originating over warm waters with wind speeds of 119 kph (74 mph) or greater

hurricane ('hər·ə·cān) a tropical cyclone forming in the Atlantic and eastern Pacific Oceans

storm surge ('stôrm 'sûrj) a wall of water that moves ashore when a hurricane strikes land

When thunderstorms occur over water, they can merge and grow into a larger storm. If winds traveling in two different directions meet, they can cause the storm to spin. When the winds of this spinning storm reach 37–61 kph (23–38 mph), it becomes known as *a tropical depression.* It is named this because of its low air pressure. If the tropical depression increases in size and strength, meteorologists upgrade the class of the storm to *a tropical storm*. They then assign it a name. This allows weather scientists to easily identify an individual storm and collect and store data regarding its size, intensity, and wind speed. As air pressure continues to drop and temperature, moisture, and wind speeds increase, the meteorologists classify the rotating storm as a tropical cyclone. The wind speed is 119 kph (74 mph) or greater at this point. Similar to tornadoes, tropical cyclones are ranked by categories ranging from 1 to 5. Tropical cyclones are affected by water currents and the Coriolis effect. These storms spin counterclockwise in the Northern Hemisphere and clockwise in the Southern Hemisphere.

What does this weather forecasting symbol represent?

Tropical Depression
Winds speeds in a group of thunderstorms reach 37–61 kph (23–38 mph).

Tropical Storm
Wind speeds increase to 62–118 kph (39–73 mph) and a name is assigned.

Tropical Cyclone
A pronounced rotation forms over the core, with wind speeds of 119 kph (74 mph) or greater.

The line indicates the pathway of this weather system. The green denotes the tropical depression, yellow signifies the tropical storm, and red represents the hurricane.

In different regions of the world, a tropical cyclone is given a different name—*hurricane*, *typhoon*, or *willy-willy*. A hurricane is a tropical cyclone that forms in the Atlantic Ocean or the eastern Pacific Ocean. When it forms in the western Pacific Ocean, it is known as a *typhoon*. A willy-willy is a tropical cyclone that occurs near Australia. These particular storm systems, characterized by heavy rain and violent winds, are the most powerful on Earth. If one of these cyclones comes ashore, a wall of water called a storm surge often results. Storm surges cause great damage and have the potential to claim many human lives.

The structure of a hurricane includes the eye, eye wall, and rain bands. The center, or eye, is a calm area. Surrounding the eye is the eye wall—a ring of cumulonimbus clouds that produce heavy rains and strong winds. The eye wall is often the most dangerous part of a storm. Rain bands are spiraling bands of clouds beyond the eye wall. As the distance from the eye wall increases, wind speed decreases. As a storm moves away from its source of moisture and warmth, it loses strength and begins to break apart.

QUICK FACT

Meteorologists give tropical cyclones names to make it easier to identify and track them. The names are selected from lists that are developed years in advance by the World Meteorological Organization. Each region has its own lists and set of rules. For example, there is a six year rotation of the names used for hurricanes in the Atlantic and eastern Pacific. In other regions including Australia, the northern Pacific, and Indian Oceans, different countries have the opportunity to suggest their own local names to be placed on that region's list. If a particular storm turns out to be extremely destructive, the name is stricken from the list and never used again.

World Meteorological Organization
Weather • Climate • Water

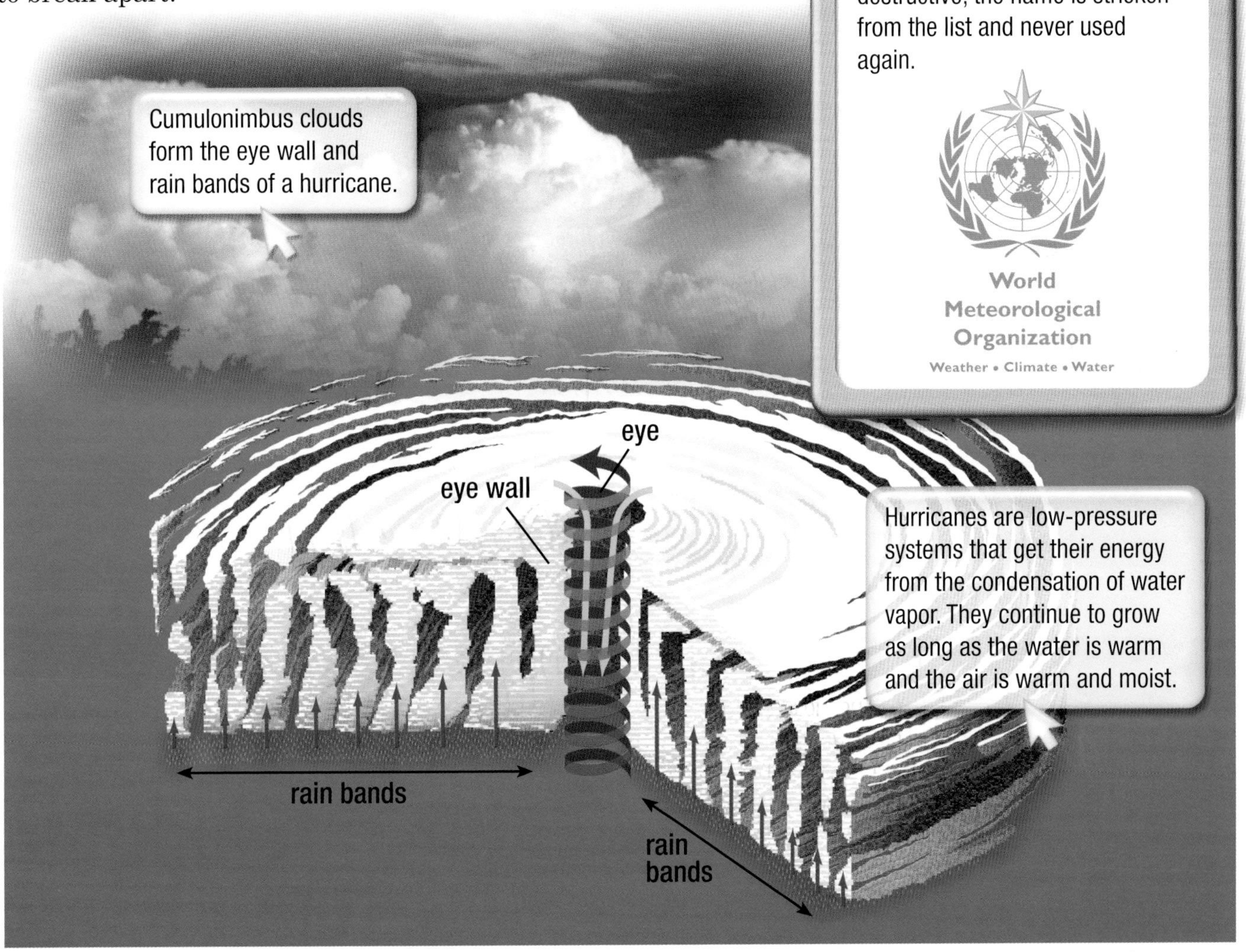

WILDFIRES

IN THE FIELD

A Hotshot Crew is a group of 20–25 individuals who have been specially trained in wildland fire suppression. They are highly skilled and can respond to any fire-related disaster. Hotshots hold integrity, duty, and respect as their core values, which have earned them high esteem. They participate in rigorous physical fitness and conditioning programs and must be available 24 hours a day, 7 days a week during fire season. The crews can be away from home for weeks at a time. Often their assignments are in remote areas with primitive living conditions. They work long hours and sleep deprivation is common. Their dedication and skill has placed them into an elite team of wildland firefighters.

Oxygen, fuel, and heat are three basic requirements for any fire to burn. The fire triangle is a visual aid commonly used to represent these factors.

Wildfires are uncontrolled fires that burn vegetation. These types of fires are one of the ways that equilibrium is maintained on the earth. Some common causes of wildfires are lightning, human carelessness, arson, volcanic activity, and smoldering underground fire. Wildfires are affected by the weather, topography, and the arrangement, size, and dryness of fuels.

Firefighters who work with wildfires need to understand how this type of natural disaster moves and changes. If a fire starts and there is no wind, the fire tends to spread out in all directions. If there is a wind, the fire will move in the direction the wind is blowing. Firefighters depend on the local weather bureau to determine if the winds will shift. A shift in wind can dramatically change the areas of safety for the firefighters.

Why do firefighters wear oxygen tanks on their backs when fighting a fire?

Wildfires can affect the weather by producing large amounts of particles in the air. This can cause different types of clouds to form, which can in turn produce more storms. The water from these storms may help firefighters put out the fires. However, the storms often produce lightning strikes, which can cause additional fires to break out.

Wildfires have occurred naturally throughout history. Many animals are able to survive wildfires by moving to new habitats or by moving to underground burrows. After a fire is put out, plants begin to grow, and ecological succession takes place. This supports animal life in that area once again. Certain types of conifers actually benefit from fires in a number of ways. Some need the heat so their cones will open up and release seeds. Wildfires also help the ground become more fertile. Plants deplete the mineral content of the soil when they absorb the nutrients. Ash helps to restore many minerals to the ground, enabling conifers to grow well. Interestingly, beautiful orange-red sunsets often result from the dust and smoke in the atmosphere from the fire.

Each year, wildfires in the United States do significant damage to homes and property.

LINKS

History Link
Research the "Year Without a Summer" of 1816. Write an essay describing the conditions that caused this, and explain how it affected the people at that time. Predict a scenario where an event like this might repeat itself.

Language Arts Link
Write a newspaper article that explains the potential problems of a hurricane hitting the New Orleans area. Include answers to the following questions: Did scientists know that a direct hit by a hurricane could cause significant damage? What man-made structures made the damage more significant in New Orleans? Could anything have been done to prevent the devastation that resulted from Hurricane Katrina in 2005?

Art Link
Research the safety precautions for thunderstorms, tornadoes, and hurricanes. Draw a poster that includes at least five safety tips for each type of storm, and arrange to have it displayed somewhere in your school.

In order to help prevent the further spread of wildfires, airplanes are used to drop fire retardant chemicals on burning or soon-to-be-affected areas. This sometimes helps to slow or even stop the spread of the fire.

CHAPTER 12

ASTRONOMY

VOCABULARY

apparent magnitude (ə·ˈper·ənt ˈmag·nə·to͞od) the measure of a celestial body's brightness as observed from the earth

KEY IDEAS

- The earth is a small, yet very significant, part of a series of much larger systems.
- There are patterns and variety in the types, positions, and motions of celestial objects.
- Stars produce light energy and exhibit changes similar to life cycles.

Stars often appear brighter and more numerous when they are viewed from a secluded place like a mountaintop, desert, or rural meadow. Actually, they are always burning brightly, even during the day. Stars only appear more brilliant at night or in certain areas because other light sources such as the sun, the moon, or city lights are not overpowering them.

The degree of brightness of a star as seen from Earth is its apparent magnitude. Since apparent magnitude is based on the perspective from Earth, it does not provide the true intensity of the star. For instance, the sun looks very radiant. However, this is not because it is larger or emits more light than other stars. It is because it is closest to Earth. In reality, the sun is only a medium-sized star.

The apparent magnitude of an object is shown with numbers. The brighter an object appears, the lower the numerical value. The fainter it is, the higher the number. Therefore, objects that have negative numbers appear brighter than objects with positive numbers. The sun has an apparent magnitude of –26.7 because it is so close to Earth. Proxima Centauri, the second closest star to Earth, has an apparent magnitude of approximately +11.

The apparent magnitude of a star, planet, or moon depends on its size and temperature as well as how close it is to Earth.

QUICK FACT

When photographing distant and faint objects, enough light has to be collected to obtain a usable image. Astronomers use computer software, special filters, and finely machined gears to focus the telescope on the object while the earth rotates. To accomplish this, a camera's shutter is open for a very long time—sometimes for more than one hour!

Strange but True

What is the name of this celestial body?

STARLIGHT

VOCABULARY

absolute magnitude
('ab·sə·lo͞ot 'mag·nə·to͞od) the actual brightness of a celestial object

QUICK FACT

The idea of apparent magnitude goes back to over a century before Christ when the Greek astronomer Hipparchus ranked the brightness of stars. A magnitude of 1 was given to the brightest stars and a magnitude of 6 was given to the faintest ones. This original classification is the basis for why greater numbers are used today for dimmer stars. With today's instruments, decimal numbers and negative numbers can be used to describe a wider and more precise range.

The actual brightness of a star affects its apparent magnitude. Stars shine because they emit light energy. This energy is produced through nuclear fusion, which is the joining together of smaller atoms to form a larger one. The fusion process releases enormous quantities of energy. Starlight is the visible product of the energy released by fusion.

Stars that produce greater amounts of energy will usually produce more light. The actual brightness of a star depends on two main factors—size and temperature. The larger the star, the more matter there is to burn. The temperature of the star's surface, measured on the Kelvin scale, reveals how much light it gives off. A star's color also depends on its temperature. Hotter stars burn more intensely and are blue or white. Cooler stars burn yellow, orange, or red.

The absolute magnitude of a star is the measurement of its actual brightness. It takes into account how bright a star is compared to all the other stars, if they were put at a standard distance of 32.6 light-years from Earth. A light-year is the length that light travels in one year inside an area that contains no matter. Scientists say this distance is around 9.46 trillion km (5.88 trillion mi). Since absolute magnitude reveals the true brightness of a star, it has an effect on how bright the star appears from Earth.

Since the sun is a star, will it eventually burn up?

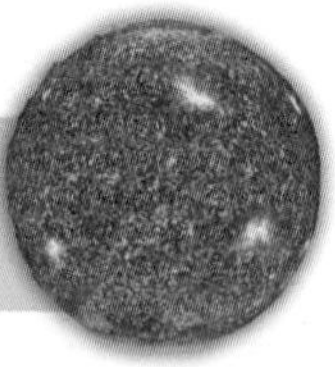

Both apparent and absolute magnitudes are calculated using the same scale. However, the two measurements can be very different for the same object.

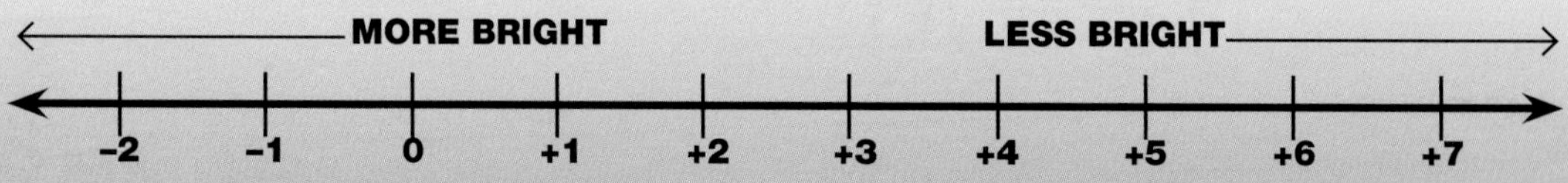

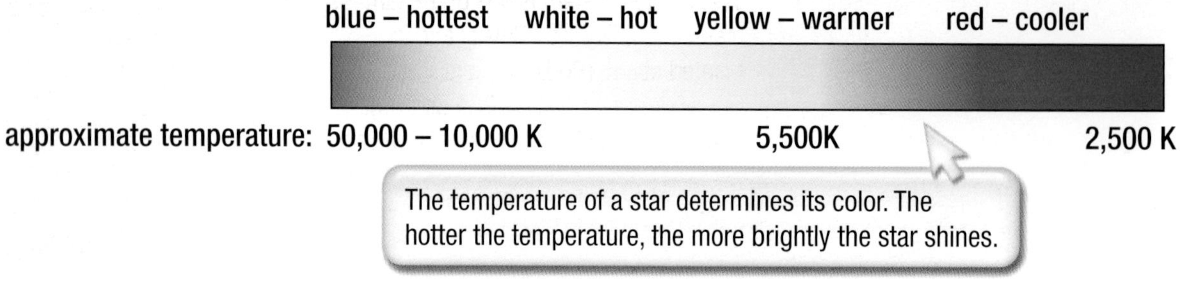

The temperature of a star determines its color. The hotter the temperature, the more brightly the star shines.

Obviously, celestial bodies are not all 32.6 light-years away. Therefore, the apparent magnitude of an object can be very different from the absolute magnitude. This is because apparent magnitude is the result of the distance from Earth, and absolute magnitude is dependent on size and temperature only. For example, the sun looks brighter than the star Antares. The sun's apparent magnitude is –26.7, but Antares' is +1. However, Antares is actually a much brighter star. Its absolute magnitude is –4.5, and the sun's is +4.8. Yet, Antares does not light up the earth's sky. This is because its distance from the earth is about 520 light-years away! Though the sun is the brightest object in the sky from Earth's perspective, if it were 32.6 light-years away, it would be barely visible. If it were as far away as Antares, people would not be able to see it without a telescope.

Stars produce their own light; however, the planets and their moons do not. Instead, they reflect the sun's light. Absolute magnitude, like apparent magnitude, is also used to describe the brightness of these reflective bodies. To be consistent, they are measured when the visible side is fully illuminated, such as during a full moon.

QUICK FACT

Antares is the brightest star in the constellation of Scorpio. It is classified as a red *supergiant*, with a diameter several hundred times larger than the sun. Even though its temperature is lower than the sun, Antares shines about 10,000 times brighter!

This cluster of stars is one of the largest inside the Milky Way Galaxy and is located about 100 light-years from the center of the galaxy. The different apparent magnitudes can easily be seen.

STAR POPULATIONS

VOCABULARY

luminosity (ˌlo͞o·mə·ˈnä·sə·tē) the amount of light radiated per second by a star

main sequence (ˈmān ˈsē·kwəns) a diagonal area on the H-R diagram in which most stars are found

white dwarf (ˈhwīt ˈdwôrf) a small, hot, very dense star

giant (ˈjī·ənt) a large, bright star with low surface temperature

A person might expect to find an even distribution of all types of stars, regardless of size or magnitude. However, just as certain organisms on Earth are more abundant than others, certain types of stars are more abundant in the heavens than others. Scientists know this from the Hertzsprung-Russell, or H-R, diagram, which two astronomers designed to chart the stars. They plotted the amount of light that stars radiate compared to their temperature. On the right side of the graph, each star's luminosity is compared to that of the sun. Luminosity is simply an amount of energy output. Absolute magnitude compares luminosity at a standard distance. The *x*-axis shows the Kelvin temperature. The absolute magnitudes of the stars are listed on the *y*-axis.

By using the H-R diagram, astronomers can estimate the size of the star. Since the size of a star is not directly observable, it must be inferred from data. Placement on the H-R diagram shows astronomers that most stars fall together in a diagonal pattern. This area is known as the main sequence. About 90% of all identified stars are main sequence stars, which are small to medium in size. The sun, yellow in color and medium in size, is a main sequence star.

If red represents hot and blue represents cold, why are the hotter stars blue or white in color?

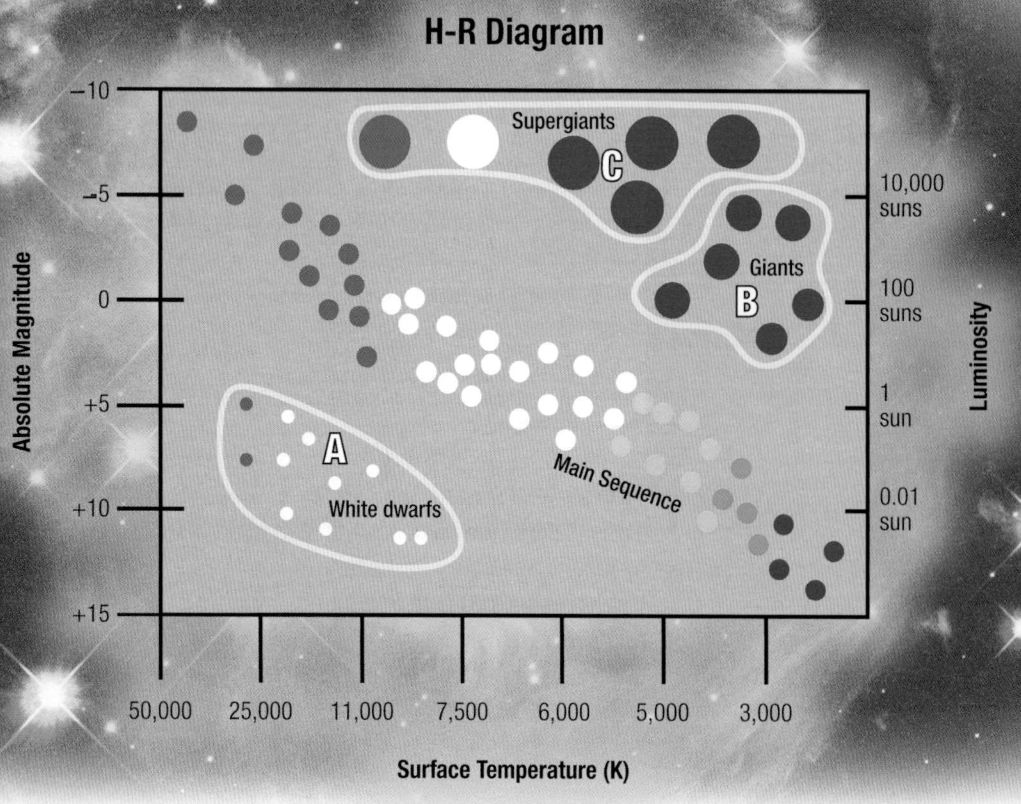

The H-R diagram also reveals three other star populations. A white dwarf found in area *A* has a fairly high temperature but a low absolute magnitude. This is because it is very small. A star plotted in area *B* is the opposite of a white dwarf. It is relatively cool, yet very bright. A cool star can burn brightly because of its great size. Each star in this population is known as a giant and is usually red in color. The population of stars found around area *C* has a greater variety of temperatures. The stars themselves are very large. These are known as *supergiants* and may be blue, yellow, or red. One of the largest known stars, Betelgeuse, is a reddish-orange supergiant.

IN THE FIELD

The H-R diagram used in astronomy is known as an *x-y scatter plot*. This type of graph is used in research of all types and shows normal relationships between two characteristics. For example, doctors use x-y scatter plots to establish normal patterns in child development. The chart displayed here shows head sizes among infants.

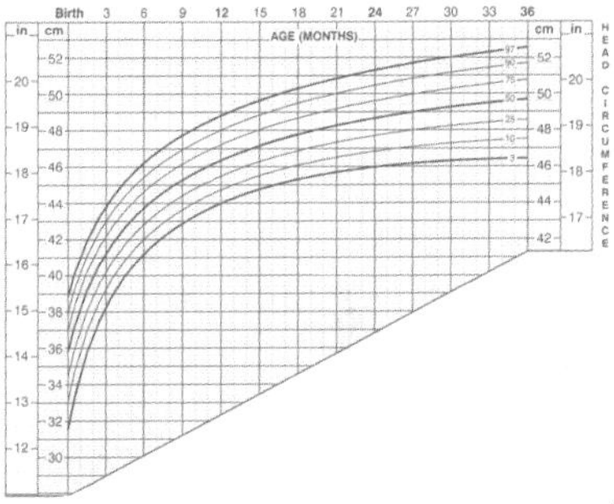

Sirius A, the brightest star in the night sky, is a main sequence star. Its tiny stellar companion Sirius B, a white dwarf, can be seen in the lower left. Sirius A and B are 8.6 light-years from Earth.

Betelgeuse, in the constellation Orion, is cooler, yet 1,000 times more massive than Earth's sun. If it were placed where Earth's sun is, it would extend beyond Jupiter's orbit!

STAR LIFE CYCLES

VOCABULARY

nebula ('ne·byə·lə) a large cloud of gas and dust in space

supernova (sōō·pər·'nō·və) the explosion of a massive star that causes a sudden increase in luminosity

neutron star ('nōō·trän 'stär) the small, dense core of a supergiant after an explosion

pulsar ('pəl·sär) a rapidly spinning neutron star that emits pulsating radio waves

The H-R diagram reveals that different populations of stars exist. Certain changes in stars have also been observed, which astronomers have theorized to be stages in a star's life cycle. The first stage begins with a nebula, which is spread out over an immense area. Gravity in the most dense part of the nebula pulls the gas and dust together. This compact cloud of gas and dust is called *a protostar*. When the protostar becomes so hot and dense that nuclear fusion begins, a star is formed.

The second and longest stage is called *the main sequence.* In it, energy is produced when hydrogen atoms fuse into helium. Stars in the main sequence population on the H-R diagram are in this stage. When a star begins to run out of fuel for fusion to take place, its core shrinks and the outer portion expands. It becomes either a giant or supergiant. A small- or medium-mass star becomes a giant. The outer portion drifts farther into space over time, forming a type of nebula. The glowing core becomes a white dwarf. The most massive stars swell into supergiants. Sometimes a supergiant explodes in an event called a supernova. The explosion is so powerful that it glows millions of times brighter for several days.

What is a black dwarf?

The Eagle Nebula is a majestic network of turbulent clouds and new stars.

During a supernova, some of the material spreads out into space and becomes one or more nebulas. The matter that becomes a nebula may contract again and become a new, yet recycled, star. Some of the other material from the explosion may become a neutron star. This happens when the matter collapses from the force of gravity. This pressure causes the electrons and protons to combine and form a neutron star. Neutron stars are smaller than white dwarfs but can have two or three times the mass of the sun. A spinning neutron star is called a pulsar. First discovered in 1967 by graduate student Jocelyn Bell Burnell, pulsars emit beams of electromagnetic radiation in regular pulses.

After a supernova explosion, an exceptionally massive star may become a black hole. The mass left over after the explosion can be more than five times that of the sun. The intense gravity of the mass pulls in the surrounding gases. Even light cannot escape this powerful force. Scientists detect black holes by observing the radiation of the swirling matter entering into the high-gravity area.

QUICK FACT

The regularity of radio waves emitting from pulsars originally baffled astronomers and made them think the signals might be coming from extraterrestrials. As a result, the first pulsar was named *LGM-1*, for little green men.

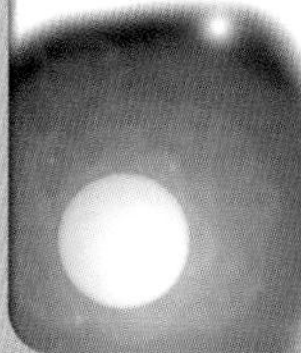

If nebulas are clouds of gas and dust that are no longer producing fusion, why are they visible?

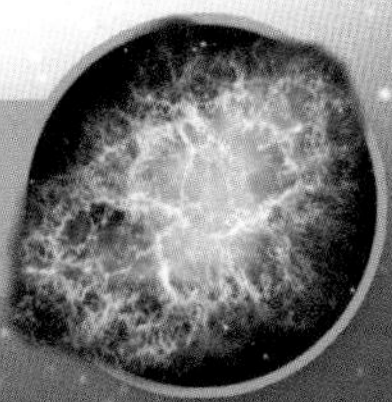

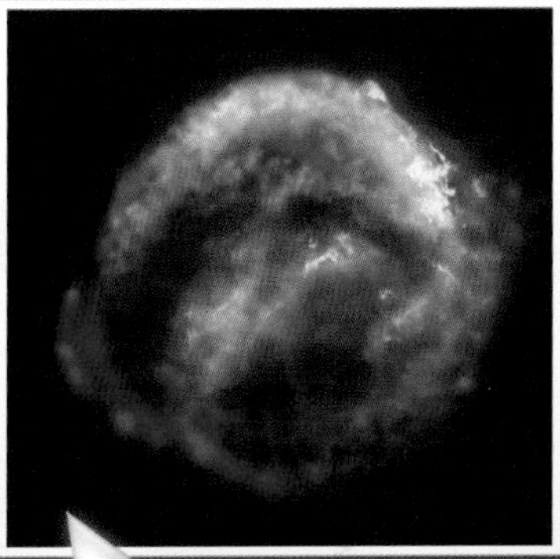

In 1604, Johannes Kepler witnessed the sudden appearance of a brilliant star in the sky. Scientists at NASA have photographed the remnants of Kepler's supernova, which is 14 light-years wide and expanding at 6 million kph (4 million mph).

Black holes are very small. Since light does not pass through them, they cannot be seen. The concept of a black hole has been depicted here by NASA.

CELESTIAL INTERACTIONS

VOCABULARY

binary star ('bī·nə·rē 'stär) a system of two stars that revolve around each other

ellipse (i·'lips) an elongated oval shape

exoplanet ('ek·sō·pla·nət) a planet orbiting a star other than Earth's sun

The movement of celestial bodies is also of interest to astronomers. Two stars that revolve around each other are called a binary star. These double stars orbit around each other's center of gravity. Interestingly, these may appear like slow pulsars, dimming when one begins to eclipse the other. Sirius A and B are binary stars. Stellar systems with three stars are called *triple stars*. Proxima Centauri is believed to be part of a triple-star system along with Alpha Centauri A and B—binary stars—as the other two companions.

Planets orbit the sun in elliptical paths. An ellipse is similar to a flattened circle. Mathematician and astronomer Johannes Kepler was the first to describe the motion of planets as ellipses. Kepler's calculations led him to formulate the Laws of Planetary Motion. The first law states that the orbit of every planet is an ellipse. Kepler's second law describes the fact that a planet travels faster when close to the sun and slows down when farther away. The relationship between a planet's distance from the sun and the time it takes to orbit the sun is explained in his third law.

Like planets, comets orbit the sun in elliptical paths.

Albireo, identified as a binary star, can be viewed with minimal magnification through a telescope. However, astronomers think that the brighter yellow star is itself a binary system, though its stars are too close together to be distinguished.

Strange but True

Although this looks like the moon, it is actually Mercury.

Because of the earth's daily rotation, stars seem to follow circular arcs. In addition, Earth's yearly orbit causes stars to appear to move across the sky. This apparent motion occurs because the dark side of Earth faces different directions on its elliptical path. To know whether stars actually move over time, astronomers compare star movements to the sun rather than to Earth. Stars change position in the sky only slightly as decades pass. Such star drift is known as *proper motion*. Since the sun itself moves within the galaxy, which also rotates and drifts, stars have very complex paths. For this reason, proper motion is the most practical description.

In addition to apparent and proper motion, some stars wobble slightly. Astronomers take special interest in this because wobbles likely result from orbiting planets. Any planet orbiting a star other than our sun is known as an exoplanet, or extra solar planet. With reflected light too dim to detect, these planets are seldom observed directly. Instead, astronomers deduce an exoplanet's existence using mathematics. Since the 1990s, astronomers have detected more than 300 exoplanets, none similar to Earth.

IN THE FIELD

The north star, also called the *polestar*, is the star that the northern end of Earth's axis points to. Egypt's ancient pyramids were aligned to true north. Yet the north star of that day was Thuban, not Polaris, as it is today. In addition to becoming the present polestar, Polaris has more than doubled in brightness since that time. In about 12,000 years, Vega, located in the constellation of Lyra, will be the most northerly star as seen from Earth.

This time-lapse photo captures the light from the stars during Earth's rotation. It illustrates the apparent circular path of stars as seen from Earth.

This image dramatizes the closest exoplanet ever detected directly. Known as *HD 189733b*, this planet orbits 30 times closer to its sun than the earth orbits its own sun. The immense heat from the star-facing side produces enough low-frequency radiation to be detected directly.

CLUSTERS AND CONSTELLATIONS

VOCABULARY

star cluster ('stär 'klus·tər) a group of stars held together by gravitational attraction

Multiple star systems orbit tightly around a central point. In addition, larger groups of tightly bound stars may be attracted to one another by the force of gravity. When this gravitational pull keeps stars together, a star cluster is formed. A star cluster is smaller than a galaxy, which is a huge collection of stars, gases, and dust clouds. Star clusters give a galaxy its distinct shape and intricate pattern. There are at least two types of star clusters. An open star cluster may contain as little as a dozen or as many as a few thousand stars. A globular star cluster is a densely packed concentration of several thousand to over a million stars.

Throughout human history, people have formed figures and shapes by visually connecting widely spaced groups of stars. These became known as *constellations*. Some well-known constellations are Ursa Major, Ursa Minor, Gemini, Capricorn, Orion, and Pisces. In astronomy, however, the term signifies areas in the sky, not just specific shapes. Today, astronomers divide the sky into 88 constellation zones with exact boundaries so that every direction or place in the sky belongs to a constellation. All modern constellation names are in Latin. The twelve most recognized ones are called the *zodiac*.

The Pleiades is a famous star cluster easily visible with binoculars. Pleiades is an open cluster of over 3,000 stars surrounded by nebulas.

Is this a flying saucer?

This globular cluster named *M55* has around 100,000 stars. It is located in the Sagittarius constellation about 20,000 light-years away.

The star patterns people see today look very similar to the ones first identified and named thousands of years ago. Over much time, patterns will change. In addition, different constellations are seen depending on a person's location on the earth as well as the orbital position of the earth. People living in one hemisphere see certain constellations that are not always visible in the other hemisphere. The apparent locations of constellations also change from season to season. Stars near the geographic poles, or circumpolar stars, can be seen at all times of the year from that hemisphere.

In the Northern Hemisphere sky, Ursa Major, or the Great Bear, contains all of the stars that make up that constellation, including the seven stars of the Big Dipper. The Little Dipper is part of the constellation Ursa Minor and has Polaris, the North Star, at the end of its handle. Visible from the Southern Hemisphere, Crux—the Southern Cross—is the smallest, yet one of the most distinctive constellations in the sky.

OUTLOOK

Galaxy clusters contain galaxies, which are themselves filled with star clusters. Galaxy clusters occur in patterns similar to huge, irregular spiderwebs. Most galaxies that are within a galaxy cluster and are along the strands of the web are about 500 million light-years apart. Evolutionary astronomers explain this as the result of sound waves early in the big bang explosion. Astronomers who believe in the biblical account of Creation believe that these patterns resulted from God's order and creativity.

Which constellations are mentioned in the Bible?

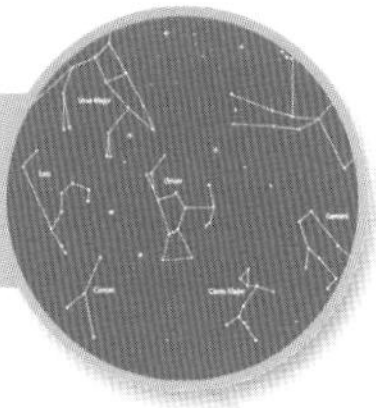

Centaurus, one of the largest constellations, is seen from the Southern Hemisphere. It contains Proxima Centauri and surrounds Crux on three sides.

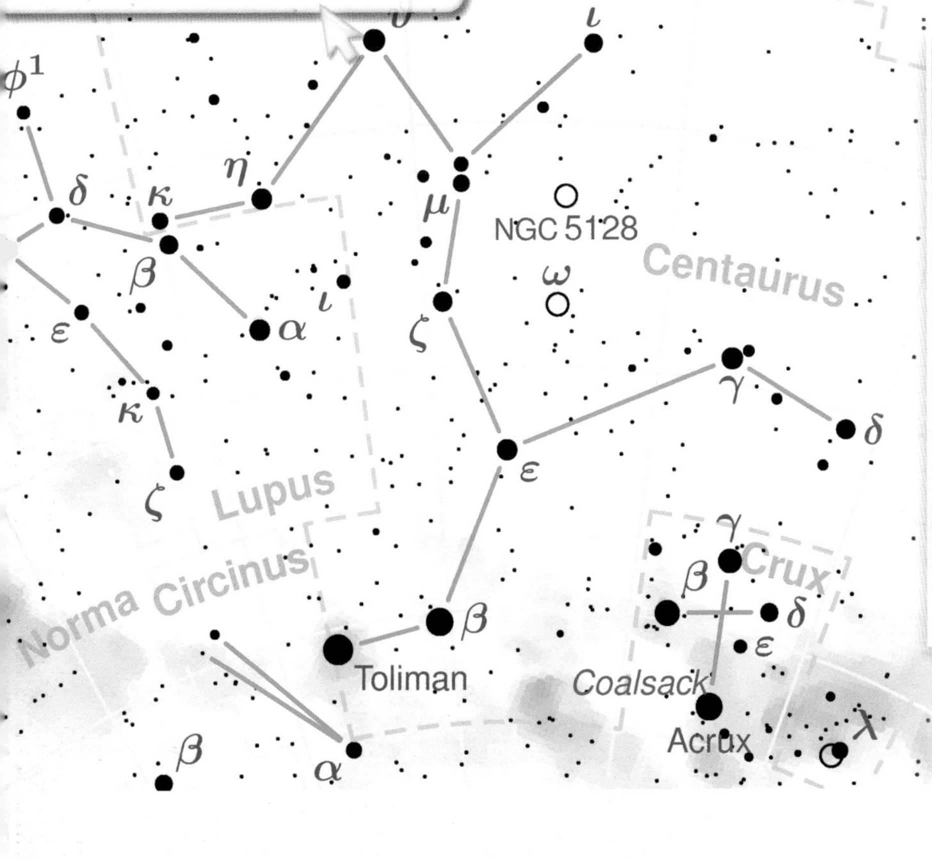

Orion, also known as *the Hunter*, is commonly visible in the northern sky. Its brightest stars are Betelgeuse and Rigel, both supergiants.

UNIT 1

LIFE SCIENCE: DIVERSITY

UNIT 2

PHYSICAL SCIENCE: STRUCTURE

UNIT 3

EARTH AND SPACE SCIENCE: PATTERNS

UNIT 4

HUMAN BODY: DECISIONS

– the study of the body as a network of systems and how to keep the body healthy

CHAPTER 13

INTERACTION OF SYSTEMS

Organization and design is shown throughout the world and universe. It can be seen in a spider spinning its symmetrical web, a caterpillar metamorphosing into a butterfly, or a delicate rose blossoming in the spring. Complex systems like these work together, allowing life to continue. As magnificent as these examples are, they fall short of God's most unique and intricate design—mankind.

KEY IDEAS

- The human body displays intricate design.
- Each body system has specific structures and functions.
- All organs and body systems are interdependent.
- Life processes occur at all cellular levels.

The adult human body is made up of trillions of cells, each with its own job. Cells work together as tissues, and different tissues make up organs. Various organs work together to form 11 major body systems. All of these systems are interdependent and unable to function entirely on their own. An example is the digestive system, which responds when the nervous system produces the feeling of hunger. Materials move through the digestive tract with help from the musculoskeletal system. Nutrients from food are transported to the cells by way of the cardiovascular system. Additionally, oxygen from the respiratory system allows the body to burn fuel and provide energy for digestion. The urinary system is involved in eliminating liquid wastes. All these body systems are remarkably engineered to carry on life processes.

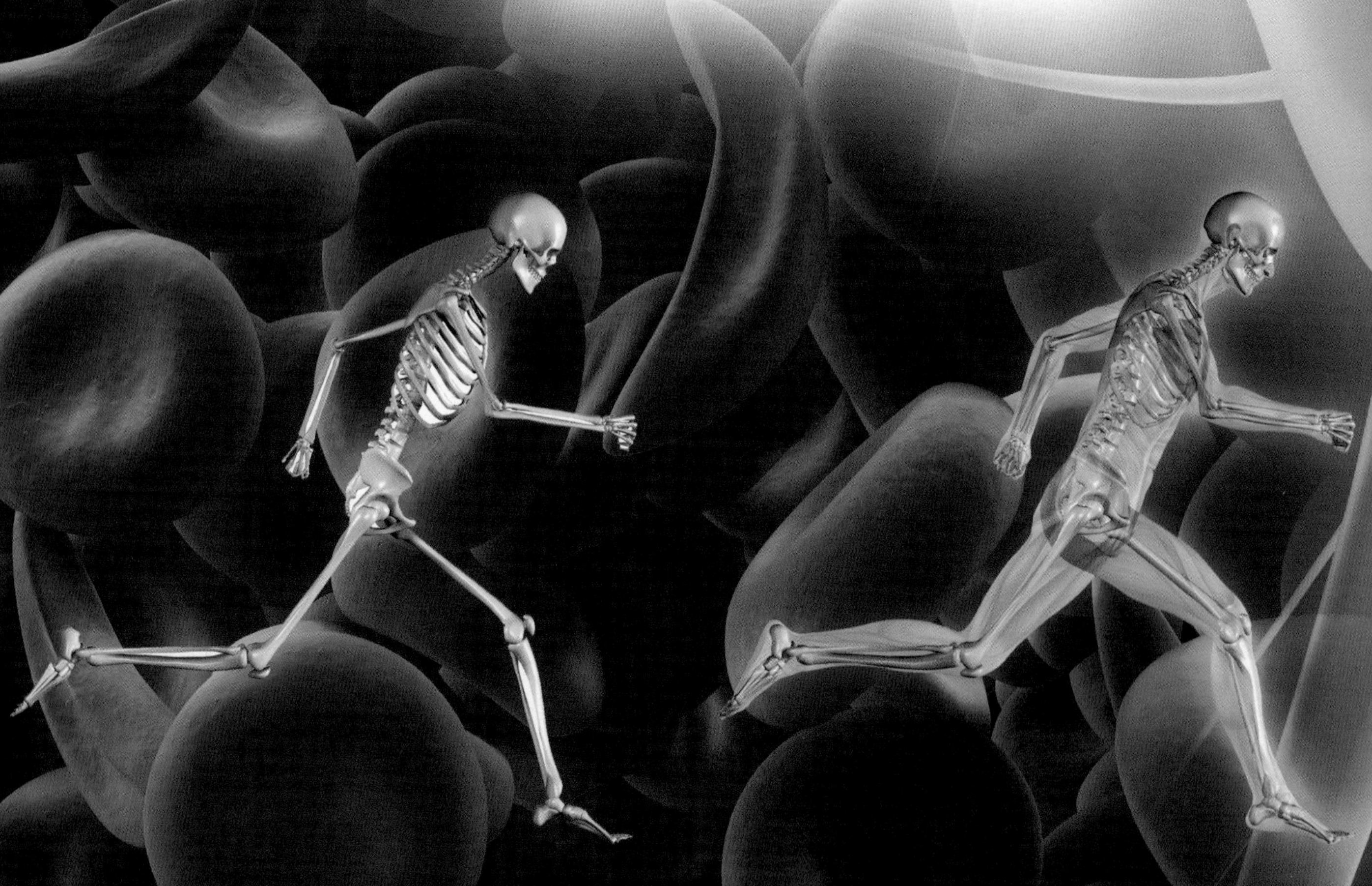

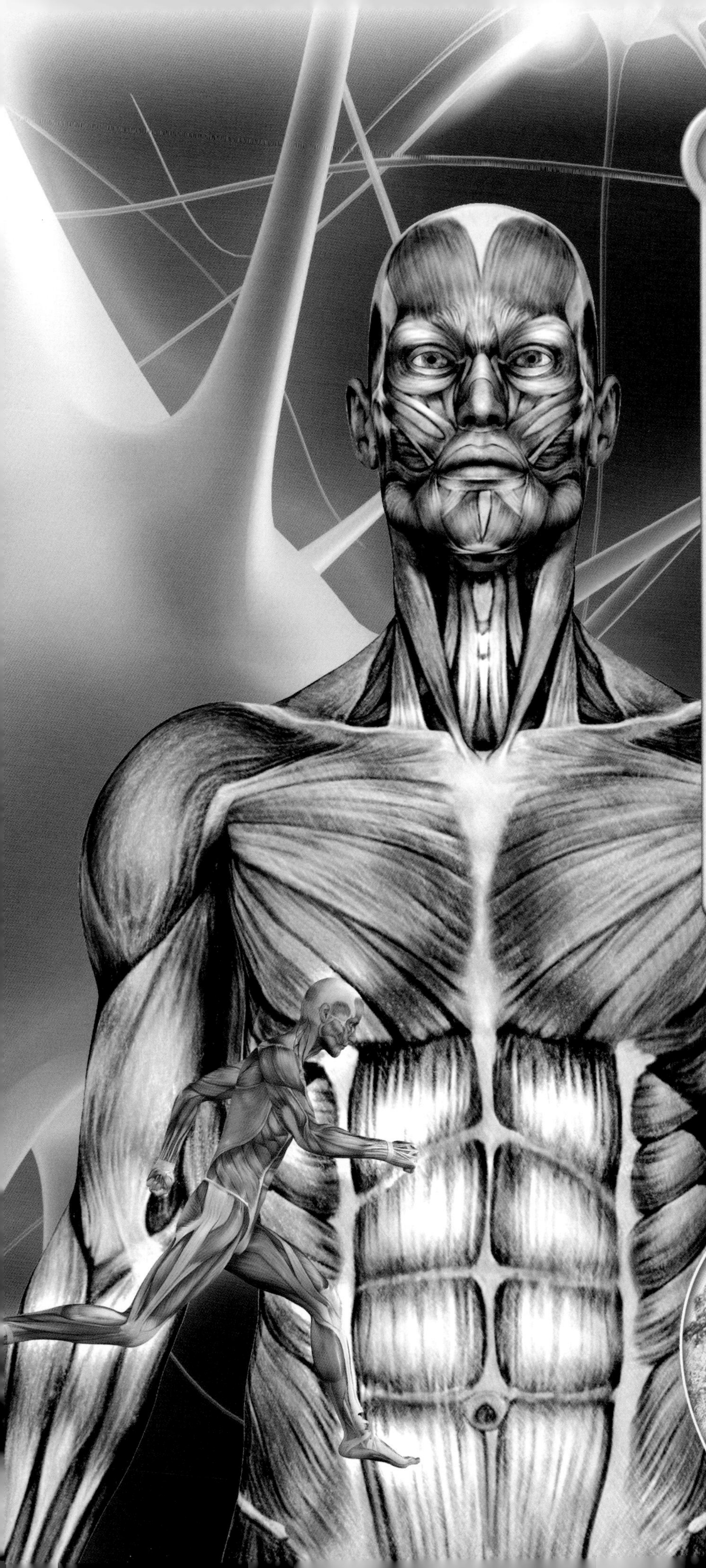

OUTLOOK

Scientists have organized all known living things into a classification system. Categories are based on physical characteristics and DNA sequencing. According to this system, humans are a part of the animal kingdom. Humans do have many common characteristics with animals; however, God has set them apart from other creatures and given them dominion over the earth. People are the only part of Creation that God breathed His breath into. God has also given people a plan of salvation through His Son, Jesus, because of His everlasting love and grace.

Strange but True

What part of the human body travels 19,000 km (12,000 mi) a day?

SYSTEMS OVERVIEW

VOCABULARY

alveoli (al·ˈvē·ə·lī) the microscopic air sacs found in the lungs

chyme (ˈkīm) the thick liquid made of partially digested food in the stomach

pyloric sphincter (pī·ˈlôr·ik ˈsfink·tər) the muscle that separates the stomach from the small intestine

villi (ˈvi·lī) the tiny fingerlike projections that line the surface of the small intestine

The cardiovascular, digestive, respiratory, and urinary systems are 4 of the 11 body systems of the human body. The cardiovascular system is the major transportation system of the body. With each beat of the heart, the aorta and other arteries carry oxygen, nutrients, and water to capillaries, which in turn transport them to cells. During cellular processes, excess water and carbon dioxide are produced. These wastes are carried back through capillaries to veins and on to the heart. Large veins have valves that prevent the blood from flowing backward. Eventually, the lungs exhale wastes from the body. Additional functions of the circulatory system include fighting disease and regulating body temperature.

The respiratory system, which includes the trachea, lungs, and diaphragm, is responsible for exchanging oxygen and carbon dioxide between the air and blood. When the muscular diaphragm contracts, it moves downward, causing the lungs to fill with air. During exhalation, it relaxes and deflates the lungs by pushing upward. The trachea branches off into bronchi, which extend into each lung. The bronchi continue branching into smaller passageways until they form alveoli. It is here that oxygen and carbon dioxide are exchanged.

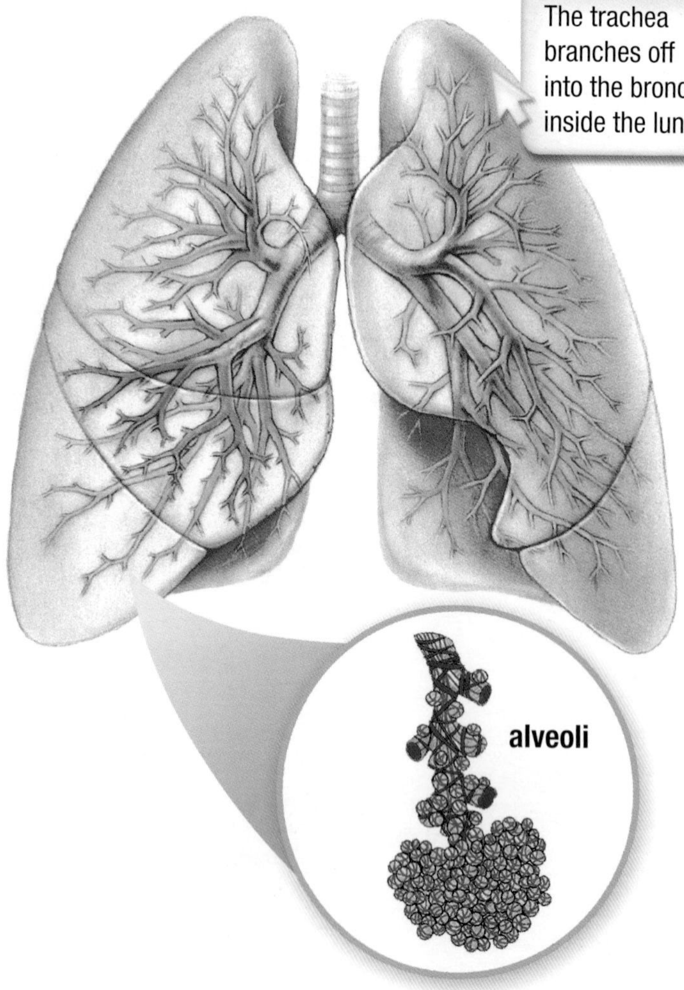

The trachea branches off into the bronchi inside the lungs.

Strange but True

In one day, the blood covers approximately 19,000 km (12,000 mi), which is equivalent to crossing the United States from coast to coast four times!

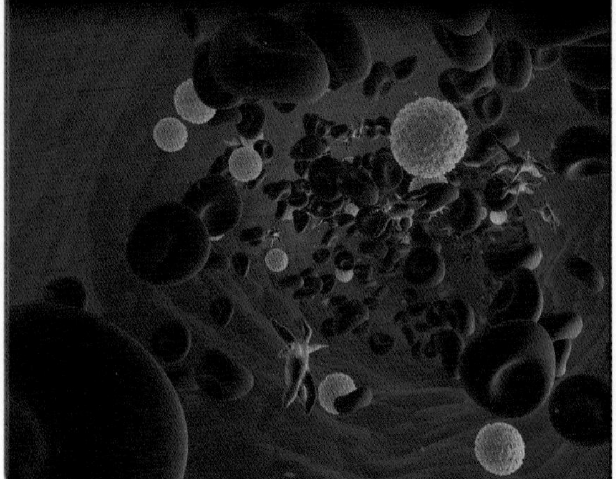

An important part of the digestive system is a long, open passageway for food digestion, known as the *alimentary canal* or the *digestive tract*. It includes organs and other structures associated with the process of digestion—the mouth, esophagus, stomach, small intestine, large intestine, rectum, and anus. Food enters the mouth, where mechanical digestion, or chewing, begins. Chemical digestion begins when enzymes in the saliva start breaking down certain nutrients. Saliva also moistens the food particles, making them easier to swallow. Once swallowed, the food travels down the muscular esophagus into the stomach, where the food mixes with stomach acid and enzymes, creating a mixture called chyme. After a few hours of mixing, chyme travels from the stomach through the pyloric sphincter into the small intestine. Enzymes from the liver and pancreas continue the digestive process. Nutrients are absorbed into the bloodstream through villi that line the intestinal wall. The nutrients are transported to individual cells, where they are used to maintain bodily functions. Undigested materials travel to the large intestine, where solid wastes, or feces, are formed. These are then discharged through the anus. Kidneys, part of the urinary system, filter the blood. Urine leaves the kidneys through the ureters and is stored in the bladder until eliminated from the body.

QUICK FACT

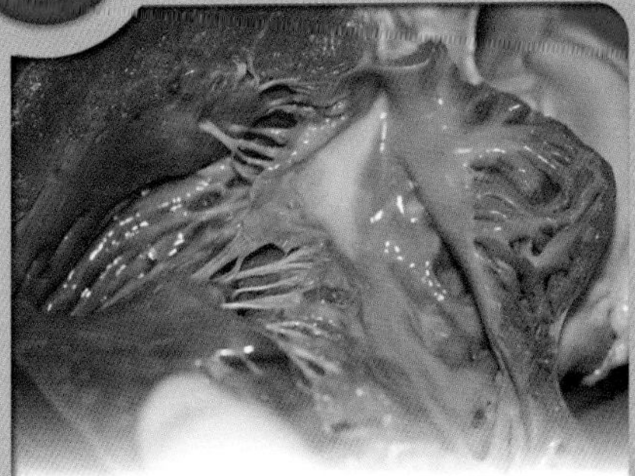

When listening to the heart, sometimes you hear a swishing noise known as *a murmur*. This occurs when a defective heart valve does not close tightly and allows a backflow of blood. A severe murmur can cause reduction of blood flow through the heart and prevent a person from carrying on normal activity. If the murmur is serious enough, the valve can be surgically replaced with an artificial valve.

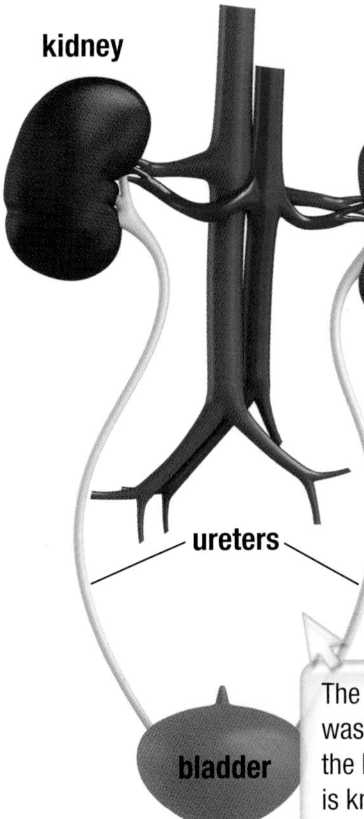

The kidneys filter wastes and toxins from the blood. This material is known as *urine*, which exits the body through the urethra.

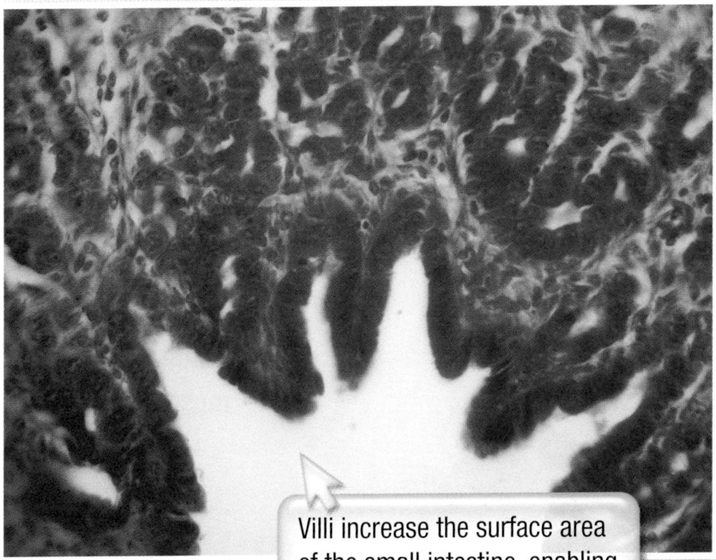

Villi increase the surface area of the small intestine, enabling it to absorb higher amounts of fluids and nutrients.

MUSCULAR SYSTEM

VOCABULARY

peristalsis (per·ə·ˈstȯl·səs) the muscular contractions that move food through the digestive tract

tendon (ˈten·dən) the connective tissue that attaches muscle to bone

The muscular system makes it possible to eat or drink something with the body upside down. Once swallowed, the food or drink moves through the digestive tract because muscles contract and relax. This involuntary, rhythmic movement is called peristalsis. Running, jumping, blinking the eyes, and breathing depend on muscle action also. In fact, whether awake or asleep, all body movement depends on many muscles working together.

There are three types of muscle tissue—skeletal, smooth, and cardiac. In the human body there are approximately 650 skeletal muscles that are attached to the bones of the skeleton. A skeletal muscle is composed of many muscle cells that appear striated, or banded. These individual cells are arranged in parallel bundles. The body of the muscle is called the *belly*. The entire muscle is wrapped in connective tissue called *fascia*. At the end of the muscle, the fascia forms a tough fibrous tendon, which attaches the muscle to a bone. The nervous system constantly sends nerve impulses along nerve cells to the skeletal muscles.

Cardiac and skeletal muscles are striated, while smooth muscle is not. Each is uniquely designed to perform specific functions.

What happens if the Achilles tendon is severed?

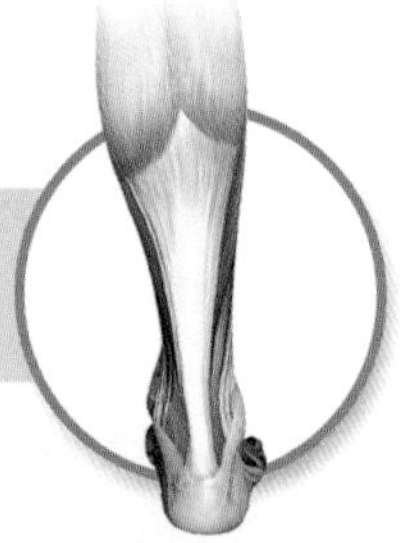

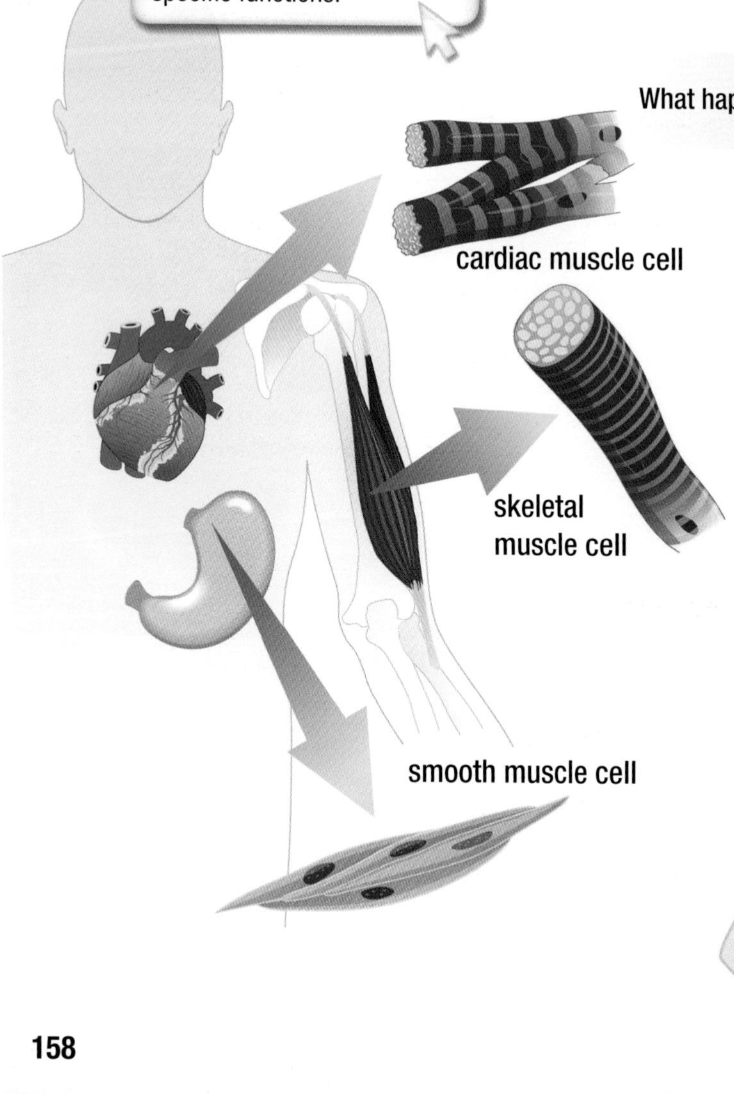

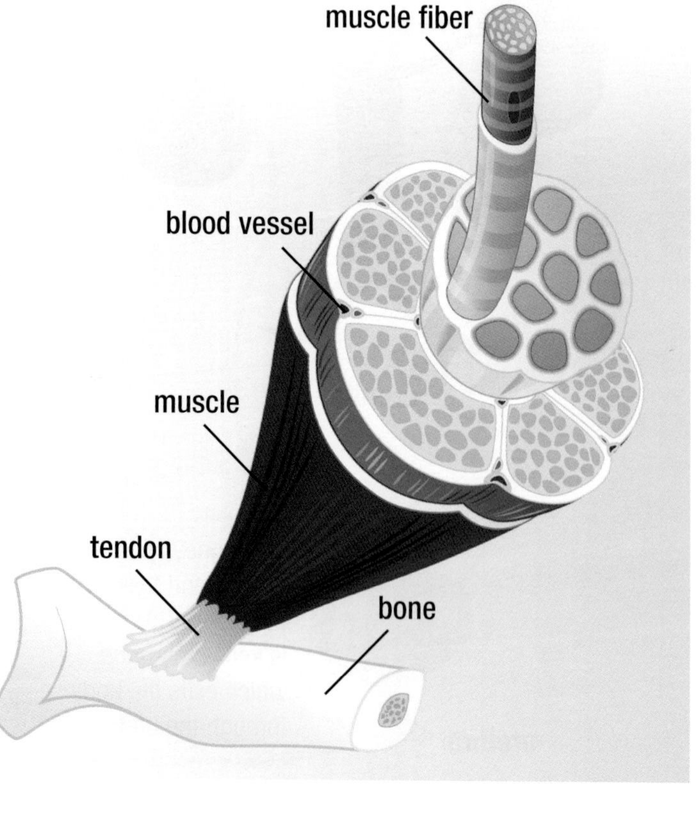

Skeletal muscles hold the skeleton together, give the body shape, and provide the force to move bones. To give joints a full range of motion, skeletal muscles exist in pairs that oppose each other. For example, as the biceps on the arm contract, the triceps relax. This results in the lower arm moving upward. Reversing this process moves the arm downward. Skeletal muscles contract quickly and voluntarily, yet can tire easily.

Smooth muscles line the digestive tract, blood vessels, bladder, and other internal organs. They contract and relax slowly and have the ability to endure long periods of work without tiring. Smooth muscles move involuntarily because the nervous system automatically controls them. For example, as the smooth muscle of the stomach contracts, food is mixed with enzymes to make chyme.

Cardiac muscle is found only in the heart. Like skeletal muscle, it is striated, and like smooth muscle, it contracts involuntarily and does not tire quickly. The involuntary contractions are responsible for the constant heartbeat.

Opposing Muscles in the Arm

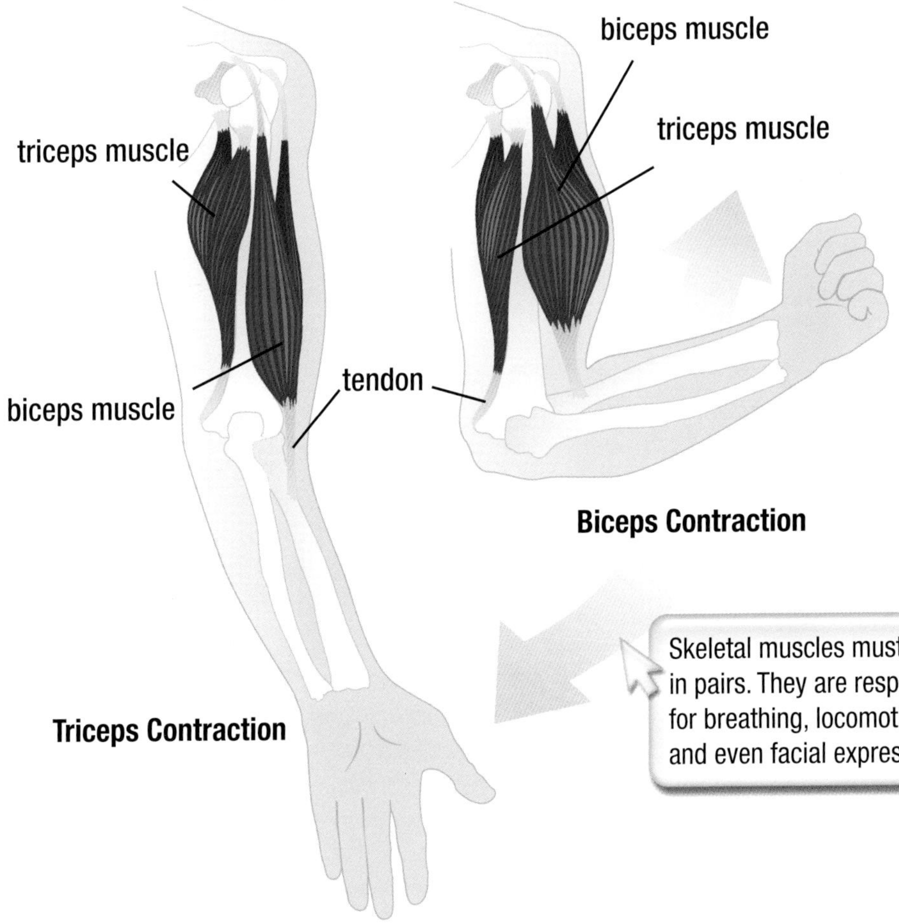

Skeletal muscles must work in pairs. They are responsible for breathing, locomotion, and even facial expressions.

IN THE FIELD

Ideas about robotics have been around throughout recorded history, although the term itself was not used until 1941. The first industrial robot became operational at the General Motors factory in 1961. Not until 1998 was the first bionic arm for humans fitted. Presently, research continues on the use of robotic assistance in the medical field. Robots have been utilized in the automotive industry, particularly in spot welding automobiles on an assembly line. In the space program, various unmanned spacecraft have gone to the moon and other planets. Robots are also used by law enforcement to dispose of bombs and carry video cameras and microphones into dangerous areas. In the military, robots help locate and destroy mines in water and on land.

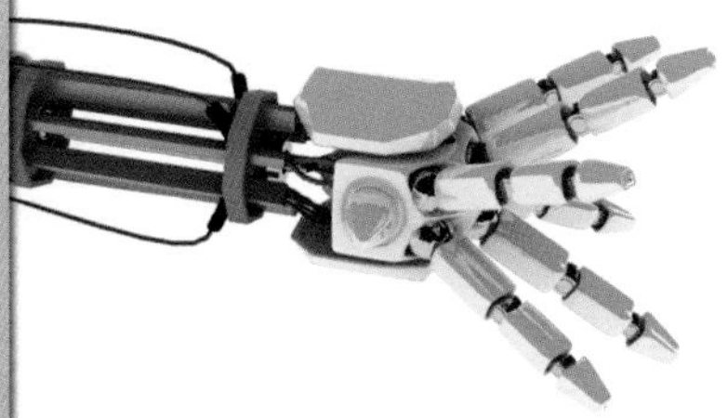

SKELETAL SYSTEM

VOCABULARY

endoskeleton (ˌen·dō·ˈske·lə·tən) the internal supporting framework of an animal or human

cartilage (ˈkär·tə·lij) the connective tissue that covers the ends of bones in a joint

sternum (ˈstər·nəm) the breastbone, located in the middle of the chest

A building without a strong foundation and internal support beams inside its walls is unable to stand upright for very long, if at all. Just as a building needs a proper support structure, so does the body. In an adult, 206 bones form the jointed endoskeleton. With their attached muscles, these bones allow movement in many directions. They give the body stability. Additionally, the skeleton protects internal organs and tissues, produces blood cells in the bone marrow, and stores calcium and other minerals.

Bone tissue in the body contains living cells. These allow the bones to grow, change shape, and repair themselves. During early development, cartilage makes up most of the skeleton. As the body grows, cartilage is replaced by bone in a process called *ossification*. It involves specialized cells that deposit calcium and other minerals into the bone. Although major growth stops soon after puberty, bone tissue is under maintenance throughout one's lifetime. New cells are continually being formed to replace old bone cells.

Which skeletal bone in the body is the largest and strongest?

IN THE FIELD

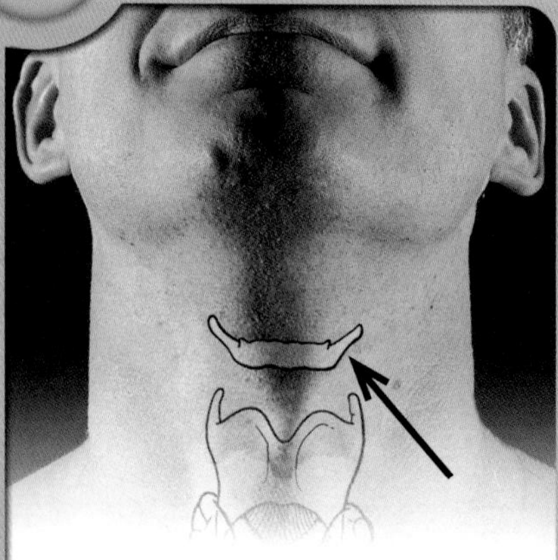

Doctors diagnose a rare but life-threatening disease called *adult acute epiglottitis* by testing the tenderness of the neck area that is in front of the hyoid bone. The human hyoid bone gives support to the tongue. Several muscles that are used in swallowing attach to the hyoid bone, which is U-shaped. It is the only bone in the body that does not connect to any other bone at a joint.

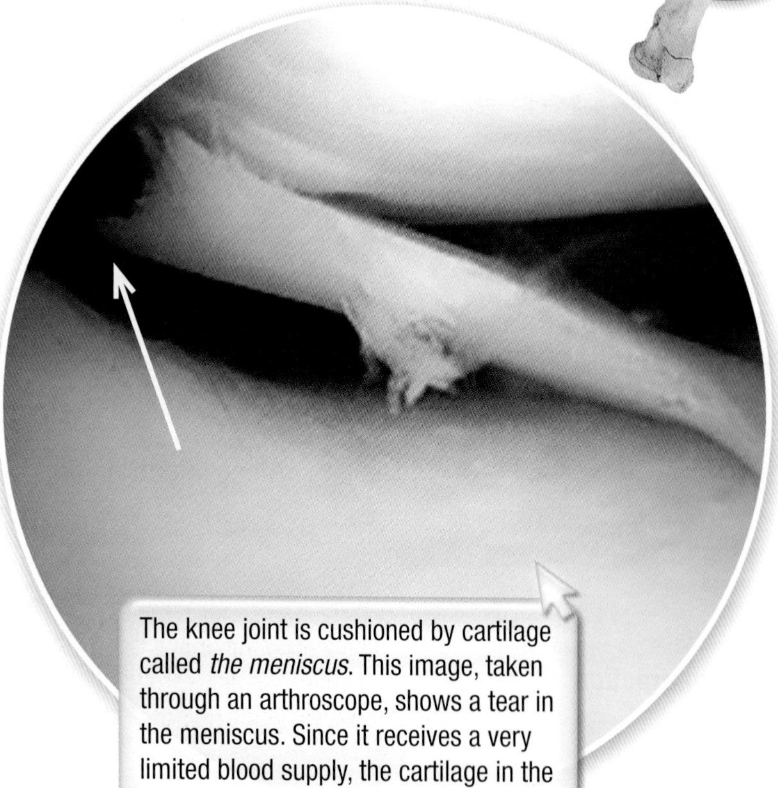

The knee joint is cushioned by cartilage called *the meniscus*. This image, taken through an arthroscope, shows a tear in the meniscus. Since it receives a very limited blood supply, the cartilage in the knee has a limited potential to heal.

The axial skeleton is the core part of the endoskeleton and protects the body's major organs. It consists of the 80 bones found in the head and trunk of the body—specifically the skull, the vertebral column, and the rib cage. The skull is made up of the facial bones and the cranium. It protects the brain. The facial bones form the jawbones, the nose, the cheeks, and the roof of the mouth. These support and house sense organs such as the eyes, ears, and nose. The vertebral column is made up of 33 vertebrae and forms the curved backbone. It extends from the skull to the pelvis and serves as an attachment site for other skeletal bones. The vertebrae safeguard the spinal cord, which runs down and through the middle. A disc of cartilage, located between each vertebra, prevents grinding of the bones and absorbs shock from body movements. The rib cage contains the sternum and 12 pairs of ribs. It provides a barrier for the vital organs such as the heart, liver, and lungs.

The appendicular skeleton consists of the body's appendages, such as the arms, legs, and girdles. The pectoral girdle consists of the shoulder bones, including the clavicle, and the pelvic girdle consists of the hip bones.

QUICK FACT

Believe it or not, giraffes and humans both have seven cervical vertebrae, or neck bones. In fact, most mammals have seven no matter the length of their neck. Exceptions include the manatee and two-toed sloth with six, and the three-toed sloth with nine cervical vertebrae.

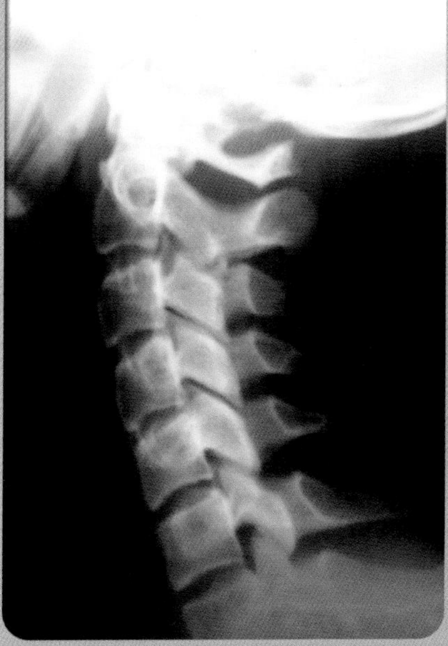

An infant's skull has soft spots that occur because the cartilage has not fully hardened into bone. This allows the skull to expand and develop a normal shape as the brain grows.

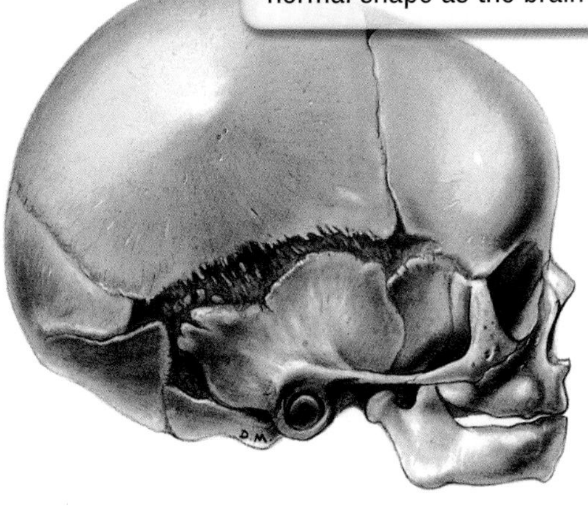

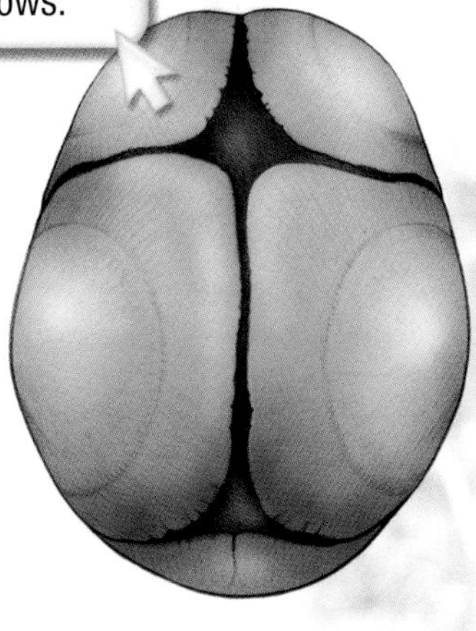

Wearing a helmet is the single most important thing a person can do to protect the brain when riding a bike.

NERVOUS SYSTEM

VOCABULARY

neuron ('nōō·rän) a nerve cell that sends messages throughout the body

medulla oblongata (mə·'du·lə ä·blȯng·'gä·tə) the lower portion of the brain stem

OUTLOOK

The elephant brain has an approximate mass of 6,000 g, the chimpanzee's is 420 g, a beagle's is 72 g, a cat's is 30 g, and the rat's brain is only 2 g. The mass of a human brain is 1,350–1,400 g. Although animals have brains of different sizes, the human brain has the most developed cerebrum. This makes it the most intricate and complex of all organisms designed by God.

The nervous system is the body's communication network. It connects the conditions inside the body with the external environment. All body functions are controlled by the nervous system. Some examples are responding to the five senses, talking, decision making, memory, and displaying emotions.

There are two main parts to the nervous system. The central nervous system (CNS) is made up of the brain and spinal cord. It receives information, processes it, and initiates responses throughout the body. The peripheral nervous system (PNS) is composed of cranial nerves and spinal nerves. There are 12 pairs of cranial nerves, which carry impulses to and from the brain. Messages to and from the spinal cord are controlled by 31 pairs of spinal nerves. The nerves in the PNS are divided into two groups—the somatic and the autonomic. The somatic division controls voluntary muscle movement. The autonomic division controls involuntary actions, such as the dilation of pupils, digestion, and the rate of heartbeats.

Billions of nerve cells called neurons make up the brain, spinal cord, and nerves. These are specialized cells that carry information throughout the nervous system to various parts of the body. A neuron consists of a long, thin axon, a cell body, and branchlike dendrites. They come in different shapes and sizes. A bundle of nerve fibers—axons and dendrites—make up a nerve.

TYPES OF NEURONS

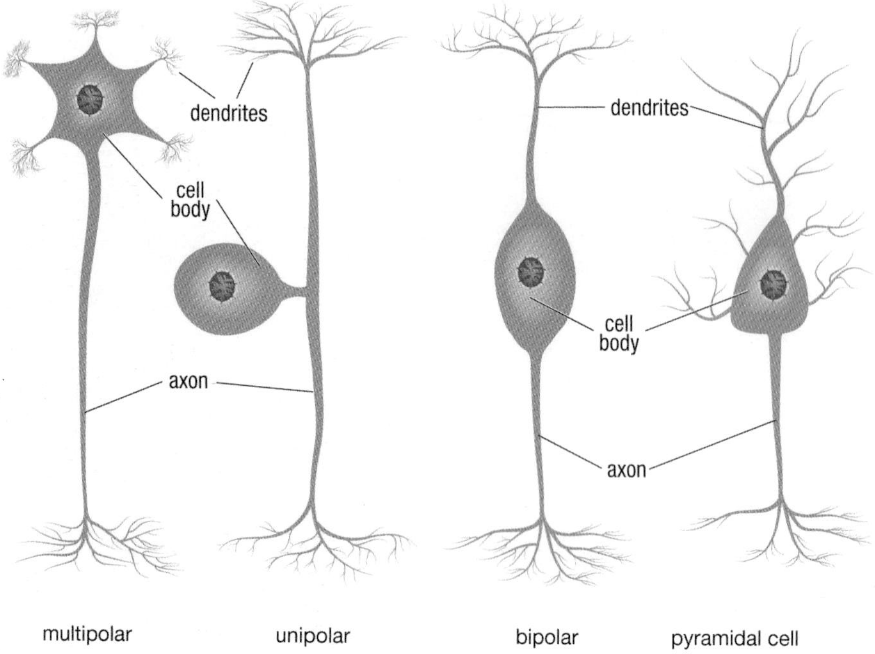

The human brain contains billions of neurons and is one of the largest organs in the body. It is protected by the cranium and three membranes. Special fluid fills empty spaces outside the brain to cushion it against jolts and vibrations. The major regions of the brain are the cerebrum, the cerebellum, and the brain stem. The cerebrum accounts for about 85% of the organ's weight. This controls the five senses, memory, learning, the ability to think, and some voluntary movements. The cerebellum, lying below and behind the cerebrum, maintains the body's sense of balance and coordinates muscular activities such as running and walking. The smallest section is known as *the brain stem*. It contains the medulla oblongata and lies just below the cerebellum, connecting the brain to the spinal cord. Basic life functions such as breathing, digestion, swallowing, and heartbeat are controlled by this region.

The spinal cord connects the spinal nerves of the PNS and the brain. It also processes messages directly without involving the brain, as in the case of a reflex action. If something sharp or hot is touched, neurons send impulses to the spinal cord, which responds by sending impulses directly back to the affected area, causing the muscles to quickly contract. Meanwhile, the brain receives sensory information as the reflex action takes place.

QUICK FACT

Why does someone get dizzy or sick on a carnival ride or when traveling on a winding mountain road? Motion receptors in the inner ear send sensory information to the cerebellum. If this data overwhelms the brain, feelings of dizziness, nausea, and sickness can occur.

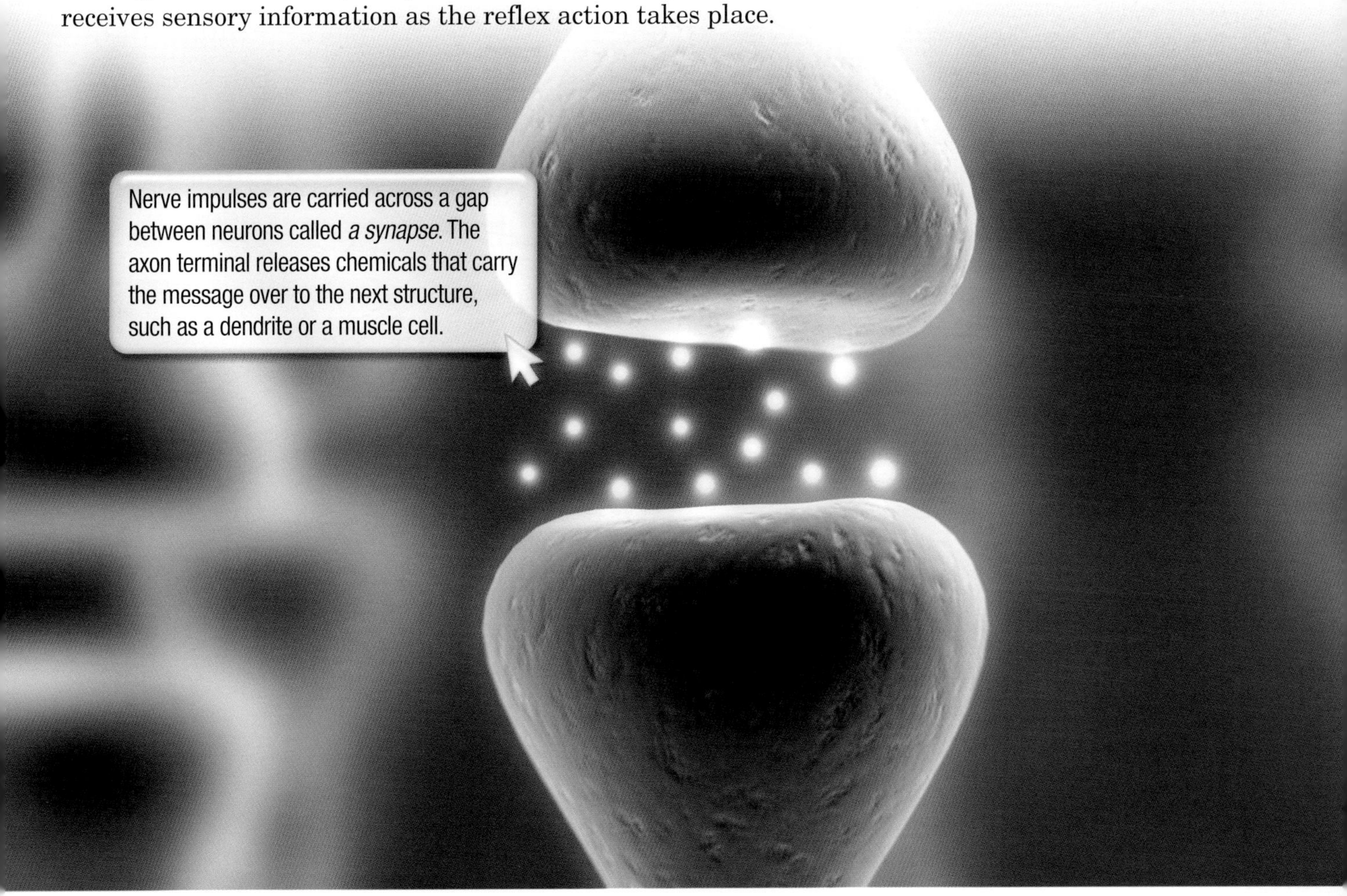

Nerve impulses are carried across a gap between neurons called *a synapse*. The axon terminal releases chemicals that carry the message over to the next structure, such as a dendrite or a muscle cell.

THE SENSES

VOCABULARY

optic nerve ('äp·tik 'nûrv) a cranial nerve that carries impulses from the retina to the brain

auditory nerve ('o·də·tôr·ē 'nûrv) a cranial nerve that carries impulses from the inner ear to the brain

QUICK FACT

The sense of touch is not centralized to a small area as the hearing, vision, taste, and smell organs are. Instead, this sense is found throughout the skin on the body. Skin is the largest single body organ and has different kinds of touch receptors located in its layers. Some receptors respond to light touch, and some respond to heavy pressure. Others sense pain and temperature. These receptors process information about the environment.

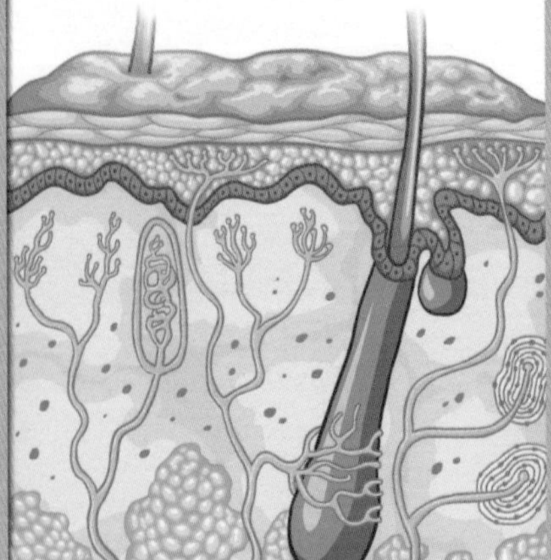

Senses play a major role in the ability to interact with the world. All the senses in the body are connected to the nervous system. Sensory neurons pick up stimuli from the environment. These stimuli are then converted into nerve impulses, which are sent to the spinal cord or brain, or both. Eyes, for example, respond to the stimulus of light. Light travels into the eye through the cornea, which is a clear tissue covering the eye, and passes through an opening called *the pupil*. The colorful iris surrounds the dark pupil and controls its size. This regulates the amount of light entering the eye. The lens focuses the light rays, which strike the retina at the back of the eye. Receptor cells called *rods* and *cones* send nerve impulses to the optic nerve, which then sends the information to the brain for interpretation.

Smell and taste are senses that work closely together. The nose and mouth identify chemicals in the air and in food. These chemical stimuli are converted into nerve impulses that travel to the brain, which interprets them as smells and tastes.

EYE

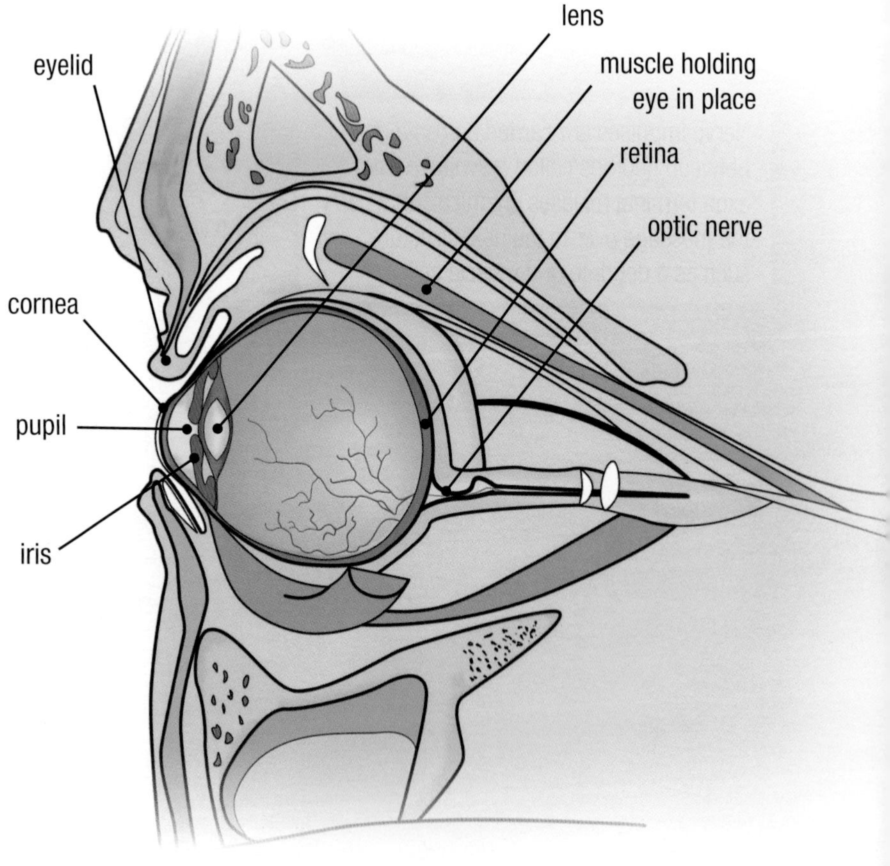

Ears respond to the stimulus of sound by converting sound energy into nerve impulses. The outer ear receives sound vibrations that travel through the ear canal to the eardrum. The eardrum is a membrane that vibrates when sound waves strike it. The vibrations pass to the bones in the middle ear—the hammer, anvil, and stirrup—and cause each of them to vibrate in a chain reaction. The stirrup then beats against the cochlea, a fluid-filled structure in the inner ear that converts the sound energy into nerve impulses. The auditory nerve carries the impulses to the brain, where they are interpreted into different sounds.

The sense of balance is controlled by the semicircular canals located in the inner ear. These canals are filled with fluid called *perilymph,* which is set into motion when the head moves. Tiny hairlike structures bend with the movement of the fluid. This produces nerve impulses that travel to the cerebellum. If the cerebellum senses that the body may be losing its balance, it sends impulses to the muscles to make adjustments.

LINKS

Art Link
Create color illustrations of three of the body systems discussed in this chapter. Label important structures, and then use them as visual aids for the class while you summarize how the body systems function.

Physical Education Link
Research the importance of balance training in athletics. Give a presentation to the class on your findings and include at least two demonstrations of balance exercises.

History Link
Write a research paper on the history of the study of anatomy. Start with the ancient Egyptians and Greeks; include medieval, early modern, and modern anatomy. Discuss some of the major technological advances that have been made through the centuries.

EAR

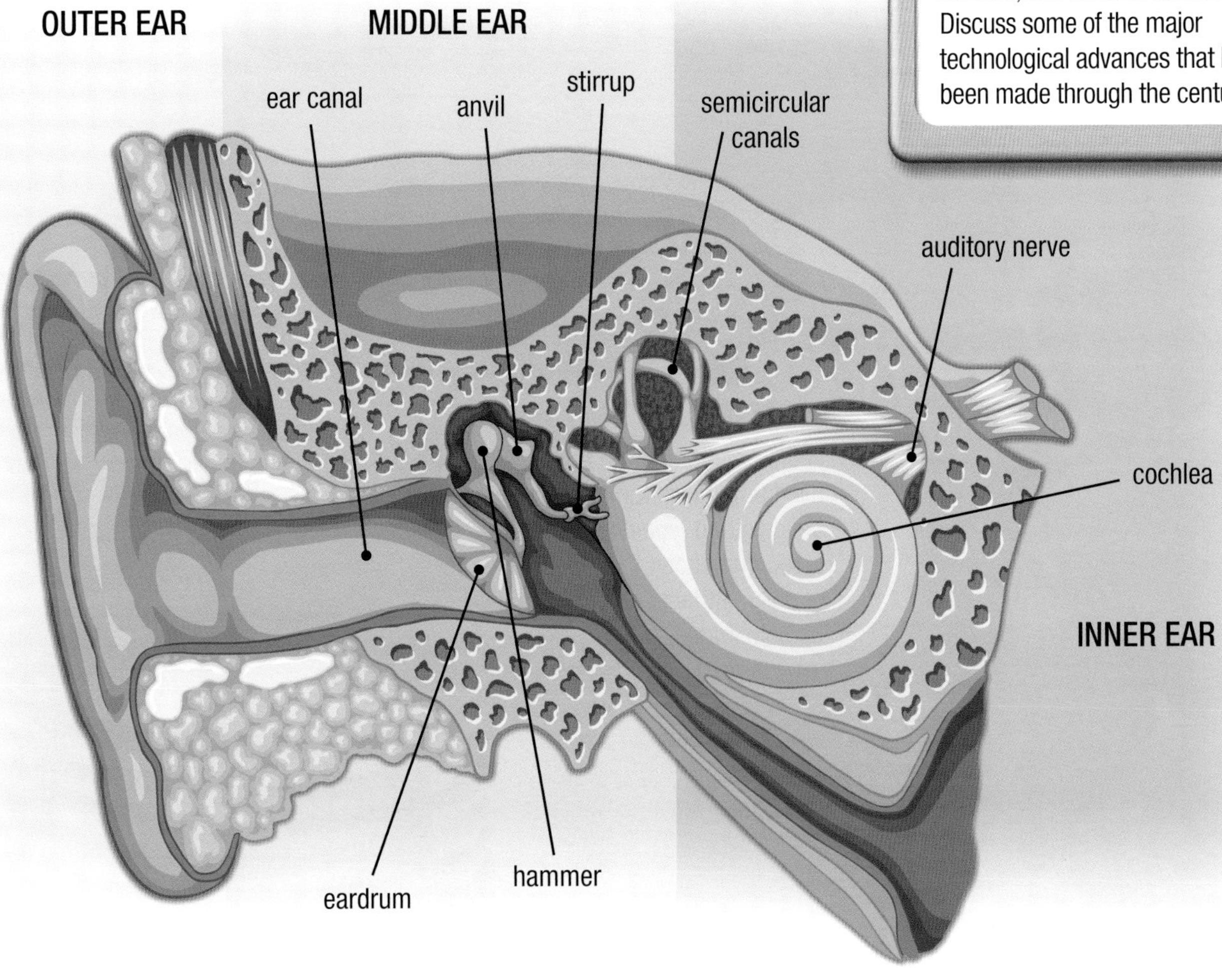

CHAPTER 14

BODY STEWARDSHIP

KEY IDEAS

- Body systems work together to keep the body healthy and functioning properly.
- Maintaining a healthy body requires a balanced diet and consistent exercise.
- Improper body maintenance increases risk of disease.

Nutrients provide the body with the raw materials and energy necessary for life processes. A balanced diet includes the following six nutrients: water, proteins, carbohydrates, fats and oils, vitamins, and minerals. A balanced diet also controls hunger. Monitoring what to eat and how much to eat is essential to the overall health of the body.

Regular exercise is also important to body health. Physical activity provides physical, psychological, and social benefits. It can improve appearance and delay the aging process as well as improve a person's quality of life.

A poor diet and lack of exercise increases the risks of developing diseases and obesity. The heart and lungs do not function as efficiently, and muscles get weak and flabby. Developing good habits at an early age has numerous long-term benefits.

Carbohydrates are a major source of energy. The energy is used to perform functions such as building and repairing tissues. It is recommended that about 50% of daily nutrient consumption be carbohydrates.

Proteins are made of smaller units called *amino acids.* These are used in forming cellular structures, growing and repairing tissues, and aiding chemical reactions. About 10–35% of a person's daily calorie intake should come from protein.

Fats and oils, also known as *lipids*, provide more than twice as much energy per gram as carbohydrates. These nutrients are also used to form cell membranes. However, because some fats are harmful in large quantities, daily intake must be limited to 20–30% of the diet.

DIET AND EXERCISE

VOCABULARY

calorie ('ka·lə·rē) a unit used to measure the energy content in food

cholesterol (kə·'les·tə·rōl) a fat-like substance produced by the liver of humans and animals

According to the World Health Organization, obesity is a worldwide epidemic. Studies show that childhood obesity frequently becomes a lifelong issue. Therefore, learning to control body weight by counting calories is a healthy decision. There are differences in the type and number of calories consumed daily. One calorie is equal to the amount of energy required to raise the temperature of 1 g of water by 1°C. Most foods contain thousands of calories. The term *Calorie*, which equals 1,000 calories, is more commonly used because of this. It has a capital *C* to avoid confusion.

There are two types of carbohydrates—sugars and starches. Sugars are simple carbohydrates, which when eaten in excess, can alter moods, lead to weight gain, and can cause blood sugar and insulin levels to spike. Over time this can lead to diabetes. Simple carbohydrates include white flour, white rice, pasta, sweetened breakfast cereals, and candy. Eating too much of these can also lead to health problems. Starches are complex carbohydrates found in high-fiber foods such as oats, brown rice, and beans.

Certain fats found in vegetable oils, nuts, whole grains, and fish are beneficial if eaten in moderate amounts. These are known as *unsaturated fats*. Saturated fats and trans fats, on the other hand, are associated with an increased risk of many diseases. Products labeled *partially hydrogenated oil* should be avoided.

Foods deep-fried in partially hydrogenated oil, commercially baked products, and some ramen noodle soups contain high levels of trans fat.

Learning to replace saturated fats with unsaturated fats and avoiding foods containing high concentrations of trans fats is a healthful approach to eating. Similarly, keeping the amounts of high-cholesterol foods to a minimum is also a good habit. Though cholesterol is needed for body functions and cell membrane composition, high levels can lead to clogged blood vessels. Overall, moderation is the important thing to remember when choosing what to eat.

During exercise, muscles rapidly use glucose, which raises the carbon dioxide and acidity levels in the blood. As the muscles contract more rapidly and forcefully, the lungs exchange gases more quickly. This is evident as the rate of breathing increases during exercise. Muscle tissue is built and maintained through physical activity, which also burns excess calories and helps limit fat storage. A sedentary person's muscle cells will gradually shrink, and the number of fat cells will increase. Unlike muscle, these cells burn very few calories. As fat cells build up, the body at rest continues to require less energy. Consequently, an increasing amount of food is stored as fat. The long-term effect of this cycle can be an overweight, unhealthy body that is more susceptible to disease.

QUICK FACT

Adolescents, as well as five- and six-year-olds, are the most likely candidates for the onset of obesity. Children between the ages of 10 and 13 who are obese have an 80% chance of remaining obese as adults. Obesity occurs when a person eats more calories than the body uses. Being physically active and monitoring calorie intake are key to avoiding this condition.

What does this corroded pipe have to do with diet and exercise?

Proper diet and exercise are beneficial throughout life.

SYSTEM OF SUPPLY

VOCABULARY

hemoglobin ('hē·mə·glō·bən) the protein in red blood cells that binds with oxygen molecules

hypertension (hī·pər·'ten·shən) the term for high blood pressure

carcinogen (kär·'si·nə·jən) a substance or agent that causes cancer

IN THE FIELD

Digitalis, a well-known heart medication, comes from the common foxglove plant. In 1799, English physician John Ferriar discovered that foxglove had a noted effect on the heart. The plant is extremely poisonous and should not be eaten. However, digitalis, an extract from the plant, causes the pulse of the heart to decrease while the force of contractions and the amount of blood pumped per heartbeat increases.

All cells in the human body need nutrients and oxygen. Cells also need to have wastes removed. The components of the cardiovascular system work together to nourish the cells. It is vital that the organs function properly. For this to happen, the right amount of nutrients must be supplied. A lack of nutrients in the diet results in an inefficient system and the possibility of major health problems.

Blood consists of red and white blood cells, plasma, and platelets. Red blood cells contain hemoglobin, a protein responsible for transporting oxygen and carbon dioxide. Iron is required to form hemoglobin. If the body does not have enough iron, a condition called *anemia* can develop. When this condition exists, the blood cannot carry enough oxygen to the cells. The heart must work harder to pump enough oxygen throughout the body. Over time, the stress on the heart can lead to erratic pulse rates, chest pain, an enlarged heart, and even heart failure.

For blood to move throughout the body properly, blood pressure must be maintained. High blood pressure over an extended period of time is not healthy and is known as hypertension. In this condition, the heart works harder than usual and may become enlarged. A diet containing too much salt can lead to hypertension.

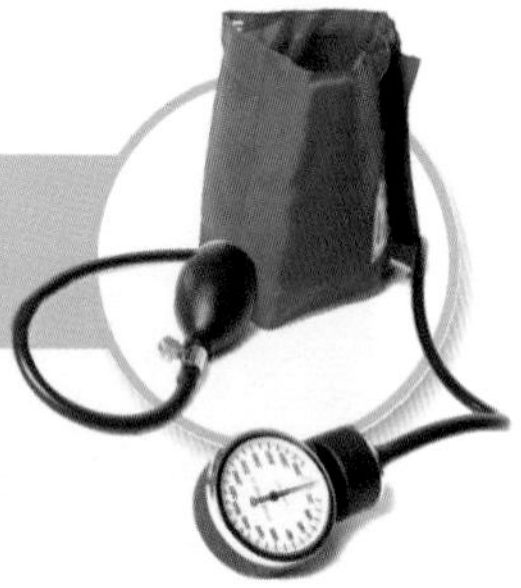

What is this instrument called?

Dried fruits, some nuts, and green leafy vegetables, such as spinach, are good sources of iron.

Hypertension can also contribute to a condition called *atherosclerosis*, which is a narrowing and hardening of arteries. Although the diameter of arteries naturally decreases with age, an advanced state contributes to heart disease.

Various nutrients help maintain a healthy cardiovascular system. Proteins are used for the manufacture of antibodies and tissues. Carbohydrates are the main source of blood glucose and the only source of energy for red blood cells. Vitamins A and C enhance the body's immunity. Vitamin C also increases the absorption of iron. B vitamins are needed for circulation, carbohydrate metabolism, and blood and antibody formation. Vitamin E is essential to the blood, preventing cell damage and protecting good cholesterol. Vitamin K helps to form and repair bone and clot blood. Calcium and potassium help regulate the heartbeat. Magnesium protects the linings of arteries. Phosphorous assists in coordinating heart contractions, and sodium is required for proper blood pH.

In addition to eating a balanced diet, it is important to stay away from substances that are carcinogens. Tobacco products and asbestos, a type of mineral used in building supplies, are well-known cancer-causing agents.

OUTLOOK

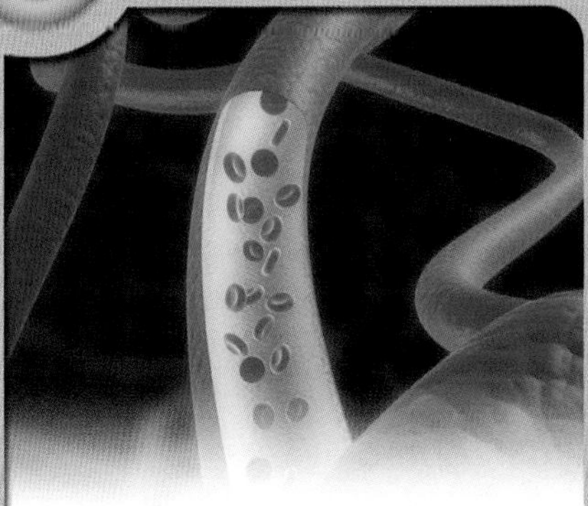

Consider how blood is the lifeline of the body, both physically and spiritually. Physically, blood carries life-sustaining nutrients to the cells and removes harmful toxins. It also defends the body from pathogens. Spiritually, the blood of Jesus enables you to have life-sustaining fellowship with God and a home in heaven. Jesus' sacrificial blood removes your sins. As you accept this sacrifice, Jesus becomes your Great Defender.

Cigarettes and other tobacco products contain over 4,000 chemical compounds. Many of these are carcinogenic or toxic in some way to the body. According to the World Health Organization, if tobacco use continues at its present rate, tobacco-related deaths worldwide will reach 8 million a year by 2030.

VOCABULARY

ligament (ˈli·gə·mənt) the tissue that connects bone to bone at movable joints

osteoporosis (ˌäs·tē·ō·pə·ˈrō·səs) a bone disease that causes a loss in bone density

IN THE FIELD

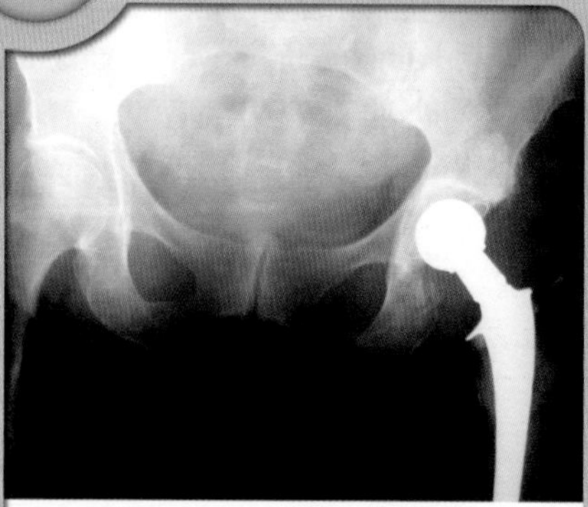

Hip and knee replacements are surgical procedures in which the hip or knee is exchanged for a prosthetic implant. Such procedures are conducted to relieve arthritis pain or to repair severe physical joint damage. Artificial hips and knees are commonly made of titanium or cobalt chrome alloys.

Muscles and bones account for much of the body's weight and appearance. Without muscles, tendons, and ligaments, the skeleton would not be able to move. By the time most individuals are in their late 20s, bone mass, strength, and density have reached their highest levels. Ninety percent of this bone tissue is present by the age of 18 in girls and 20 in boys. Therefore, youth is the time when diet and exercise programs should start. Proper nutrition and regular physical activity build strong bones and muscles. Calcium and vitamin D are essential for healthy bones too. Eating foods such as low-fat cheese, dark-green leafy vegetables, calcium-enriched juice, and yogurt can provide necessary calcium. Sunlight and fortified milk provide vitamin D.

Consistent exercise not only builds strong bones, but also strengthens muscles and increases muscle endurance. Keeping muscles, ligaments, and joints toned and flexible is important for maintaining proper movement and posture. Weight-bearing exercises, like running and walking, help keep bones strong and prevent calcium loss. Good exercises that help build bone mass include walking, jogging, hiking, climbing stairs, playing sports, skiing, and weight training. If strong bones are built when a person is young, he or she will experience the benefits later in life.

What is the common name of the condition when ligaments are abnormally loose?

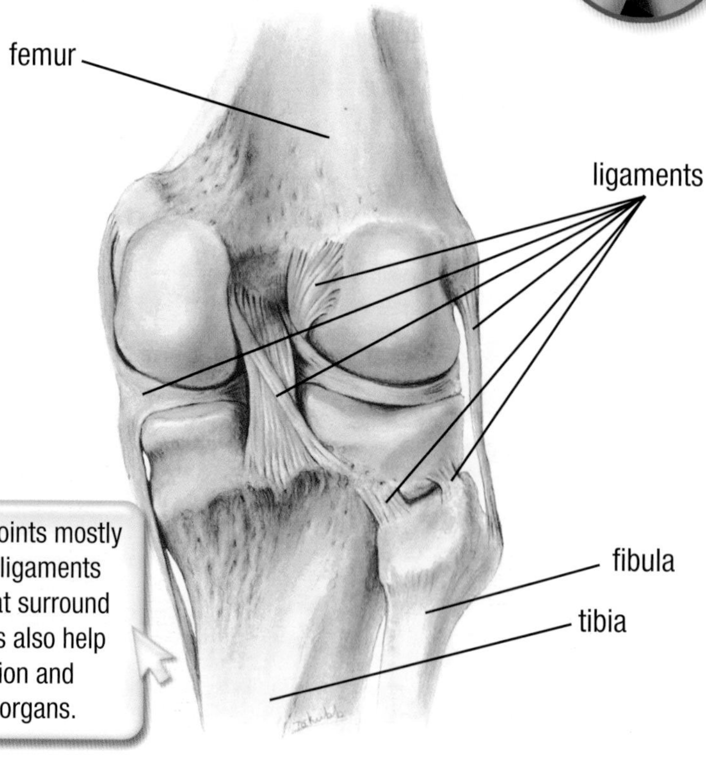

The stability of joints mostly depends on the ligaments and muscles that surround them. Ligaments also help prevent dislocation and support various organs.

Several conditions can result if a person fails to eat and exercise properly. Osteoporosis is a chronic disease that usually shows up in adulthood and can cause bones to weaken and break more easily. It is characterized by a severe loss in bone mass. Osteoarthritis is a disease that causes the cartilage between bones to disintegrate. The rough and irregular bones cause pain as they rub together. In rheumatoid arthritis, the lining of the joint thickens, becomes inflamed, and breaks down. The joint can become very stiff and painful. Many people suffer when vertebral discs become worn down, slip, or rupture. Pain results if the disc presses against the spinal cord or the spinal nerves. Over time, simple daily tasks can become virtually impossible to do.

Even though sports and recreational activities are important, there is always the possibility of having musculoskeletal accidents and injuries. Fractured bones, dislocations, sprains, and tears in muscles, cartilage, and ligaments are common. Additional injuries may affect teeth, shoulders, ribs, ankles, and knees. A common knee injury is torn or worn cartilage, which causes pain, discomfort, and immobility. It is important to begin healthy habits at a young age to prevent and minimize the risks of disease and injury when older.

OUTLOOK

The phrase *use it or lose it* has various applications. From birth, muscles and bones are growing and changing. As the body matures, muscles and bone cells increase in size and strength. Coordination and muscle control improve as the nervous system matures. In older adults, muscles and bone begin to lose some of their mass. Muscles undergo gradual loss of size, strength, and endurance. Bones begin losing calcium and phosphate and become more brittle. Research has shown that many of these changes due to aging can be delayed by incorporating a healthy nutritional diet and good exercise habits. This is similar to our effectiveness as Christians. Consistent study of the Word, prayer, and obedience keeps us strong witnesses, fulfilling the purpose of glorifying God's name.

What type of doctor specializes in bone injuries?

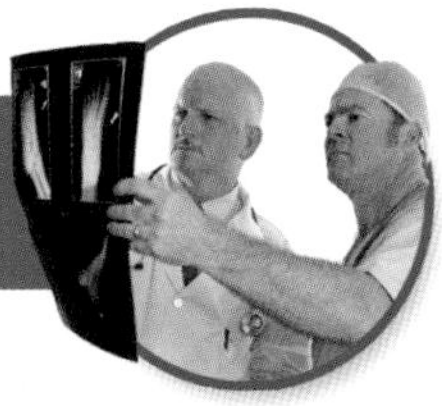

Bone density significantly decreases in individuals with osteoporosis. In serious cases, even simple activities, such as bending over, tying a shoe, or sneezing, can cause a fracture.

SYSTEM OF CONTROL

VOCABULARY

dendrite ('den·drīt) a highly branched extension of the neuron's cell body

axon ('ak·sän) a single, long projection that extends from the neuron's cell body

myelin ('mī·ə·lən) a fatty substance that surrounds the axon

synapse ('si·naps) a tiny gap between one neuron and another

electrolyte (i·'lek·trə·līt) a substance that forms ions in a solution and conducts electric currents

The basic unit of the nervous system is the neuron. It relays information throughout the body. This is accomplished by transmitting impulses from one nerve cell to another or to a muscle or gland. Although neurons vary in size and shape, every neuron has a cell body that is similar to other cells. It contains organelles and performs regular cell functions. Attached to the cell body are many dendrites that branch out. A dendrite transmits information toward the cell body.

The axon is also attached to the cell body. It is a single, long extension that carries information away from the cell body. The far end of the axon branches into axon terminals. Many axons throughout the nervous system are covered with a fatty substance called myelin. The myelin sheath, or covering, acts as an insulator. It affects the transmission rate of electrical impulses. The speed of nerve impulses is faster along myelinated axons than those that are not myelinated. This is important when, for example, your finger accidentally touches a hot stove. The reflex time needs to be extremely short to prevent injury. Damaged myelin may cause an impulse transmission to short circuit. When impulses are transmitted from one neuron to another, they cross a microscopic area called a synapse.

What is a Schwann cell?

Electrical impulses travel from one neuron to the next. The impulse stimulates the release of neurotransmitters, which enable the impulse to be transmitted across the synapse.

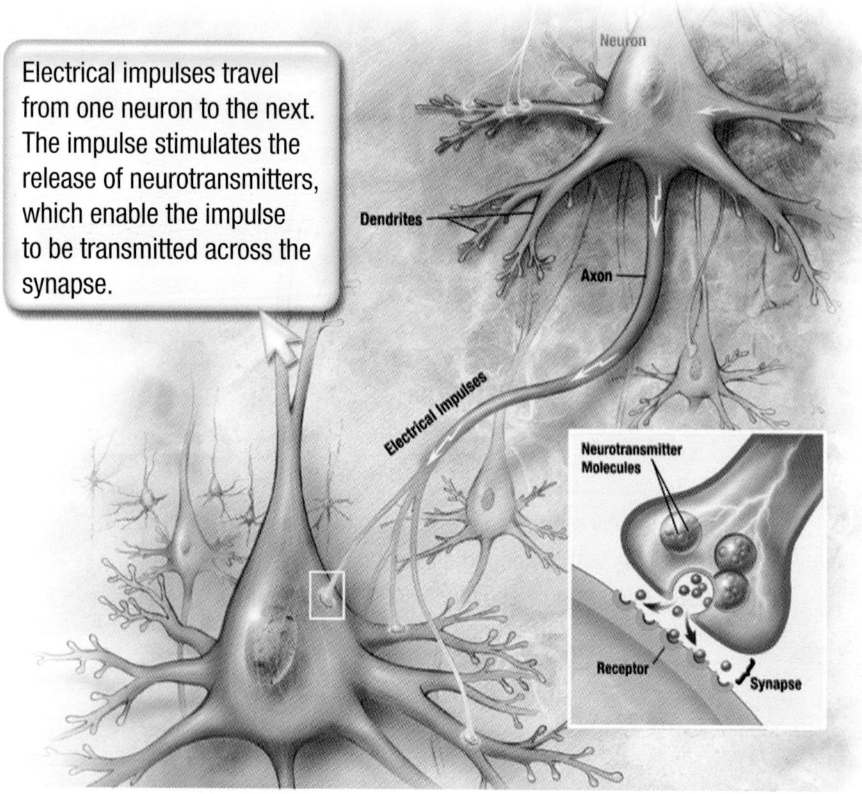

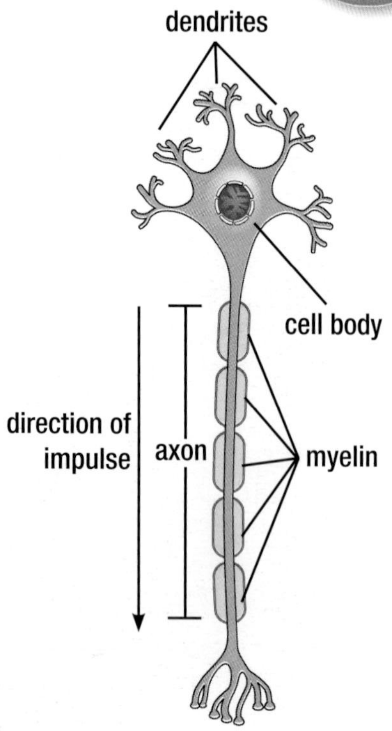

Typically, an axon terminal will form a synapse with the dendrite of another neuron, muscle, or gland. This allows many connections between the axon and other neurons. A nerve impulse crosses a synapse with the aid of chemical messengers called *neurotransmitters*.

Certain nutrients are required by the nervous system to function properly. The body uses sodium and potassium as electrolytes to conduct electrical currents and to carry out functions within cells. B vitamins help maintain nerve health and muscle tone. For example, vitamin B_1 aids in learning capacity. Niacin, which is also known as *vitamin* B_3, helps the overall functioning of the nervous system. The body uses vitamin B_5 to help produce neurotransmitters. Vitamin B_6 maintains sodium and potassium balance to continue normal brain function.

A deficiency in any of these nutrients can result in several disorders. In addition, a lack of vitamin E can cause nerve damage. Muscle cramps are often the result of an electrolyte imbalance. Multiple sclerosis is a disease that attacks the central nervous system by damaging the myelin sheath on neurons. However, the effects of this disease can be lessened by a proper diet.

QUICK FACT

Botulism toxin, produced by the *C. botulinum* bacterium, can inhibit the contraction of muscles. The neurotoxin gets into the neuron and interferes with the release of the transmitter that is responsible for carrying information across the synapse. As a result, the nerve cannot stimulate the muscle. Unless the nerve can generate a new axon, the damage is permanent.

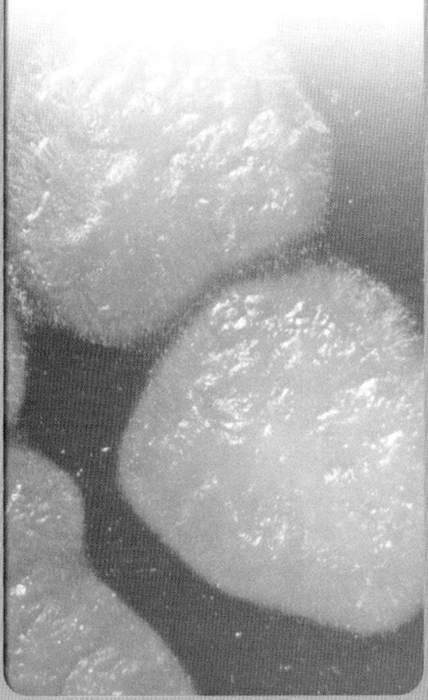

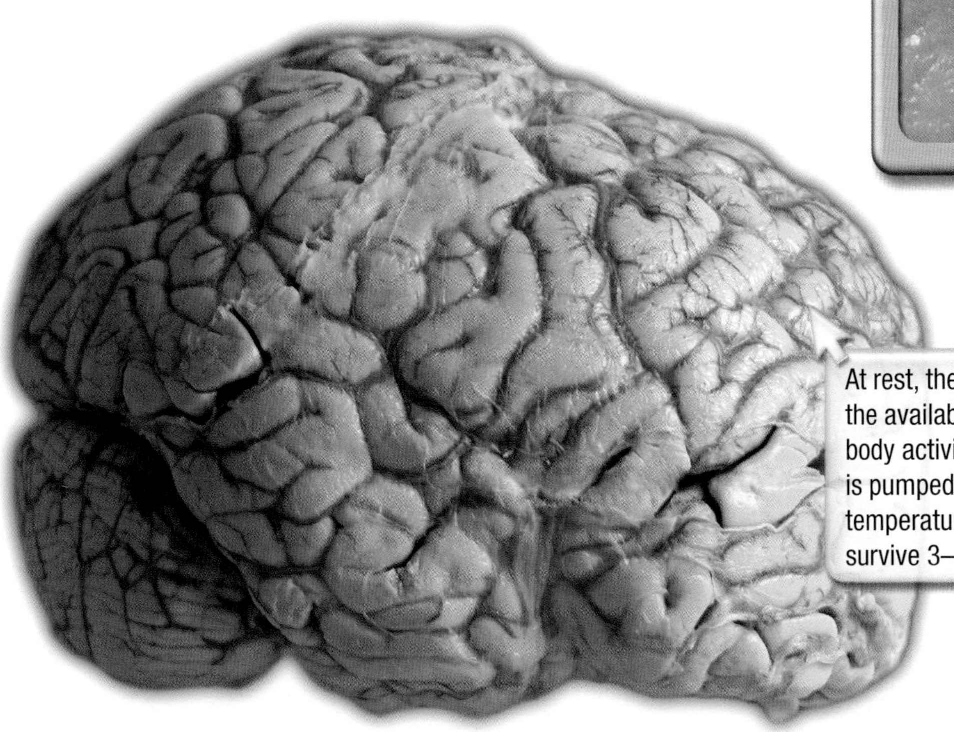

At rest, the brain uses about 20% of the available oxygen in the blood. As body activity increases, more blood is pumped to the brain. At room temperature, brain cells can only survive 3–5 minutes without oxygen.

LINKS

History Link
Research the history of sugar. Create a time line illustrating the earliest cultivation of sugar in America and any significant events leading up to present day. Display the time line in class or get permission to hang it on a school wall.

Technology Link
Learn how sugar is processed and refined. Develop and illustrate a computer-generated flowchart, beginning with sugarcane or sugar beets in the field and ending with sugar as an ingredient in a purchased or homemade food item. Present the flowchart on a poster board, and give a presentation to the class.

Language Arts Link
Pick a food item that is advertised on television or in a magazine. Summarize what the advertisement is saying and what claims are being made. Describe the techniques used by the companies to entice viewers or readers, particularly children, to want their products. Locate the item in a store, and read the food label for its contents. Note the amount of protein, carbohydrates, fats, vitamins, and minerals. Describe how this food item is or is not beneficial to the body. Report your findings.

There is truth to the statement *You are what you eat*. The food and drink that a person consumes become the raw materials the body uses to function and grow. Scientific research shows that eating healthful foods in moderate amounts contributes to a longer, healthier life. In addition, nutritionists promote healthful cooking as a way to increase health benefits. Choosing a healthful method of food preparation does not mean giving up the great tastes of foods. Rather, it can provide a rich flavor while keeping health-risky fats and sugars to a minimum.

Selecting a better method of cooking can be as simple as using lemon juice, fruit juice, vinegar, or water to cook in instead of oil. If oil is necessary, applying it in spray form or with a pastry brush can reduce the amount needed for the cooking process. Yogurt or cornstarch can be used as a thickener in a recipe instead of heavy cream, which is high in fat. Grilling vegetables in place of frying them in a pan is also a healthful choice.

It is important to make healthful food and cooking choices early in life.

Strange but True

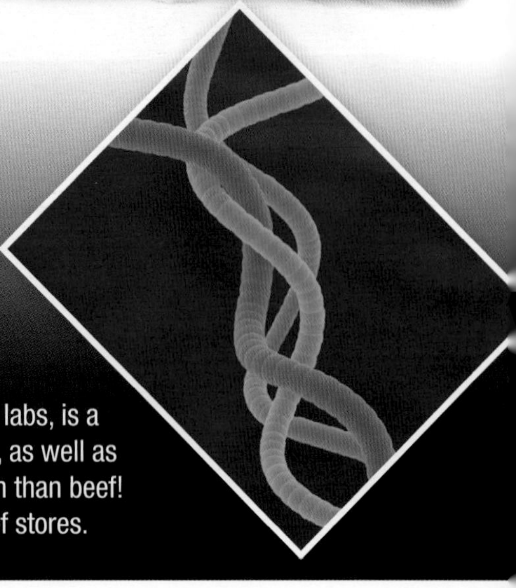

Spirulina, a cyanobacterium that can grow in lakes or be cultivated in labs, is a rich source of nutrients. It contains high concentrations of vitamin B_{12}, as well as many other vitamins, minerals, and enzymes. It even has more protein than beef! Spirulina is sold in powder and capsule form in health food sections of stores.

Cooking Methods

poach	Involves water or liquid just under the boiling point; includes constant basting or self-basting.
steam	Involves steam; use regular heat under a double boiler of water with a steamer basket inset.
boil/simmer	Boil/simmer food submerged in boiling water with heat turned down for simmering; overcooking can reduce the amounts of nutrients.
bake	Cook food in a pan or dish with or without lid; all surfaces of food are exposed to a heat source; sometimes involves a minimal amount of fat to prevent sticking.
broil/grill	Cook food dry except for possible marinade; only one side of food at a time is exposed to radiant heat; includes outdoor grilling.
roast	Cook in deep dish without lid in oven; usually food item is basted; all surfaces of food are exposed to heat source; involves oil, butter, own juices for basting; health factor depends on basting; using olive oil is better than using butter.
sauté	Cook rapidly with small amount of hot fat; used to sear thinly sliced food; should not create steam; food often floured or breaded; involves oil, butter, breading; using oil is more healthy than using butter.
fry	Cook with fat in a shallow pan using moderate heat; food is often floured or breaded; involves shortening, oil or butter, breading; unhealthy on a regular basis; better to use oil than shortening or butter.
deep-fat fry	Submerge food into fat (oil or shortening) inside a deep pan or kettle; using oil is more healthy than using shortening.
cream	Make a cream sauce using dairy products such as milk, butter, and cheese; unhealthy on a regular basis; better if low-fat milk products are used.

Key: [light grey] = most healthy, [white] = fairly healthy, [dark grey] = least healthy

GLOSSARY

A

absolute magnitude the actual brightness of a celestial object (page 142)

absolute zero the lowest possible temperature at which matter has no remaining thermal or heat energy (page 68)

acceleration the change in an object's velocity over a period of time (page 94)

acid a substance with a pH less than 7.0 (page 72)

airfoil an object whose shape contributes to lift (page 84)

air pressure the force exerted by air (page 82)

air resistance the action of friction caused by air (page 96)

allele a different form of a single gene that controls an inherited characteristic (page 42)

alveoli the microscopic air sacs found in the lungs (page 156)

angiosperm a vascular plant that bears flowers and fruit (page 10)

apparent magnitude the measure of a celestial body's brightness as observed from the earth (page 140)

appendage an external structure that extends from the main body (page 16)

Archimedes' principle a submerged object is pushed upward by a force equal to the weight of the fluid it displaces (page 80)

arthropod an invertebrate that has a segmented body, jointed appendages, and usually an exoskeleton (page 20)

atomic mass the number of protons plus the number of neutrons in one atom (page 54)

atomic number the number of protons in one atom of a particular element (page 54)

auditory nerve a cranial nerve that carries impulses from the inner ear to the brain (page 164)

autotroph an organism that produces its own food (page 6)

average speed the total distance traveled divided by the total travel time (page 92)

axon a single, long projection that extends from the neuron's cell body (page 174)

B

base a substance with a pH greater than 7.0 (page 72)

benthos the organisms that inhabit the ocean floor (page 110)

Bernoulli's principle pressure decreases as a fluid speeds up (page 82)

binary fission a type of asexual reproduction in which a cell divides into two parts (page 36)

binary star a system of two stars that revolve around each other (page 148)

binomial nomenclature a two-part naming system that consists of genus and species (page 4)

bioluminescence the production of light by living organisms (page 110)

biome a large region that has a particular climate and specific plants and animals (page 24)

brine pool an area of water on the ocean floor that has high salinity (page 112)

budding a type of asexual reproduction that involves the outgrowth of a small part of the parent, which develops into a new organism (page 36)

buoyant force the upward force exerted by a fluid (page 80)

C

calorie a unit used to measure the energy content in food (page 168)

carcinogen a substance or agent that causes cancer (page 170)

cartilage the connective tissue that covers the ends of bones in a joint (page 160)

chemical family a group of elements that have similar properties (page 58)

cholesterol a fat-like substance produced by the liver of humans and animals (page 168)

chordate an animal that has the beginnings of a backbone during one or more stages of development (page 14)

chromatid one of the two strands of a duplicated chromosome (page 34)

chyme the thick liquid made of partially digested food in the stomach (page 156)

cinder cone a steeply sloped volcano made of pyroclastic material from explosive eruptions (page 132)

cnidarian an invertebrate with radial symmetry, a soft body, and tentacles with stinging capability (page 22)

codominance the condition in which both alleles of a gene are actively expressed and neither is dominant or recessive (page 46)

composite volcano a tall, cone-shaped mountain made of alternating layers of lava and pyroclastic material (page 132)

continental shelf a gently sloping area of the ocean floor that extends outward from the shoreline (page 108)

creationist one who believes in the biblical account of Creation (page 124)

crustacean a mainly aquatic arthropod that has a hard exoskeleton and two pairs of antennae (page 20)

current the continuous flow of ocean water in a certain direction (page 104)

D

dendrite a highly branched microscopic extension of the neuron's cell body (page 174)

deposition the change from a gas to a solid without passing through the liquid state (page 66); the process in which sediment is laid down (page 120)

dicot a plant having an embryo with two cotyledons (page 10)

diffusion the movement of molecules from an area of higher concentration to an area of lower concentration (page 32)

dominant allele the allele that hides the effects of another allele (page 42)

drag the backward force on an aircraft caused by friction (page 84)

E

echinoderm an invertebrate that exhibits radial symmetry and a tough, spiny skin (page 20)

ectotherm a cold-blooded animal whose body temperature fluctuates with the temperature of its environment (page 16)

electrolyte a substance that forms ions when in solution and conducts electric currents (page 174)

electron dot diagram a figure in which dots around an element's symbol represent valence electrons (page 60)

electron energy level a location of electrons surrounding the nucleus in the atom (page 56)

electrostatic charge a property of matter that can be either positive, negative, or neutral (page 54)

ellipse an elongated oval shape (page 148)

endoplasmic reticulum a network of passageways within a cell that transports materials (page 28)

endoskeleton the internal supporting framework of an animal or human (page 160)

endotherm a warm-blooded animal that maintains a constant internal temperature (page 18)

epicenter the point on the earth's surface directly above the focus (page 130)

eukaryote an organism composed of one or more cells containing a visible nucleus and organelles (page 8)

evolutionist one who believes in the theory of evolution (page 124)

exoplanet a planet orbiting a star other than Earth's sun (page 148)

exoskeleton a hard, external covering of an animal (page 14)

F

fermentation the process in which cells break down molecules without the use of oxygen (page 30)

focus the point beneath Earth's surface where rock breaks and causes an earthquake (page 130)

foliated a layered appearance caused by the parallel arrangement of grains (page 116)

force a push or a pull on an object (page 90)

friction the force that resists motion between two surfaces in contact with one another (page 96)

Fujita scale a scale used to rate tornado intensity (page 134)

G

gamete a mature male or female reproductive cell (page 34)

genotype the set of genes that make up an organism (page 40)

geologic column a vertical sequence of strata that provides a historical record of Earth's eras and periods (page 126)

geologic time scale a chart or diagram that describes the events of Earth's history in chronological order (page 126)

giant a large, bright star with low surface temperature (page 144)

glucose the simplest form of sugar, used as a source of energy (page 30)

grain the minerals or rock particles that give rock its texture (page 116)

gymnosperm a vascular cone-bearing plant whose seeds are not enclosed (page 10)

H

heat capacity the ability to store and release heat energy (page 68)

hemoglobin the protein in red blood cells that binds with oxygen molecules (page 170)

heredity the passing of traits from parent to offspring (page 38)

heterotroph an organism that obtains food from an outside source (page 6)

heterozygous having the presence of two different alleles for the same gene (page 44)

homozygous having the presence of the same two alleles for the same gene (page 44)

hurricane a tropical cyclone forming in the Atlantic and eastern and central Pacific Oceans (page 136)

hybrid an organism that has two different alleles for a particular trait (page 42)

hydraulic system a system that uses fluids to increase or transfer forces (page 80)

hydrogen bond a weak bond that connects hydrogen-containing molecules at polar areas (page 70)

hypertension the term for high blood pressure (page 170)

I

incomplete dominance the condition in which both alleles are partially expressed in a blended appearance of the trait (page 46)

inertia the resistance to a change in motion (page 90)

intertidal relating to an ocean zone located between high- and low-tide lines (page 108)

ion an atom that has gained or lost one or more electrons (page 66)

K

Kelvin scale a temperature scale that begins at absolute zero (page 68)

keratin a strong, structural protein found in skin, hair, nails, and feathers (page 18)

kinetic friction the force that resists the motion of a moving object (page 96)

L

lift the force that pushes an aircraft up (page 84)

ligament the tissue that connects bone to bone at movable joints (page 172)

load the dissolved or suspended matter in a body of water (page 118)

longshore current a movement of water caused by waves that strike the shore at an angle (page 106)

luminosity the amount of light radiated per second by a star (page 144)

M

main sequence a diagonal area on the H-R diagram in which most stars are found (page 144)

medulla oblongata the lower portion of the brain stem (page 162)

meiosis the type of cell division that produces reproductive cells (page 34)

metal an element that is typically shiny and hard and a good conductor of heat and electricity (page 58)

mitochondrion an organelle that produces energy from food (page 28)

mold fossil the shape of a previously living organism preserved in sediment (page 122)

mollusk an invertebrate with a soft body that is typically enclosed in a shell (page 20)

momentum the property of a moving object that causes it to tend to keep moving (page 94)

monocot a plant having an embryo with a single cotyledon (page 10)

myelin a fatty substance that surrounds the axon (page 174)

N

nebula a large cloud of gas and dust in space (page 146)

nekton the free-swimming organisms (page 110)

neritic relating to the area of the ocean that extends from the low-tide line out to the edge of the continental shelf (page 108)

neuron a nerve cell that sends messages throughout the body (page 162)

neutron star the small, dense core of a supergiant after an explosion (page 146)

newton the standard metric unit for the measurement of force (page 94)

nonmetal an element that is typically dull and brittle and a poor conductor of heat and electricity (page 58)

O

oceanic relating to the zone that extends from the edge of the continental shelf and covers the entire open ocean (page 108)

optic nerve a cranial nerve that carries impulses from the retina to the brain (page 164)

osmosis the diffusion of water through a membrane that allows specific substances to pass through (page 32)

osteoporosis a bone disease that causes a loss in bone density (page 172)

ostia the small pores through which water and nutrients enter a sponge (page 22)

P

Pascal's principle pressure is transferred equally throughout a fluid in all directions (page 80)

pedigree a record that shows a pattern of genetic inheritance in a family (page 44)

period a horizontal row of the periodic table (page 56)

periodic table a chart that arranges elements having similar properties into the same groups (page 52)

peristalsis the muscular contractions that move food through the digestive tract (page 158)

perpetual motion motion that continues endlessly (page 98)

petrifaction the process by which an organism is completely replaced by minerals (page 122)

phenotype the observable characteristics of an organism's genotype (page 40)

pH scale a range of values from 0 to 14 that indicates the concentration of hydrogen ions in a solution (page 72)

plankton the tiny algae and animals that float in the surface zone (page 110)

plasma a superheated gas composed of electrically charged particles (page 66)

polarity the quality of having opposite charges for different points of a molecule (page 70)

poriferan an invertebrate with a porous, asymmetrical body that pumps and filters water (page 22)

pressure the amount of force exerted on a certain area (page 78)

prokaryote a unicellular microorganism that lacks a distinct nucleus (page 6)

pulsar a rapidly spinning neutron star that emits pulsating radio waves (page 146)

Punnett square a diagram used to show all the possible allele combinations of a genetic cross (page 44)

purebred an organism with identical alleles for a particular trait (page 42)

P wave a type of seismic wave that compresses and expands (page 130)

pyloric sphincter the muscle that separates the stomach from the small intestine (page 156)

R

recessive allele the allele whose effect is hidden when paired with a dominant allele (page 42)

resin fossil a small organism preserved in fossilized tree sap (page 122)

ribosome an organelle responsible for protein synthesis (page 28)

rip current A strong flow of water that returns seaward perpendicular to the shore (page 106)

S

shield volcano a gently sloping mountain made of lava released from nonexplosive eruptions (page 132)

solubility the ability of one substance to dissolve in another (page 70)

somatic cell a body cell other than a reproductive cell (page 34)

squall line a row of severe thunderstorms (page 134)

star cluster a group of stars held together by gravitational attraction (page 150)

static friction the force that resists movement of an object at rest (page 96)

sternum the breastbone located in the middle of the chest (page 160)

storm surge a wall of water that moves ashore when a hurricane strikes land (page 136)

strong force the attractive force that holds the nucleus of an atom together (page 54)

sublimation the change from a solid to a gas without passing through the liquid state (page 66)

supernova the explosion of a massive star that causes a sudden increase in luminosity (page 146)

surface tension the elastic property of liquids that allows drops to form and creates the smallest area possible at the surface of a liquid (page 70)

S wave a type of seismic wave that moves side to side or up and down (page 130)

synapse a tiny gap between one neuron and another (page 174)

T

taxonomy the science of classifying organisms (page 2)

tendon the connective tissue that attaches muscle to bone (page 158)

thermodynamics the scientific study of how energy transfers from one place to another and from one form to another (page 98)

thrust the force that pushes an aircraft forward (page 84)

tornado a rapidly rotating column of air that extends from a cumulonimbus cloud and touches the ground (page 134)

trace fossil the preserved remains of footprints, eggs, burrows, or droppings (page 122)

trait a characteristic that is inherited (page 38)

tropical cyclone a rotating storm system originating over warm waters with wind speeds of 119 kph (74 mph) or greater (page 136)

tropism a positive or negative involuntary reaction of a plant to a stimulus (page 12)

V

vacuole a membrane-bound sac within a cell or tissues that stores water or other materials (page 28)

valence electron an electron in the outermost energy level of an atom (page 58)

vascular having a system of tubes to transport water and nutrients (page 10)

velocity the measure of an object's speed and direction (page 92)

vent the opening in a volcano through which magma and gases escape (page 132)

villi the tiny fingerlike projections that line the surface of the small intestine (page 156)

viscosity the resistance of a liquid to flow (page 70)

W

wave a movement that transfers energy from point to point through matter (page 104)

weight the downward force on an object caused by gravity (page 84)

white dwarf a small, hot, very dense star (page 144)

INDEX

Boldfaced page numbers indicate the location of vocabulary word definitions.

A

abrasion 119
absolute magnitude 142, 143–145
absolute zero 68
acceleration 94
acid 72, 73
active transport 32–33
adult acute epiglottitis 160
aerobic 7
  respiration 31
African elephant 19
Age of Exploration 4
air conditioner 75
aircraft carrier 80
airfoil 84, 85–86
air pressure 82
air resistance 96, 95, 97
Albireo 148
algae 8, 10
allele 42, 43–44, 46–47
Alpha Centauri 148
alveoli 156
amino acid 27, 167
ammonia 60, 99
amoeba 8
amphibian 14, 16–17, 23
  types 17
anaerobic 7
  respiration 31
anemia 170
angiosperm 10, 11
Angkor Wat 13
animal breeding 48–49
animalcules 6
animal kingdom 14–15
annelid 14, 23
Antares 143
apparent magnitude 140, 141–143
appendage 16, 20, 161
arachnid 20
Archaea Domain 2, 5, 7
Archimedes' principle 80, 76
architect 131
argon 63
Aristotle 3, 88, 90
arthropod 20, 14
  classes 20
arthroscope 160
asexual reproduction 36–37
atherosclerosis 171
athlete's foot 9
atom 52–54, 59–61, 64–65, 76
atomic mass 54, 53, 55
atomic model 57–58
atomic number 54, 53, 55
auditory nerve 164, 165
auto mechanic 81
autotroph 6, 7–8, 10
average speed 92
axon 174, 162, 175

B

bacteria 6–7, 73
  shapes 6
bacteria domain 2, 5
Bakewell, Robert 48–49
bald eagle 15
ball bearing 97
Banff National Park 118
Banyan tree 13
base 72, 73
Bauhin, Caspar 11
Bauhinia variegata 11
bee hummingbird 18
benthos 110
Bernoulli, Daniel 82
Bernoulli's principle 82, 83–84, 86
Betelgeuse 145, 151
Big Bang 151
Big Dipper 151
binary fission 36
binary star 148
binomial nomenclature 4, 11
bioluminescence 110, 111
biome 24, 25
bird 14, 18, 25
  blue-footed 18
  characteristics 18
  feathers 18
Black Butte 133
black dwarf 146
black hole 147
black smoker 111
blimp 57, 80
blood sugar 30
blood type 46
blue whale 19
body system
  cardiovascular 154, 156, 170–171
  digestive 154, 156–157
  muscular 158–159
  musculoskeletal 154, 172–173
  nervous 154, 162–163, 174–175
  respiratory 154, 156
  skeletal 160–161, 172–173
  urinary 154, 156–157
body wave 130
boomerang 86
Bose-Einstein Condensate 67
Bose, Satyendra 67
botulism 175
brain 175
  regions 163
  sizes 162
brakes 81
brine pool 112
Bryce Canyon 119
budding 36, 37
buffer 73
bull shark 113
bumblebee bat 19
buoyancy 80, 112,
buoyant force 80,
Burnell, Jocelyn 147

C

calorie 168, 167, 169
Calypso 112
Cambrian explosion 126
carbohydrate 166–168
carbon 58, 61
carbon dioxide 66, 71, 105
carcinogen 170, 171
Carnegie Mellon University 98
carrion 23
cartilage 160, 161
catastrophism 121–122
C. botulinum 175
cell 26, 28, 158–159
  bone 160
  cycle 26, 34
  division 34–35
  membrane 32–33
  muscle 163
  nerve 162–163
  organelles 26–29
  receptor 164
  reproduction 36–37
  respiration 30–31
cellular respiration 26, 30–31
cellulose 28
Celsius, Anders 68
Celsius scale 68
Centaurus 151
centromere 34–35
cervical vertebrae 161
chemical family 58, 59
chemical property 56
chicken 46
Chiclet 12
chlorine 61, 63
chloroplast 10, 28
cholesterol 168, 169
chordate 14, 15
chromatid 34, 35
chromosome 34–35, 38, 45
chyme 156, 157
cicada 20
cigarette 171
cinder cone 132, 133
classification 2, 10, 15
cnidarian 22, 14, 37
codominance 46, 47
Coelopleurus exquisitus 21
Cohn, Ferdinand 6
color-blindness 45
combustion engine 74
comet 148
composite volcano 132, 133
condensation 79
cones 164
conifer 10, 139
constellation 149–151
continental crust 114
continental margin 108–109
continental rise 108–109
continental shelf 108, 109
cooking method 176–177
cooling curve 66
cooling system 75
copper 56
coprolite 122
coral reef 109, 111
Coriolis effect 105, 136
Corynebacterium diphtheriae 6
cotyledon 11
Cousteau, Jacques 112
crater 132
Creation 121, 124, 151
creationist 124, 126
creosote bush 10
crossbedding 121
crustacean 20
Crux 151
cryologist 69
cumulonimbus cloud 134–135, 137
current 104, 102, 105, 136
  deep 106–107
  surface 106
Curtis, John 12
cyanobacterium 176
Cyathus olla 9
cytoplasm 26, 28, 30–31, 34

D

decomposer 9
Deep Space 1 91
deflation 119
de Honnecourt, Villard 99
dendrite 174, 162–163, 175
density 102, 105, 107
deposition 66, **120**, 121–122, 126
diabetes 30
diatom 8
dicot 10, 11
diet 73, 166, 170–171
diffusion 32, 33
digestion 157
digitalis 170
dinoflagellate 8
Dioscorides 3
DNA 27, 36, 38, 40, 48
dog breeding 48–49
dominant allele 42, 43–44, 46
donkey 39
downwelling 107
drag 84, 76, 85, 97
drifter 106
dry ice 66
dust devil 134

E

ear 165
Earth 128, 140–143
  crust 114
earthquake 130–131
echinoderm 20, 14, 21
  types 21
ectotherm 16
Einstein, Albert 67
electrolyte 174, 175
electron 53–63, 67
electron dot diagram 60, 61
electron energy level 56, 57–58, 62–63
electrostatic charge 54

element 52–53, 56, 58–59
of life 61
ellipse 148
El Niño 107
endoplasmic reticulum 28, 29
endoskeleton 160, 161
endotherm 18
energy 64–69, 74, 130–131
engineer 131
epicenter 130
equilibrium 32, 128–130
era 126
erosion 119
Etruscan shrew 19
eukarya domain 2, 4–5, 8–10, 15
eukaryote 8, 30
Euphorbia pulcherrima 4
European Space Agency 23
evolution 125
evolutionist 124, 125
exercise 73, 166, 169, 172–173
exoplanet 148, 149
exoskeleton 14, 20
extremophile 113
eye 164

F

facilitated diffusion 33
Fahrenheit, Daniel 68
Fahrenheit scale 68
fascia 158
fat 168–169
saturated 168–169
trans 168–169
unsaturated 168–169
fermentation 30, 26, 31
fern 10
Ferriar, John 170
ferrum 55
fingerprint 39, 44
fire
basic requirements 138
retardant 139
triangle 138
fish 14, 16
flight 76–77, 84–85
fluid 73, 76, 79–83
fluorine 63
flying wing 84
focus 130
foliated 116, 117
force 90, 91, 94
fossil 122–123
friction 96, 86, 95, 97–98
types 96
Fujita scale 134, 135
fungus kingdom 5, 9
fusion 142, 146

G

galaxy cluster 151
Galileo 68, 88, 90
gamete 34, 35
Gamgee, John 99
gene 38, 44–45
genetic disorder 35, 45, 47
genetic engineer 36
genetic engineering 48
geneticist 38, 40, 42
genetics 38
genotype 40, 41, 43–44, 47
geologic column 126
geologic time scale 126, 127
giant 144, 145–146
Ginko biloba 11
girdle 161
glider 85
global warming theory 105
globular cluster 150
glucose 30, 28, 31, 33, 169
Golgi body 28–29
grain 116, 117
Gram, Hans 6
Gram's stain 6
gravitropism 13
gravity 12–13, 98–99, 119, 147–148
Great Debate 125
great ocean conveyor belt 107
green tree python 17
gymnosperm 10, 11
gyre 106

H

hail 135
halite 114
Hawaiian Islands 132–133
HD 189733b 149
heart
murmur 157
muscle 158–159
heat capacity 68, 69, 102
heat energy 74–76
heat engine 74
heating curve 66
hedgehog 19
helicopter 86
helium 57
hemoglobin 170
hemophilia 45
heredity 38
herpetologist 17
heterotroph 6, 7–9
heterozygous 44
hinny 39
Hipparchus 142
homozygous 44
hooded seal 19
hoodoo 119
horse 39
horse breeding 49
Hot Shot Crew 138
hot spot 132
H–R diagram 144–146
hurricane 136, 137
eye 137
eyewall 137
rain bands 137
Hurricane Katrina 118
hybrid 42, 43–44
hydraulic system 80, 76, 81–82
hydrogen 60, 70, 72

hydrogenated oil 168
hydrogen bond **70**, 71
hydrogen chloride 61
hydrologic cycle 102
hydrothermal vent 111, 113
hydrotropism 12
hydroxide 72
hypertension **170**, 171
hypoglycemia 30

I

ice cap 109
igneous 114, 116
  extrusive 116
  intrusive 116
inbreeding 48
incomplete dominance **46**, 47
inertia **90**
insect 20, 25
insulin 30, 36
intertidal **108**, 109–110
invertebrate 14, 20–23
ion **66**, 67, 72–73
iron 55, 170
Isaiah 5

J

joint 172–173
jumping spider 20
Jupiter 145

K

karyotype 35
kelp forest 109, 111
Kelvin scale **68**, 142, 144
Kepler, Johannes 147–148
keratin **18**
kinetic friction **96**
King Clone 10
kingdom 2
King Hezekiah 5
Komodo dragon 24

L

lactic acid 31
Lake Nicaragua 113
Lake Powell 114–115
laminated rubber bearing 131
La Niña 107
Late-Cretaceous mass extinction 126
law of conservation of energy 82–83
law of conservation of momentum 95
laws of motion 88, 90–91
laws of planetary motion 148
laws of thermodynamics 98
leaven 9
Legionella pneumophila 6
LGM-1 147
lichen 118
lift **84**, 76, 85–87
ligament **172**, 173
light energy 142
lightning 65, 67, 134, 138–139
light year 142–143
Lingulodinium polyedrum 8
Linnaeus, Carolus 4, 11
lion 19, 25
lion's mane jellyfish 22
lipid 167
lithium 55, 57, 62
Little Dipper 151
liverwort 10
load **118**
Loetscher, Ila 17
longshore current **106**
lotus plant 71
luminosity **144**
Lyra 149
lysosome 28–29, 33

M

Magellan, Ferdinand 4
main sequence **144**, 145–146
mammal 14, 19, 25
  characteristics 19
Manilkara zapota 12
marine fireworm 23
Mauna Kea 133
medulla oblongata **162**, 163
meerkat 25
meiosis **34**, 35
Mendel, Gregor 40, 43, 46–47
Mendel's laws 40
meniscus 70, 160
Mercalli scale 131
metal **58**, 53, 59, 62–63, 69
metalloid 53, 59
metamorphic 114, 116–117
meteorologist 136–137
methane 61
Methanocaldococcus janaschii 5
microscope 6
Milky Way Galaxy 143
Mimosa pudica 13
mineral 114, 116, 166
mitochondrion **28**, 29–30
mitosis 26, 34–35
Mohave Desert 10
mold fossil **122**
mollusk **20**, 14, 21, 112
  classes 21
Moment Magnitude scale 131
momentum **94**, 95
Monkey Trial 125
monocot **10**, 11
Morning Glory Pool 7
moss 10
motion 88–95
  laws 87–88, 90–91
  perpetual 98–99
  receptors 163

Mount Fuji 133
Mount Saint Helens 133
Mount Vesuvius 133
mule 39
multiple sclerosis 175
muscle 172–173
belly 158
cramps 175
tissue 158
types 158–159
myelin 174, 175

N

NASA 23, 91, 147
natural selection 125
nebula 146, 147
Eagle 146
nectarine 42
nekton 110, 111
nematode 14, 23
neo-catastrophism 121
neon 63
neritic 108, 109
neuron 162, 163, 174–175
neurotransmitter 174–175
neutron 53–54
neutron star 146, 147
newton 94
Newton's cradle 95
Newton, Sir Isaac 88, 90, 92
Newton's laws 86–88, 90–91, 94
nitrogen 57
bases 27
nitrous oxide 59
nonmetal 58, 53, 59, 63
north star 149, 151
notochord 14
nucleolus 28
nucleus 5, 8, 28–29
nutrient 154, 166, 170–171, 175
nutritionist 176

O

obesity 169
oceanic 108, 109, 111
oceanic crust 114
ocean zone 108–111
ochre pits 127
omnivore 25
optic nerve 164
organic chemistry 59
organ system
cardiovascular 154, 156, 170–171
digestive 154, 156–157
muscular 158–159
musculoskeletal 154, 172–173
nervous 154, 162–163, 174–175
respiratory 154, 156
skeletal 154, 160–161, 172–173
urinary 154, 156–157
Orion 145, 150–151
ornithologist 18
osmosis 32
ossification 160
osteoporosis 172, 173
ostia 22
oxygen 30–31, 56, 60, 71–72, 138

P

paleontologist 126
pangolin 90
parasite 9
Paraliparis devriesi 16
paramecium 8
Pascal's principle 80, 76, 81
passive transport 32
pea plant 40–43, 47
pectoral girdle 161
pedigree 44, 45
pelvic girdle 161
penguin 18
penicillin 9
perilymph 165
period 56, 57
periodic table 52, 53, 58
peristalsis 158
perpetual motion 98, 99
petrifaction 122, 123
Peyto Lake 118
phagocytosis 26–27, 33
phenotype 40, 41, 43, 46, 48
phosphorus 58
photosynthesis 28, 30
phototropism 12
pH scale 72, 64, 73
physical property 56, 59
pipe 132
planarian 23
plankton 110, 8, 107
plant kingdom 2, 5, 10–11
plasma 66, 64, 67
Platyhelminthes 14, 23
Pleiades 150
poinsettia 4
poison ivy 43
polar bear 24
Polaris 149, 151
polarity 70
polestar 149
poriferan 22, 14
potassium 33, 62
pressure 78, 79, 81–83
differential 83
primary wave 131
prokaryote 6, 7, 30
proper motion 149
protein 38, 47, 166–167, 170
transport 33
protist kingdom 2, 5
ciliated 36
types 8
proton 53–55, 58
protostar 146
protozoa 8
Proxima Centauri 140, 148, 151
pseudopod 8
pulsar 146, 147
Punnett square 44, 45

purebred 42, 43–44, 49
PVC 56
P wave 130, 131
pyloric sphincter 156, 157
pyroclastic material 132–133

R

radiocarbon dating 123, 126
Ray, John 4
recessive allele 42, 43–44, 46
red-gilled sea slug 5
reflex action 163
refrigerant 75
refrigerator 75
reptile 14, 16–17, 25
  types 17
repulsion 54, 56
resin fossil 122, 123
rheumatoid arthritis 173
ribosome 28, 29
Richter scale 131
Rigel 151
Ring of Fire 133
rip current 106
robotics 81, 159
rock
  breakdown 118–119
  cycle 114
  types 116–117
rods 164
rose 43

S

Sagittarius 150
salinity 105, 108
saliva 73
sandbar 106
sandblasting 119
scaly anteater 90
scatter plot 145
Schwann cell 174
Scopes trial 125
scuba 108, 112
sea anemone 22
sea cucumber 21, 109
sea urchin 21
secondary wave 131
sedimentary 114, 116–117
sedimentation
  chemical 117
  physical 117
seismologist 131
selectively permeable 31–32
senses 162–165
sexual reproduction 36, 38
shape 78–79
shield volcano 132, 133
sickle cell anemia 45, 47
Siemens Westinghouse 98
silicon 58, 61
silicon dioxide 60
silicon hydride 61
Sirius A 145, 148
Sirius B 145, 148
skin 164
sky diver 93, 97
snapdragon 47
snottite 7
soap 72
sodium 33, 57, 62
  chloride 114
solubility 70, 71
somatic cell 34, 35
species 4, 14–16, 20, 39
speed 92–95
spirulina 176
sponge 22, 37
spore 36
squall line 134
staphylococci 6
star
  cluster 150
  color 142
  drift 149
  life cycle 146–147
  light 142–143
  populations 144–145
  size 141–142
  temperature 141–142, 144–145
starch 168
state change 66–69, 74–75
state of matter 64–67, 76–78
static friction 96
Stealth Bomber 85
Stereocidaris granularis 21
sternum 160, 161
storm surge 136, 137
stratovolcano 133
strong force 54
sublimation 66
sugar 61, 168, 176
sun 140, 142–145, 149
supercell 134
supergiant 143–146
supernova 146, 147
surface tension 70
surface wave 130–131
S wave 130, 131
synapse 174, 163, 175
syncytium 36
Systema Naturae 4

T

taxonomy 2
temperature 76
  layers 108–109
tendon 158, 159, 172
  Achilles 158
Theophrastus 3
theory of plate tectonics 114
thermal 85
thermocline 108
thermodynamics 98
thermometer type 68
thermoscope 68
thigmotropism 13
Thomson, Sir William 68
thrust 84, 76, 85
Thuban 149
thunderhead 134

thunderstorm 134, 136
tide 102, 104
tissue 154, 160
bone 160
muscle 158
titanium 59
toad 17
topspin 87
tornado 134, 135
Tornado Alley 135
tortoise 17
touch receptor 164
Toxocara canis 23
trace fossil 122
trait 38, 40, 42, 45
triple star 148
tropical
depression 136
storm 136
tropical cyclone 136, 137
tropism 12, 13
types 12–13
trumpeter swan 18
tsunami 104
tuberculosis 5
tube worm 111
turtle 17
Kemp's Ridley 17
Leatherback 22
twin 45
typhoon 137

U

uniformitarianism 120–121
universal solvent 71–72
upwelling 107
Ursa Major 150–151
Ursa Minor 150–151

V

vacuole 28, 29, 33
valence electron 58, 59, 61–63
van Leeuwenhoek, Antonie 6
varve 121
vascular 10, 11
Vega 149
velocity 92, 93
vent 132
venturi 83
vertebrate 14, 16–17
villi 156, 157
viscosity 70, 64, 71
vitamin 166, 171–172, 175–176
volcano 71, 80, 103, 113
activity 132–133
types 132–133
volcanologist 133
volume 78–79

W

wall cloud 135
water 60, 66, 76–77
boiling point 68
currents 106–107
freezing point 68
level 104
movement 102–105
pH 72
properties 64, 76–77, 105
spout 134
states 66, 68–69, 76–77
uniqueness 70–71
wave 104, 102, 105
body 130–131
seismic 130
surface 130–131
weather balloon 79
weathering 118–119
weight 84, 76, 80, 85
welder 67
white dwarf 144, 145–146
whooping cough 6
wildfire 138–139
Willoughby, Francis 4
willy-willy 137
Woese, Carl 7
wood louse 20
woolly mammoth 123
World Meteorological Organization 137
worm 23

X

xenon 91

Y

yeast 9, 31
Yellowstone National Park 7, 113

Z

zodiac 150
zygote 36

CREDITS

Chapter 1
Snottites, **pages 3 and 7**, Daniel S. Jones/Penn State
Tuberculosis, **page 5**, Janice Carr/CDC
Methanocaldococcus jannaschii, **page 5**, Dr. Reinhard Rachel/Universitaet Regensburg
Gram-positive photo of *Corynebacterium diphtheriae*, **page 6**, CDC
Gram-negative photo of *Legionella pneumophila*, **page 6**, Dr. William Cherry/CDC
Bioluminescence, **page 8**, J. Michael Sauder, Carlsbad, CA (http://www.flickr.com/photos/msauder)
Diatoms, **page 8**, courtesy of Mark B. Edlund
Downy mildew, **page 8**, by Dr. James Correll/Department of Plant Pathology/University of Arkansas
Amoeba capturing bacterium, **page 8**, CDC
Creosote bush, **page 10**, Gary A. Monroe/USDA-NRCS PLANTS Database
Banyan tree, **page 13**, courtesy of Justin Watt
Mimosa pudica, **page 13**, courtesy of H. Zell

Chapter 2
Antifreeze fish, **pages 15 and 16**, Melanie Conner, National Science Foundation (NSF)
Hooded seal, **page 19**, courtesy of The Scottish Sea Life Sanctuary, www.sealsanctuary.co.uk
Sea urchin tests, **page 21**, courtesy of Steve Jurvetson, who does not sponsor, authorize, or endorse this textbook. This image file is licensed under Creative Commons Attribution 2.0 License.
Nematode, **page 23**, courtesy of Joel Mills, who does not sponsor, authorize, or endorse this textbook. The image file is licensed under the terms of the GNU Free Documentation License, Version 1.2 or any later version, as well as the Creative Commons Attribution ShareAlike 2.5, Attribution ShareAlike 2.0, and Attribution ShareAlike 1.0 License.

Chapter 3
Neuroglia, **pages 26 and 27**, © Dennis Kunkel Microscopy, Inc.
Syncytium, **pages 27 and 36**, National Institutes of Health (NIH)
Cell interior, **page 28**, Nicole Rager Fuller, NSF
Mitochondrion, **page 30**, Nicole Rager Fuller, NSF
Phagocytosis, **page 33**, Dr. Volker Brinkmann/Max Planck Institute for Infection Biology, Berlin
African lily mitosis images, **page 34**, National Institute of General Medical Sciences
Karyotype, **page 35**, in memory of Paul A. Behr
Binary fission, **page 36**, courtesy of Ron Meumeyer, www.microimaging.ca

Chapter 4
Polydactyly, **page 45**, DrGnu23, GNU Free Documentation License, Version 1.2 or any later version. Provider of image does not necessarily endorse, sponsor, or authorize this textbook.

Chapter 5
Carbonado, **pages 53 and 58**, courtesy of Dr. Stephen E. Haggerty, Florida International University
Lithium and potassium, **page 62**, courtesy of Pat Blackburn/CSCS, Colorado Springs, CO
Chlorine gas, **page 63**, courtesy of James L. Marshall, University of North Texas, "Walking Tour of the Elements"

Chapter 6
Bose-Einstein condensate, **page 67**, Marshall Space Flight Center/NASA
Stellar babies, **page 68**, NASA/JPL/University of Arizona
Clayton Anderson, **page 70**, NASA

Chapter 8
Pangolin, **page 90**, courtesy of www.creationism.org
DS1, **page 91**, NASA
M. C. Escher's Waterfall, **page 98**, © 2008 The M.C. Escher Company-Holland. All rights reserved. www.mcesher.com
SOHO spacecraft, **page 99**, SOHO/ESA and NASA

Chapter 9
Tube worms, **pages 103 and 111**, Woods Hole Oceanographic Institution
Tidal gauges, **page 104**, NOAA Central Library Historical Imagery/National Oceanic and Atmospheric Administration/Department of Commerce
Drifter and its deployment, **page 106**, Diane Stanitski/Global Drifter Program and Adopt a Drifter Program/NOAA
Rip current, **page 106**, Dennis Decker/WCM, NWS/NOAA
La Niña, **page 107**, NASA Goddard Space Flight Center (NASA-GSFC)
El Niño, **page 107**, NASA/JPL
Plankton, **page 110**, U.S. EPA Great Lakes National Program office
Hydrothermal vent, **page 111**, P. Rona, OAR/National Undersea Research Program (NURP)/NOAA

Mussels, **page 112**, NOAA/http://oceanexplorer.noaa.gov/explorations/02mexico/logs/oct17/media/mussels.html
Mud pool, **page 113**, R. G. Johnsson/NPS

Chapter 10
Ochre pits, **pages 115 and 127**, Eric Christian/NASA
Gabbro, **page 116**, F.C. Calkins/USGS
Fault breccia, **page 117**, courtesy of Tina R. Hill
Breccia, **page 117**, USGS
Quelccaya Ice Cap, **page 120**, Lonnie Thompson/Byrd Polar Research Center/ The Ohio State University
Varves, **page 121**, USGS
Crossbedding, **page 121**, David Rubin/USGS
Bryozoan, **page 125**, NOAA
Brachiopod, **page 125**, courtesy of Dr. James E. Lawson, Jr./Oklahoma Geological Survey Observatory

Chapter 11
Tornado, **pages 129 and 135**, NOAA, OAR/ERL/ National Severe Storms Laboratory (NSSL)
Vocanologists, **page 133**, Thomas J. Casadevall/USGS
Mauna Kea, **page 133**, courtesy of www.volcanovillage.com
Waterspout, **page 134**, Dr. Joseph Golden, NOAA
Cumulonimbus cloud, **page 134**, NOAA's National Weather Service (NWS) Collection
Weather system, **page 136**, CPHC/NWS/NOAA
WMO logo, **page 137**, World Meteorological Organization
Fire retardant, **page 139**, Bob McMillan/FEMA

Chapter 12
Mercury, **pages 141 and 148**, NASA/Johns Hopkins Applied Physics Laboratory/Carnegie Institution of Washington
Bluish nebula, **pages 140 and 141**, D. Gouliermis/ NASA/ESA and the Hubble Heritage Team (STScI/ AURA)
Antares, **page 143**, courtesy of Creative Commons Attribution 3.0 License. Copyright holder does not sponsor, authorize, or endorse this textbook.
Star cluster of the Milky Way Galaxy, **page 143**, by Don Figer/NASA/STScI
Head circumference chart, **page 145**, CDC
Sirius A and B, **page 145**, NASA, H.E. Bond and E. Nelan (Space Telescope Science Institute, Baltimore, Md.); M. Barstow and M. Burleigh (University of Leicester, U.K.); and J.B. Holberg (University of Arizona)
[illegible]lgeuse, **page 145**, NASA, A. Dupree/CfA and [illegible]land/STScI
Eagle Nebula, **page 146**, NASA/JPL-Caltech/Institut d'Astrophysique Spatiale
Black dwarf, **page 146**, NASA/JPL-Caltech
Pulsar, **page 146**, Maggie Masetti, NASA
Kepler's supernova, **page 147**, NASA/ESA, R. Sankrit and W. Blair (Johns Hopkins University)
Crab nebula, **page 147**, NASA/ESA/CXC/JPL-Caltech, J. Hester and A. Loll (Arizona State Univ.), R. Gehrz (Univ. Minn.), and STScI
Black hole, **page 147**, NASA
Kepler's supernova, **page 147**, NASA, ESA, R. Sankrit and W. Blair (Johns Hopkins University)
Red supergiant, **page 147**, NASA/ESA and H.E. Bond (STScI)
Halley's comet, **page 148**, by W. Liller, Easter Island, part of the International Halley Watch (IHW) Large Scale Phenomena Network/NASA
Albireo, **page 148**, © 2005 Richard Yandrick
HD 189733b, **page 149**, NASA/ESA
Warped spiral galaxy, **page 150**, Hubble Heritage Team (STScI/AURA), C. Conselice (U. Wisconsin/ STScI) et al./NASA
M55, **page 150**, Canada-France-Hawaii Telescope/ Coelum
Galaxy cluster, **page 151**, W. Couch (University of New South Wales), R. Ellis (Cambridge University), NASA
Centaurus constellation, **page 151**, © 2003 Torsten Bronger. The image is licensed under the terms of the GNU Free Documentation License, Version 1.2 or any later version published by the Free Software Foundation; with no Invariant Sections, no Front-Cover Texts, and no Back-Cover Texts. Torsten Bronger does not sponsor, authorize, or endorse this textbook.

Chapter 14
Spirulina, **pages 167 and 176**, © Dennis Kunkel Microscopy, Inc.
Electrical impulses, **page 174**, courtesy of National Institute on Aging
C. botulinum, **page 175**, CDC

Cover, page v, Unit 1 Divider page
Macrophage, lymphoctyes, and human red blood cells image, © Dennis Kunkel Microscopy, Inc.